BARRY LONG, born an ordinary man, raised in country towns in New South Wales and without much education, became an inspiration to thousands of men and women and recognised around the world as one of the foremost spiritual masters of the 20th century.

Coming from no religious tradition or school, he had no credentials to offer – other than the truth he spoke. Yet what he said had the power to change lives. How does such power and authority arise? The clues are in this spiritual autobiography, describing a life lived in the fullness of the spirit; a life of love and truth.

This is his own extraordinary story, told in detail for the first time and now published posthumously.

The story begins with his early career as a journalist. He becomes the youngest editor of a Sydney Sunday paper, *The Truth* (later the *Sunday Mirror*). But the daily reflection of the spirit supplants all ambition and he leaves that world for the real truth, which beckons him to India. There, after travelling across the subcontinent in a van, he finds himself alone in the foothills of the Himalayas and passes through a mystic death, his realisation of immortality.

The story continues in London where he meets the woman who takes a central role in the unfolding drama. Their life together produces profound spiritual realisations and the biography then reaches out beyond normal experience to encounters with powers from deep inner space.

We see a master being made. But before he can enter the world stage there are severe tests to be undergone, culminating in the death of his beloved.

Packed with incident, acutely observed and honestly told, this is not just the story of one life but a revelation of the way destiny works when the life is guided by truth.

# Barry Long

---

# MY LIFE OF LOVE AND TRUTH

## *A Spiritual Autobiography*

BARRY LONG BOOKS

Published by
The Barry Long Foundation International 2013

© The Barry Long Trust

BARRY LONG BOOKS

www.barrylongbooks.com
www.barrylong.org

Email:  contact@barrylong.org

Library of Congress Catalog Card Number:  2012954203
ISBN:  978-1-899324-19-4

Cover photo and design by Rita Newman
Cover photo © Rita Newman / www.newman.at
All other photographs © The Barry Long Trust

Printed by C & C Offset Printing Co., Ltd., Hong Kong

# CONTENTS

# PUBLISHER'S NOTE

Barry Long began writing his autobiography in the 1970s and continued writing and revising it in the years and months before his death in December 2003.

He occasionally spoke in public about his life but generally only to demonstrate a point in his spiritual teaching. He was not concerned with drawing attention to himself or his story if that would detract from his message, which is essentially that divine truth and love reside in a direct experience accessible to every one of us in our own lives now.

As long as he lived, he was living proof of his own teachings; he lived what he taught. In death he leaves us an account of his life which puts his other published works in that living context. It is a testament to the extraordinary way God, truth and love worked in Barry Long; and by his example we are inspired to look to the underlying purpose of our own lives.

This book is Barry Long's story up to 1982 and describes the making of a spiritual master. It is an honest account and for the most part names and facts have not been concealed or changed. Where Barry Long makes use of writings by other people, permission to quote them has been sought and given. Letters have had customary pleasantries and personal details removed.

Barry Long's autobiography survives him as proof and a reminder that the authentic spiritual or divine life is original and informed by a living power of which we are normally unaware. As this is not a normal life, some aspects of the story may offend expectations or appear incredible. To get the most from the book, please read it with a still mind.

# ABOUT TRUTH

Everything in this autobiography is necessarily written from my viewpoint – with a few exceptions where people tell their own stories. As there is no universal viewpoint in recounting anything, it is possible from another's point of view, and over a span of so many years, that I may offend, misrepresent or misquote. If so, it is not intentional; I have endeavoured to tell the life straight as I perceived it.

Throughout the book I also present the spiritual truth behind the events and experiences described. Truth, unlike viewpoints, is universal, which means there can be no dispute in truth. Nonetheless, there may be a difficulty. Many people have realisations of truth, right up to what could be called the ultimate. But no realisation is complete – it remains partial – until actually lived in the world. A popular concept is that after, say, God-realisation ("Self-realisation" in the East), the whole life is instant bliss. This, like all assumptions, is not true. Moreover, the error seems to have been fostered by so-called "realised" men and women. God-realisation does indeed induce a constant untroubled equilibrium in a man or woman. But what is not commonly known is that there then follows an external testing of the inner equilibrium. Circumstances and situations that previously would have caused concern, disturbance or distress have to be faced to affirm that the equilibrium is real. This may

1

take many years. The deeper the realisation, the more provoking or demanding the circumstances are likely to be.

Also not commonly known is that there are multiple descending levels within of God or truth realisation. Which explains why there are so many teachers each convinced that their way is right. Real knowledge of God at any level is right. But the profundity and extent of the knowledge depends on the depth of the realisation – and the living of it. People realise things and don't make them real. As the levels of realisation deepen, and the circumstances demanded by each are lived through, the outer life improves. Finally, the inner state is known to have been perfected; and the perfection (which has nothing to do with the man or woman) is reflected in the harmony of the external life. All is solved; all is provided. The life is free of problematical circumstances. There are no conflicting relationships. The lovelife is trouble-free. Work and fulfilment have come together.

In all that I've just said there is no certainty of continuity. Truth is always moving. Nothing remains static. Anything is possible in the moment.

All this of course describes an extraordinary depth of God or truth-realisation often referred to as enlightenment. Bringing such realisation into the world is the same as bringing God into the world. And God knows, the world needs it – but only God knows in whom.

When I present the truth in this book there may be room for doubt in a reader who has not realised the same depth of truth and lived it through. I accept that. But it doesn't alter the truth.

# I MUST GO...

In 1962, at the age of 36, I was having lunch with my wife and two young children at my father's home near Sydney, Australia. Six of us were around a table in the kitchen nook. It was a bit cramped and I had an increasing feeling of being closed in, stifled. The sensation became most unpleasant. I knew I had to get outside. Mumbling my apologies I hurriedly left, and once outdoors immediately felt better. As I strolled up the road, words and then a tune began to compose themselves in my head. I walked along singing them to myself, the chorus first:

> Stand back, stand back
> Stand back forever.
> Stand back, stand back
> Stand back, it's now or never.

Then came the first verse:

> I must go where the tall trees grow
> Where the giants stand alone,
> And there I will be

Made eternally free
For I am going home.

The chorus about "standing back" certainly described exactly what I'd felt. The sentiment was not directed at my family or anyone in particular. It was just a statement that was completely right for me at that moment. The words of the verse were a mystery. Tall trees? Giants? Home? What they meant, if anything, I had no idea. It was just another poem. By then I'd had four or five years of growing awareness of the truth, or developing consciousness, and spontaneous poetic expression was not new to me. The song caught on in the family and for the next year or so the four of us would sing it around the house together.

Three years after writing the song I was living in the foothills of the Himalayas in northern India, having left my family and thrown in a job as manager of a Sydney public relations company. On the 11th of November 1965, still in India and after six dreadful weeks of catharsis and confusion, I realised immortality. At last I knew the truth – that truth, anyway. It was irrevocable, beyond doubt and could never be erased from my consciousness. It was not a matter of memory. I had participated in the living fact. I had been made free – freed forever of the fear of death.

As I stood on the open verandah of the stone bungalow where I was living, an isolated place notched into the side of a hill a 1,000 feet above a winding valley, the meaning of the words of the song gently dawned on me. It was morning. The air was crisp, clear and clean – the ever-aspiring dust of the plains nearly a mile below, was temporarily beaten back to earth by the recent monsoon deluge. Every smell and image was sharp and distinct like single notes played on a piano. The senses, glazed by months of relentless Indian sun, broke out afresh in the earthiness of autumn. Up and around the mountain crept the smell of charcoal breakfast fires; huge high-flying hawks glided almost arm's-length away past my eyrie. And as my eyes followed the scent of pine sap, I turned and faced a forest of tall pine trees forming a half-circle up the mountainside in front of me – 1,000s of them, all 40 and 50 feet high!

In the other direction, 15 to 20 miles away but still dwarfing everything in sight in majesty and size, were two magnificent Himalayan snow peaks – comely Trisul, always heavily ermined in snow, and jutting, black-faced, angry Nanda Devi – both giants, both standing superbly alone.

The second verse of the song then immediately wrote itself:

> I must go where the four winds blow
> Where the spirit speaks to its own
> For now I am free
> Like the wind I must be
> And help the others home.

That sums up what this book is about. It is the story of some of the experiences and adventures of an ordinary family man, successfully established in a good career, who at the age of 31 suddenly found himself undergoing a fundamental change in consciousness which was to wrench him away, revolutionise his normal values – and change the lives of many people. It could be anyone, could happen to anyone. And it is happening in one way or another to innumerable ordinary people at this moment. It is a compelling story of destiny at work behind the clamour of circumstances and human expectations. And some of it is unbelievable and fantastic by normal standards. But it is all true. And anyone who is undergoing this vast change in consciousness, which wrecks the hopes and lives of men and women, will recognise what is described and not be quite so much alone as they may have thought.

# CHAPTER 1

# THE FIRST TEST

T he first symptom of inner change occurred around 1957 when I was 31. I was a sub-editor on *Truth*, one of Sydney's three Sunday papers. Instead of drinking with the other journalists in the pub at lunchtime, or sitting around chatting idly, I went walking in the parks. The chief sub-editor, a gentle man, sometimes joined me. But soon I found I had to be alone more and more.

In the winter the only secluded places I could find in that busy extroverted city were the churches. There I could sit undisturbed. If there was a lunchtime service I would go to another church. It was rare for anyone to come in otherwise.

I wasn't the praying type. I wasn't at all religious in the usual sense. In the beginning I didn't know anything about the practice of meditation (which clearly was happening in me) which I had probably derided or dismissed at sometime in my brash, stampeding fashion. I was very sure of myself. I still am – only in a different way. I wasn't the quiet or introspective type you'd normally expect to "go spiritual". And I certainly was neither modest nor self-effacing. If anyone personified the ebullient, outspoken, self-asserting, boastful, energetic "you are my sunshine" Leo character, I did. I loved glamour, the limelight and being a newspaperman, especially when I was a hot-shot reporter. I had started at 15 as a copyboy on the Sydney *Daily Mirror*, then owned with *Truth* by Ezra Norton, one of the last of the old-style eccentric newspaper barons. I would even go into the office on my days off to travel around with the reporters and photographers. I was a keen, thrusting young man, aggressively ambitious and extremely self-confident.

Yet now in the maturity of my 30s something new was happening to me inside. I was retreating, not from the world, but from the certainty of myself. Out in the world I was punching on as hard as ever, determined to clamber towards the top and actually succeeding. But within, inexorably, I was taking a pause without realising it. I needed some radical space inside from which to start looking at myself – a new perspective. The next couple of years were going to make sure I got it.

At 32 I was appointed editor of *Truth*. It was being phased out and I was to be the first editor of its successor, the new Sydney *Sunday Mirror*, later acquired by the Rupert Murdoch organisation. It was here in the editor's chair that I learned however high you manage to climb, there is always someone over you – and sooner or later he will let you know it. You can never really be free out there. This is hardly a great discovery; but it is a potent realisation. It takes the demon out of ambition. For myself, I invented the saying, "Everybody has his Baume."

Eric Baume was the editorial director of Ezra Norton's Australia-wide newspaper group. He was a forceful, flamboyant man in his late 50s, known throughout the country for his provocative television and radio broadcasts – *This I Believe* and *I'm on Your Side* – a self-appointed public defender and champion, and very impressive too. Over six foot tall, well built, commandingly upright and with a bristling black moustache which he stroked incessantly, Eric Baume's steamrolling presence emitted shock-waves that instantly polarised others' emotions. Apart from verbalising, he never really did much at all. Yet he managed to galvanise half the public of Australia into furies of impotent reaction as they read his newspaper columns or listened to his off-the-cuff panaceas for the social and political malaise. They hated him. The other half loved him. It had to be one or the other. He couldn't be ignored; and he wouldn't go away. Through his columns and broadcasts he was a powerful political force.

As editor I was directly responsible to Baume. In a way I was his protégé. He had noticed me back in 1950 when I was a reporter on the

*Daily Mirror* and applied to him to go to Korea as a war correspondent. He turned me down – sending an older and more experienced man – and delighted in calling me WC for months after.

For nearly 12 months as editor, Baume gave me hell. When appointing me he had said, 'I'm going to break you if I can. If I break you, you're no good to me. If I don't, you'll be the best editor this city's ever had.' Baume was exceedingly proud that at 28 he had been 'the youngest editor ever' of the *Sun*, Sydney's other big afternoon daily. Now he was going to try to re-live the experience through me.

This was only an opening event in a long process to bring about a change of consciousness, and someone had to have the task of hammering out of me my identification with newspapers. Any hang-up or driving desire has to be depersonalised. And Baume was just the man for the job. I had to be taught the fatuity of ambition and its reflexive desire for power and fame. Through him I was to learn to stand strong in the face of professional humiliation, ridicule, insult – but not with the strength of defiance. I had discovered the first chink of intelligent spiritual space in me and with it the strength that comes from surrendering to what is, to what can't be changed because it is right for you.

It is all very clear now. But it wasn't then. I just knew I must hold on – hold on to that space which I was beginning to call the "Lord". This was not the Lord of any church or religion. No priest, parson, man or doctrine could infiltrate it; it was my Lord, my individual strength of knowing something I couldn't define or formulate, although I did try. One such attempt was my first "song". Most individuals undergoing a change in consciousness try to express the inspiration in poetry or song, the essence of delight and artistic response. In that moment of truth each of us is an artist in his or her own way, although we may not be in the next. We fumble for adequate expression.

My first experience of spontaneous song after the spirit started to enter me was a devotional one, a song of praise, a paean to the Most High. It represented the first faint sensing of universal unity – that which is greater and behind all appearance.

> I believe, I believe, Oh I believe,
> I believe, I believe, Oh I believe.
> I believe, Oh I believe, I believe,

> I believe, Oh I believe, I believe.
> Harmony, Harmony, Harmony,
> I believe, all is one, all's harmony,
> Part of you, part of me, all's harmony,
> I believe, all is one, all's harmony.

Meanwhile back at the office, Baume never let up on me. At midnight on Saturdays, just before the final clean-up edition was ready to go to press, he would sometimes phone from a downtown nightclub and say he didn't like the look of page one (even though he'd seen it hours before). 'Remake it,' he'd bark in the old Hollywood style, and I could imagine the head waiter, or some captive guests sitting around his table, being terribly impressed. Baume knew exactly what was in every edition of the paper because he had copies rushed to him by radio car wherever he happened to be entertaining.

One Saturday evening he swept into my office snorting with rage. It was 40 minutes before the first-edition deadline. On the drive back from his club, the Sports Club, a taxi in front had suddenly stopped to pick up a fare and Baume's chauffeur just managed to avoid an accident.

'I've got a new front page lead for you.'

'We'll be late.' (Editors can't afford late editions.)

'I don't care. Bloody taxi drivers… nearly killed us.'

He buzzed for his secretary and dictated a mishmash of editorial comment on the dangerous habits of taxi drivers while the chief sub-editor and myself sent it out paragraph by paragraph to the printers for setting. We published 15 minutes late, missed several train connections and probably lost a few thousand sales. The story was so limp it nearly fell off the page.

On Wednesday mornings Baume would ask to see the story I intended to lead the paper with the following Sunday! Often on a Saturday morning he would kill an article or an investigation we had been working on all week and leave us scrambling for news. You can't run and edit a newspaper like that. But that was my problem, not Baume's. He wanted me to live my job seven days a week.

The editor of a Sunday paper always has a news editor or associate editor, a number two, to direct the reporters, devise ideas for stories, coordinate news collection and look after innumerable other operational details. Baume insisted I didn't need any assistance. The two opposition Sunday papers had assistant editors, chiefs of staff as well as news editors. My small staff and I, he confided, were "brilliant" enough to handle it all. It was a non-stop circus which we aptly named "The Sunday Miracle". The buck of course was mine.

He kept cutting back the staff and insisting on irritating economies, even reducing the number of radio cars available for reporters.

'Why don't you quit?' he would say when I protested. 'You haven't got the guts, have you?'

'You fire me.' (That would have cost him a packet: I had a three-year contract and a 12 year severance provision.)

Then he'd try getting at me through my loyalties to my staff.

'I want Plummer fired.' (Jack Plummer, the chief sub-editor was an outstanding journalist who later became editor of the *Sun*.)

'No.'

'Give me your recommendation and I'll do it for you.'

'No.'

'You'll regret it.'

I didn't. It was all pretty awful while it lasted but unconsciously I was using his harrowing pressure to strengthen my knowledge of myself. I wasn't humble or saintly in my attitude. I'm sure I never gave anyone that impression. I was a pretty tough newspaperman; you had to be to get into that league and stay there. And besides, "surrender to what is" is not submission to the oppressor. For me, surrender is surrender to the greater Being within. What happens outside is habit, circumstance and appearance – another battlefield altogether. I never stopped complaining about Baume to my family and friends. They all knew from my lips what a swine I thought he was. I never saw myself as a good example to others. The simple fact is, I wasn't.

After 12 months of Baume's unrelenting harassment, my wife Betty and I agreed that I must quit as editor. The next morning when I walked into the office my letter of resignation was in my pocket. My secretary informed me I was required downstairs in the office of my colleague, the editor of the *Daily Mirror*, Jack Toohey. There I was introduced to two men. They were the managing director and the editor in chief of one of the opposition newspaper groups which owned the *Sydney Morning Herald*. Our company had been sold.

'You are to take no more instructions from Baume,' said the managing director. 'You are responsible to Mr Clinch here. He is the new editorial director.' (Lindsay Clinch was one of Sydney's most famous newspapermen.)

It was a miracle, the kind of personal miracle that occurs when the consciousness is being guided intensely towards the truth. When the lesson is learned there is no necessity, and no time, for the particular circumstances to continue. The difficulty is you can never anticipate the miracle. You have to hold on and on and on until you are released by circumstance or you know within yourself with unshakeable conviction that the ordeal is over. It might take 12 months, or it might take a lifetime, depending on the depth of the identification or unconsciousness. Right surrender is the feeling that you can't possibly bear another minute while knowing you can wait forever.

As I returned to my office, Baume's head appeared around his door, which was next to mine.

'Hey Barry, have you got a minute?'

His change of manner was quite comical. He ushered me in charmingly, invited me to be seated and sat down at his desk.

'Barry,' he said, leaning forward confidentially, 'have you heard anything?'

'Yes.'

'Official?'

'My word.'

'What?'

'You're out!'

I had always imagined this would be a delicious moment but it wasn't. He must have known about the sale. It was incredible that they hadn't informed him officially. There had been rumours going around for months but no one had suspected the old fox would be ousted if there was a takeover. He had a fabulous contract with four years to run. It would have cost a fortune to buy him out.

Baume nodded and went quiet. Then with magnificent aplomb he drew himself up in his chair.

'Me out!' he exploded. He was his old self and it suited him much better. He slammed his fist down on the desk. 'Dear boy,' (one of his favourite expressions) 'they'll never get *me* out.' This he believed.

But they did. And they gave *him* the treatment. It took three months of the most punishing isolation to get him to vacate, to quit voluntarily. They took his personal chauffeur, then his company car, and then denied him access to the transport pool. They reassigned his personal assistant and removed his two private secretaries. His bank of phones never rang officially, no one knocked on his door. His free newspapers and magazines were stopped and the copyboys didn't answer his buzzer.

Even Baume had his Baume.

Baume wasn't a bad guy. He was stiff medicine that helped to cure me of some of my early delusions. We had our laughs. I respected him for what he was. And there was an extraordinary sequel a year later.

After the new company took over, I was informed they would be bringing in one of their own editors, Ray Beckett of the *Sun*, and I was invited to stay on as news editor, which I did.

But my great desire as a youth to be a newspaperman had been sated by 20 years experience, from copyboy to editor. So in 1960 I resigned. I moved to Parliament House, Sydney, as Press Secretary to the new Leader of the New South Wales Opposition party, Robert Askin (later Sir Robert Askin, the Liberal Premier). The job had been offered to me before it was advertised. Later I asked Askin, who I had not known personally before, what made him finally choose me.

'Eric Baume,' he said. 'He gave you a wonderful recommendation.'

# CHAPTER 2

# ALL IS PROVIDED

I worked for Askin for the following two years at Parliament House, in Macquarie Street. This was the next stage in my spiritual preparation – an intensive study period incredibly coincidental with my rather mundane job. It was a dream opportunity that anyone with a raging thirst for truth will appreciate. I was given the time and facilities to read through the very extensive and selective philosophy and metaphysics section of the Parliamentary Library, one of the finest libraries in Australia – while at the same time being paid a top salary.

By a further coincidence, the librarian, who was just retiring as I arrived, happened to be personally active in psychic research and was something of a theosophist with an absorbing interest in Eastern philosophies! Naturally, these subjects were more than well represented on the shelves. His successor, Russell Cope, also was a deeply studious man who happened to be interested in every aspect of philosophy and religion. He became a personal friend and would inform me whenever "interesting" new books were coming in.

With discrimination, I read everything. I read the histories of the religions, great and obscure, and especially the words attributed to their founders, actual and traditional. As a rule, only the original sources of truth are meaningful, seldom the versions and commentaries of followers. Anyone who quotes another person on fundamentals, or to make his or her point, usually has no real knowledge. I read the lives of the saints, the philosophers ancient and modern, Eastern and Western, Persian, Arabian and all the worthwhile writers on metaphysics. I also read every old and recent account of mystical and psychic experience acceptable to my developing discrimination. (Discrimination in this sense is a power that manifests in the genuinely expanding psyche, enabling rubbish or helpful material to be distinguished at a glance.)

Intellectual writers I avoided like the plague. These are the authors who have not experienced first-hand the things they write about. They quote and copy others, expound beliefs and draw conclusions that are only rationally valid. They are sincere, clever and yet often harmful to the earnest seeker because their arguments are so convincing. The discriminating consciousness can identify an intellectual as soon as he or she speaks, or from a couple of written sentences. Truth is quick, simple, straightforward and instantly recognisable. Contrary to popular belief, it does not create, build, persuade or involve. It dissolves the only things that real knowledge can – doubt and argument.

When I joined Askin he had only recently been appointed Leader of the Opposition. Two years remained before the next general election. His policy was to proceed quietly. The Labor Party had been in government in New South Wales for 16 years. Askin and his party were vulnerable to accusations of inexperience in government. The two things he wanted to avoid most were, first, the temptation for opposition leaders to comment on every tinpot issue to please the sensationalist media, and second, acquiring a reputation for criticising anything the government proposed, just to show he was around.

Askin had a superb flair for publicity. He had always written his own speeches, was smoothly articulate, shrewd and in many ways a lone wolf. He had worked hard over the years as a backbencher, building up close personal relationships with the most influential lobby journalists. Like all successful politicians, he leaked stories even against his own party members if he thought it necessary. As far as he and I were concerned, Askin decided he would continue to look after the main metropolitan press lobby and I would keep the publicity going to the 120 provincial and suburban newspapers and radio stations throughout the rest of the state.

This involved my continued presence in the Parliamentary Library checking file copies of newspapers as they came in for important local issues for Askin to comment on. Apart from preparing and sending out these stories, we could only issue one statewide press release every couple of weeks for fear that editors would start discarding them as political propaganda. I tried to do more in several other ways but couldn't. So my job was almost a sinecure and took relatively little of my time.

My personal relationship with Askin was most amicable. But the fact was that Bob needed a buddy, not a press officer. He got one a couple of years after I left in Alan Green, a man about his own age with similar interests and who, incidentally, had hired me as a young reporter when I joined the *Daily Mirror* in 1948. When Alan Green died, Askin, who was then Premier, gave him a state funeral. They were that close.

So by the huge coincidence that has been my life, I had several hours to spare during most days of those two years to read and absorb, without neglecting the work for which I was being paid. The Party's gift to me when I left was Bertrand Russell's *The History of Western Philosophy* – signed by Askin and many of the members of Parliament.

Years later, when Askin died after ten years as Premier (in 1981), it was reported in various media that he had been corrupt – a friend and protector of organised crime and criminals, a taker of bribes – and that he had even sold knighthoods for $60,000 apiece. I saw no sign of this in the man who lived with his wife (no children) in an ordinary apartment at Collaroy, a northern beach-side suburb. All I observed in him was the desire to do something really effective for the good of the state and its people. To this purpose and to pay for his election promises, his secret agenda in opposition (to which I was privy) was to substantially extend the licensing of poker machines and the tax on them. This policy, dependent on gambling, could have been the source of any rot when he came to power.


For an individual whose consciousness is in the process of being spiritually expanded, all the circumstances needed to aid and impel him or her are provided. Mine is a classic case. But all cases are classic in their way, if the individual's story is ever told or reviewed. In retrospect, the truth of the life reveals itself. In the early years the essential cohesive purpose is rarely apparent, except in flashes, because we are then still so identified with our personal confusion and conflicting emotional values. But this thread of incomprehensible purpose which makes the life individually significant and meaningful is what is traditionally known as "the way of the spiritual life".

In writing this book my endeavour is to show this thread linking and shaping the salient events in my life, so that others similarly engaged may be encouraged to look back and see its indelible tracing in their own lives. Looking back and beginning to understand the fantastic precision of it all, is in itself a necessary exercise in the long struggle to disidentify with the human illusion of personal control.

Reading and hearing the truth is a particularly important part of the process. Before a person can proceed beyond the first stages of conscious catharsis such as I have so far described, it is necessary to have been exposed to the religious idea. The religious idea is inculcated into everyone in some form or other in childhood. So we all have it. Whatever culture the individual is born into, there is also always present the superstitions and magical notions of the parents, tribe or society which he or she just can't avoid being exposed to; these are all part of the universal religious idea.

To disown these concepts in adulthood is irrelevant; the religious idea is a potency and, once encountered as conditioning, is in the individual to stay. And just as well. For when he or she has weird dreams, or psychic experiences due to energies beyond sensory understanding, these can take comprehensible form in the mind as visions and voices of saints, Christ, UFOs, Buddha, the Virgin Mary, angels, demons, the devil, gods and all the rest of the superstitious or spiritual hierarchy including "God".

When a person is firmly spiritually orientated, the elementary conditioned religious idea is "updated", refined by meditation and conscious discriminative practices. The earlier imaginative images and superstitions are transformed and a more sensitive and less formal comprehension remains. The person then finds himself or herself reading or listening to traditional metaphysical or philosophical ideas with new understanding.

The scales do literally fall from the eyes. The Old and New Testaments and the Eastern religions seem to hold vivid and vibrant new meaning. Familiar phrases and passages become filled with esoteric significance. Revelations that mean nothing at all to others leap out of the pages. Even the occult and pseudo sciences, such as astrology, may seem to embody that same element of truth so avidly and insatiably pursued. In the intellect and in the blood throbs a new pitch of excitement as though for the first time the individual is beginning to know what it is to learn and to live.

But from there on the process is more and more demanding. The purpose of this penetrating new knowledge is to prepare the mind for the approaching change of consciousness so that it can withstand the accompanying pressure and chaos without cracking.

Mind and consciousness are not identical. Mind has no knowledge of its own – it is a reaction to experience and memory. It can become unhinged in frightening or terrifying circumstances when it can't name what is happening; when it can't relate to familiar patterns, it dreads its own extinction. This dread the mind often apprehends as madness.

Consciousness, on the other hand, is behind the mind. It is forever still, unmoving. The spiritual life is about gradually reducing the robotic and emotional movements of the mind until it becomes as still as the consciousness behind it. Immediately this happens there is either a deep insight, a realisation or, in the case of a permanent cessation, the illuminating state and knowledge of immortal life. Only the human mind and emotions stand in the way.

The expansion of individual consciousness is an acutely traumatic process. No precedent for it exists in experience, in memory or instinct. It is too original, radical and truly subjective to be approximated by thought or emotion. The separation from the mind leaves the mind suspended in an unstable and seemingly isolated condition. Fortunately, in the vast majority of cases the separation is very gradual.

The process of awakening towards enlightenment involves encounters with forces and energies that are quite horrific at times (as well as transcendentally beautiful). The person's life – if he or she is to receive a permanent illumination – is literally turned upside down. Relationships are smashed or rearranged to obliterate the claims of the past; the values, attachments, prejudices, expectations, assumptions, sentiments, the layers of the years of conditioning and the secretions of habit must all go into the dissolving fire of conscious scrutiny. The foundations of the psychological self have to be given the acid test to find out what is essential and what is not. The emotional upheaval can be devastating.

It is a long, long, wearying affair. The mind, so unassailably sure of its independent existence among the solid comfortable roots of sense-perception and its conditioned responses, starts to panic at the first weird creaks, as consciousness starts to shine through. No longer able to perceive one tangible world, it senses the presence of an oddly more powerful reality within. Here the mind of relationships has no frame of reference as there are no relationships in reality. All the mind possesses to fall back on is its knowledge of the religious idea. This is just enough to lean on – if you don't go crazy – until the mind attunes to the increasing subtlety of its own consciousness.

# CHAPTER 3

# GOD-MAD

etty and I had been married in 1951 when I was 25 and she was
23. Our daughter Annette was born the following year and
Scott two years later. At that time there was nothing overtly
spiritual in our lives. Betty was attractive and like myself a very strong
personality, a Leo. We got along pretty well together. Did I love her? I
thought I did. I had never loved anyone more, anyway. I liked living
with her. It took us a while to get sexually attuned but after that we were
physically well suited.

In 1960 when I went to work for Askin, Betty and I and the children
moved into a new bungalow we'd built at Wahroonga, one of Sydney's
lovely northern suburbs featuring a profusion of trees, parks and natural
forest. I was doing well. The home was designed for us by the architect
Harry Seidler, his last private house before he went on to establish an
international reputation. It was very comfortably furnished to our taste,
and we bought a new car every 18 months or so. Betty's parents were
comfortably off and had retired early to their seaside property at
Narooma on the south coast of New South Wales. The 150 acre estate
was the most beautiful place I had ever known. We used to go there for
our holidays, either staying with friends in our "shack" or with my par-
ents-in-law in the large house.

The property had its own white sand beach and the climate was so mild it was possible for us to swim eight months of the year. The four of us and our dog Clementine used to spend most of the days on the beach and swimming in the rock pools. That was when I wasn't fishing up the river two miles away, or from an old wooden rowing boat I used to launch, not so intrepidly, through the breakers from the beach. To me it was idyllic. A three week holiday I spent there with my family and Clementine before the turmoil started was perfect in every respect. I remember telling my friends repeatedly at the time that I was the luckiest man in the world. I had everything. And I *did* have everything. I knew I did. It is not uncommon when the consciousness is about to undergo a radical change for the life being left behind to be experienced as relative perfection, the ideal.

That was the signal for the beginning of the end of the personality called Barry Long. The process had speeded up when we moved to Wahroonga. By then an exceptional love of life had dawned in me, not as a particular activity but as a whole, a state. It was not a blind faith but an intrinsic knowledge of life's rightness. To me, life was a vaster thing than mere living and dying. It still is. Life today I know is consciousness. Living is the external reality, the relationship, the conflict. In those days I expressed my knowledge in this song:

> My friend Life is death and birth
> My friend Life is the whole wide earth.
> My friend Life is sorrow and a tear
> But my friend Life does not know fear.
> All the people would drag me down
> But not while my friend Life's around.
> My friend Life is change and pain
> But that's all part of my friend's game.
> Play the game and it can be fun
> Fight to win and the fun's all done.
> My friend Life is an outstretched hand
> It's your friend too if you grab it, Man.

I know now this love of life was a formal aspect of my love of God. The love of God is the love of no-thing. Such love is the pressure on the mind of the pure religious idea without image or concept. It carries with it the desire to be good, to be of service to others, to shrink from thanks, to take no credit for the good you might appear to do. I don't remember ever asking God at that time for anything; that would have been an absurdity when there is no thing to ask of or for. But I was continuously pouring out my thanks in a wordless passion. Thanks for what? I don't know. That is the subtlety of it.

My love of God has now all gone as something apart from my life and it is impossible to reproduce these separative emotions as they were then. But the simple fact was I could not get enough of God; and when the divine energy came in brief moments between my awful longing, I was radiant to myself. My desire for this indescribable nothingness was as insatiable as it seemed unnatural. For a long time I was literally God-mad. Yet it did not affect my working life, mostly because it was a positive expression. I worked with my passion for God, in my passion for God. I did everything for God. I lived for God.

In India, the God-mad phenomenon is relatively well known. There they have a name for these people – *masts*. In many cases the mast is so God-mad that he can't work; work just doesn't exist for him because in his love of God he has everything, and there is no other desire even to exist or survive. One of India's great sages, Meher Baba, who died in 1969, was himself once God-mad. After his enlightenment he founded an ashram with special quarters for masts where they could eat and sleep without having to pay. Inevitably, he found himself inundated with impostors and had to abandon the scheme.

It was either Meher Baba or another famous Indian master, Ramakrishna, who told the story of a mast who didn't bother to leave when his hut caught fire and he had to be dragged out, his face horribly burnt but still alight with the rapture of devotion. He refused to acknowledge his burns. 'It is God's face,' he said. The next morning the burns had healed. The point I'm making is not about the reputed miracle but the fact that obsessive God-love is a distinct human phenomenon accepted by other cultures. A *sannyasin* who gives up everything to find God is seldom, in his wanderings, turned away from an Indian household. But in the West it is usually a case of God help anyone who is incapacitated by this strange spiritual passion and can't cope.

God-madness of course is well recorded in history in the writings of people like St Teresa, Kierkegaard, Boehme, Meister Eckhart, St John of the Cross, Thomas à Kempis, St Augustine and even the Roman emperor Marcus Aurelius. One of the extraordinary facts that emerges from these works is the way the inspirational utterances and insights of God-loving saints like Teresa had to be "modified" to satisfy the religious forms and ideas laid down by very worldly Roman Catholic primates and priests.

Obviously, there must be many people who are God-mad in this generation, too. Where are they, I wonder? And especially, where are the borderline cases who reject the old religious connotations but still can't rid themselves of the inexplicable divine longing? It seems to me that something of this obscure love-obsession is behind the modern malaise of young people searching so desperately for new values and new significance, and sometimes finding it for a while in the love-obliterating substitute world of drugs or sex.

My love of God did not happen suddenly. It was a graduated surge that kept mounting and mounting as I read, meditated and wept. The weeping was unbelievable. The emotion would suddenly seize me – infinite longing over cosmic distances of separation from all that I could ever desire – and I would sob with a spasm of unspeakable emptiness and loneliness. It would happen in public, in buses, trains, anywhere. I would have to race out of a business meeting or conference into the washroom to let the torrent flow.

A poem I wrote while walking along the beach sums up the desolation I sometimes felt.

> Cry seabird
> Sharp and doleful cry
> Yours should be a happy song.
> Sky, wind, sea and sand
> Here the sweetest notes belong.
> Cry again seabird
> Or could it be
> That the sadness I hear
> Is only in me?

As I have said, my spiritual process did not affect my ability to cope with the external world. Not that I am aware of, anyway. I never got carpeted or had my work criticised; on the contrary, I always seemed to be promoted. I was in fact becoming more and more alert and aware. I couldn't help but notice an amazing capacity developing in me for seeing the fact. My power to destroy arguments and contentions based on false premises made it more and more difficult for others to have a simple conversation with me. I could not tolerate an idle or unconscious statement.

At no time was I driven to try to change the world. But I was impelled to change or destroy attitudes in people, leaving them nothing but the vacuum of their own uncertainty. I was cruel and pitiless in my new-found intensity and strength. I noticed I spoke with an authority that I had never dreamed of possessing. I was right; that was the problem when others tried to refute or criticise. I was right – not because I said so, but because the point was self-evident and incontestable on any but emotional grounds. And emotion is incapable of producing the fact.

Before this I had never been sure of my opinions. I used to memorise what I read or thought sounded convincing and repeat those views. I think I could say I had no mind of my own in this respect and had to rely a good deal on my personality. I remember distinctly the uneasiness I felt in having no real values to relate my impressions to. There was the usual "right" and "wrong" that had been instilled in me since childhood – but is this really enough? For me it wasn't. Conventional values I knew to be inadequate but I had nothing to substitute for them and they did seem to work to everyone else's satisfaction. This amazed me as it was clearly a double-value world, a sham of appearances based on emotional criteria – not on what was the fact. It was like a huge conspiracy in which everyone had tacitly agreed not to mention what was wrong so they could live a collective lie. Why they should want to, I could never work out. They were certainly not happy. It was life to them. To me it was plain delusion.

Later, when the awakening began, I was to write this song:

> How do you write the story of a million years
> How do you write the story of a river of tears
> How do you write the story of eternity
> How do you write the mystery of you and me?
> O, the whole world's agroaning and travailing in agony
> Aweeping and afearing as it shuffles towards its destiny.

25

> How do you write the story of this tragic throng
> How do you write
> How do you write
> How can you right what's wrong?

Obviously in my first 30 years of living I was "lost" without really knowing it. I couldn't admit my uncertainty to anyone without evoking the double-standard reflex which insists that the double-standard is the rule and, what's more, is right! The camouflage for my own uncertainties was all I had. With the coming of the spirit I discovered that the camouflage was all the others had too, deep down. It was then that I began refusing to acknowledge the double-standard – unless it suited me. Now I spoke, not in opinions and beliefs, which are the index of emotionalism and double-standards, but in incontestable fact – power.

For the first time I knew what I was talking about. I didn't know it as personal erudition; only that it came through me. It was of me but not me. Neither personal cleverness nor any exalted ability to sway others with oratory or argument was involved – only the simple fact that what was said was true. Every discussion I had with another about the fundamentals of life ended in silence. If others had made the same points, silence would still have ensued. For the fact is universal. It is not personal. The difficulty is in facing up to it; if you can't face it, you can't find it.

My poor mother, who always loved me far beyond anything I deserved as a son, thought I was going mad, though she would never say it. She asked me in a most gentle, anxious way to visit a psychiatrist, the best in Sydney, and she would arrange it. I said I would if she could produce from among her numerous friends and acquaintances one person who could dispute the truth of what I said.

To me, any diagnosed condition or analysis of the mind of an individual who speaks or writes the truth is irrelevant. The only substantive question is: Is what is being said true? If it is, I must listen and learn even from the fool. If that is not the proper question then I might be tempted by the same reasoning to forbid the brilliant surgeon from operating because he is left-handed.

In those early days of the spirit, the cold, detached, naked fact or truth was a terrible weapon in my hand. The trouble with the truth is it destroys the lie in the individual, and most of our relationships and values are built on this euphoric and flimsy stuff. I made husbands and wives examine their relationships with terrible results; churchmen stare at their pretence, fathers at their doting selfishness, mothers at their own crying need which they called love.

In my professional life I was able to accept and participate in the traditional conventions and double-standards, so there was no conflict there. I drank, sometimes to excess, ate what I wished, swore when I did, lied as I thought necessary and did most things that most other human beings do. The point is I wasn't different from any other "sinner", though perhaps a bit worse than some. In my experience, the spirit is not a reward for goodness defined by a double-standard ethic. All I can say is I was aware of what I did. That is not an excuse for me or for anyone. It is just a fact.

In my business relationships I behaved "normally" – I was not moved to interfere with these. Double-standards are the essence of business technique. If you don't observe the rules of the game you can't play – and by the way of things I wasn't a monk or a saint, I was a player. Only where the unconscious personal emotion of individual business associates impinged on my solar plexus did I "speak the truth" to them. This sensation of sensing the emotion in another is extremely subtle and produces in me a kind of impersonal concern that indicates they have a need for some self-truth to be revealed.

Meanwhile, my torturing and emotionally incinerating love of God persisted. It was dreadful for Betty. She had no understanding of the truth whatever. I might have been speaking another language. Try as I did, I could not penetrate her consciousness. We clashed and quarrelled incessantly. I used to provoke her with my perception and she would retaliate with the fury of sheer uncomprehending intransigence – as well as fear. In the beginning she had gone along with my enthusiasm but it was becoming a threat to our marriage, not to mention my sanity which she must often have doubted.

The dear, poor woman started to despise (I make that judgment only to convey a reaction) whatever it was that I loved with such all-consuming devotion. I used to get up in the middle of the night to meditate – I was actually woken, made to get up – and we'd have a blazing row about my coming down to earth. At weekends I'd bury myself in my spiritual books and share nothing because there was nothing to share. She hid the books. I had to hide others under the house and creep down to read them when I was supposed to be in the garden.

She was flagellating me as much as I was her. Each of us was torturing the other. Inwardly, I was being taught to turn the other cheek. This was only for me of course; to her I must have seemed incredibly selfish and callous. Betty used to find me weeping and sobbing in my chair and would gaze at me with disbelief and inconsolable misery. The search for truth is a selfish search. Couples can only go so far together. In the end you must die alone and you must be reborn alone. Still, this stage of Betty's terrible travail of which I was the instrument was to end, again in a "small" miracle, which I shall describe in its place.

During those years I was indeed God-mad. As I have said, God-madness is not uncommon in the history of mystical experience, but it is relatively rare, especially in the West. On many occasions Betty had to witness my rolling on the bedroom floor in an agony of longing for this unnameable formless love.

CHAPTER 4

# SPIRITUAL EXPERIENCES

Everything I did in those early days at Wahroonga was related to the spirit. My creativity seemed to be a direct line to the centre of my being. Everything I said and wrote had to it the ring of eternals.

Annette, my daughter, wanted a poem to put on the cover of a school project book she was preparing about lighthouses. It came instantly. There was only one lighthouse to me, the truth; and one darkness – unconsciousness.

> Who stands alone by day and night
> By day a rather pointless sight
> By night a restless living light
> Despoiler of the dark's delight?
> The lighthouse.
> Who in this world of man and time
> Is given essence best to shine
> Towards horizon's jesting line
> Lighting naught but the anxious mind?
> The lighthouse.

By this time my spiritual process had revealed to me the pernicious action of all thought. I knew that everyone who persisted in associative and discursive thinking – and that added up to everyone – could not be free or see the truth; that is, could not see the world as it really is. The world as we see it most of the time consists of the past. We look at it through the eye of emotion.

> The cry of the sinking heart
> Is the sigh of the thinking heart
> For if you think
> Then you must drink
> At the place of the sinking heart.
> Your thought is but spawn of the past
> Caught on memory's treacherous cast
> And if you think
> Then you must drink
> At the place of the sinking heart.

My spiritual experiences were frequent. One night I was sitting in the bathroom reading Aurobindo's commentary on the *Bhagavad Gita* (Song of the Blessed One) when I had my first experience of what I'd heard called the *kundalini shakti* power. It shot up my spine without warning, whipped my body as erect as a poker and rolled my eyeballs up until I felt they must have been looking into the top of my head. Tears streamed down my cheeks in emotionless poise. All was still, very still. Something was said by the energy but I can't remember it now.

Another day I was standing in the lounge room when I realised I "knew" something. No one else was in the room. I said, 'I am the light of the world. Even if I remain in this one spot forever they will flock to me.' This is the universal consciousness which appears in some form or other on the way to enlightenment. It does not necessarily have to manifest as such again; no real experience of truth needs to be repeated. Once is enough. Only in the circumstantial world does experience have to be repeated to produce an expert. To yearn for repetition of spiritual revelation or upliftment is a desire of the mind and emotions. It is best to leave these things to that which initiated them.

Compassion is another form of love that was shown to me. It was different from the usual notion of compassion. It happened to me three times, once in Australia and twice in India. The first occasion was after I had interviewed some of Askin's constituents one Saturday morning at an office near his home. When Askin had official appointments, or his private secretary was unavailable, I used to fill in. In the summer, Betty and I would pack the kids and some lunch into the car and drive 15 miles across to the coast. About midday, after finishing the interviews, I'd join them on the beach.

On this particular Saturday I was walking towards the beach past a hospital for crippled children. The youngsters were sitting on the lawn and in wheelchairs. I stopped and leant on the wooden fence gazing at them. I felt nothing. I was not a sentimentalist. The fact had forced me to accept life as it was – unless I was moved to do something about it – and that included the reality of suffering and crippled children.

The passion hit me without warning. I doubled up, almost hitting my head on the railing. My whole being collapsed in a paroxysm of infinite compassion that was not of me. My body sobbed and shook in the depths of every cell. My weeping for God had never been anything like this. That was an outgoing, an e-motion. This was an incoming, a silent cry of all-knowing, sharing in all-present pain and infirmity. Mine were the eyes through which it looked into the world. Then it was gone. No lingering sadness. Nothing. All that was left was me. But I was cleaner.

In India it happened while I was watching a young goat grazing contentedly on the side of a hill. 'Poor little goat,' I sobbed in a convulsion of knowing the pain of not-knowing, the fragile trust and bewilderment of awakening consciousness which throbs in all living things. The next time was for a young Indian boy happily striding down a track with his dog trotting beside him. Again my being sobbed with the same unbelievable profundity of understanding. Poor little boy; poor little goat. My God, how I loved them.

On both these occasions only normalcy and no apparent suffering appeared in the subjects – but that all-knowing compassionate sublimity that was not of me knew better. I know now that it was divine compassion for all that is born, for to be born is to be born into inevitable pain or suffering.

At Wahroonga I used to be woken up at night and taught how to breathe. I had never practised breathing methods. I must have read about them in books on yoga but not with sufficient impact to make me want

31

to practise. The first time was uncanny but not frightening. There was the
knowledge that it was "being done" for me, that I was only the observer
and that if I could do anything about it I would only get in the way.

I woke up on my back and watched my body being gently forced to
exhale and inhale with deliberate precision. My breathing was varied
dramatically so that gradually I became aware of the action of breathing
and all that it involved instead of it being just an instinctive, habitual
process which hitherto had just "happened". The phenomenon repeated
itself most nights for several weeks. It produced among other things a
remarkable feeling of well-being and an increased sense of participation
in my own existence. (Betty lying beside me was never aware of what
was going on, to my knowledge.)

The same breathing pattern then began happening during the day.
I didn't have the problem of "forgetting to remember"; it would just start
up. As it became part of my waking life the nightly tuition ceased. I
would suddenly find myself "breathing" in meditation in the bus, train,
car or cinema. It became more and more my natural way of breathing:
I breathed to a pattern that was no pattern – a pattern that was set and
changed every moment.

When I took a breath I didn't know how long I would hold it, or if I
would hold it; nor did I know at what rate I would release it or at what
stage of exhalation I would breathe in again. I learned to breathe without expectation so that there was no grabbing, no panic, no mind
interference. It seemed I was prepared to hold my breath till I died if
necessary.

The body itself is a consciousness that has to be raised. Every body is
in a different stage of consciousness. New dimensions of breathing introduce new awareness and help to break up old cellular and neural
patterns. Also gawkish and clumsy walking, slovenly eating habits,
excessive slackness in speaking, are all possible indicators of unconscious areas that may have to be consciously addressed and refined.

The lightness of the weight or feel of the body is another noticeable
feature of developing spiritual consciousness. I was first made aware of
this by Betty who frequently remarked that she could not feel the weight
of my leg, arm or body when it lay across her. As the spiritual life
deepens, a certain grace and lightness of movement seems to appear
in the body actions. I'm moved to relate this in the world to the artistry

and the fluidity of movement of the exceptional dancer, ice skater, gymnast and the like.

Art and beauty in all their forms are really the expression of the spirit, though the performing artist need not necessarily be aware of the divine origins of his or her artistry. But the art of the spiritual life is the final realisation of the source of all art and beauty both in the world and beyond it. In other words, the art of art is the realisation of God or supreme truth.

# CHAPTER 5

# MASTERS

E verybody seriously engaged in the spiritual process is eventually provided with a teacher or a master (guru). It is not haphazard; the teacher must come when the man or woman is ready. There is no need to search for him. And his teaching is always exactly what is required for the individual to take the next step towards greater self-discovery.

The unknown quantity is the stage of the person's "readiness". Most people who read this book will have reached a certain stage of self-knowledge because they will be recognising some of what is said and described as being identical with their own experiences. Truth is proved, not by argument or persuasion, but in your own experience. Truth or self-knowledge is beyond purely academic and intellectual minds because those minds are concerned with acquired learning and not with the person's own experience.

A spiritual teacher theoretically needs only a little more knowledge (power) than the person he is teaching. As the aspirant's self-knowledge deepens he or she is likely to move on to another, more perceptive teacher. And finally he or she will find themselves in front of a true master or guru, a God-realised teacher.

Such masters are distinguished by the fact that their knowledge of truth is original and unlimited in relation to their students. The paradox of all God-realised masters is that they don't know anything "themselves"; they have been raised above the mind's knowing practice and have instantaneous access to the truth required in any moment. By not "knowing" anything they have ceased to exist as persons (in relation to truth) and have merged with and realised the one Consciousness behind all.

Masters are conscious of their role and immediately responsive to the unconscious needs of truth in others. They can teach anyone at any level even by their presence – the power of the master's realised Consciousness. (God-realisation does not necessarily invest the master with tantric power, which means he will not be able to teach wholly at the sexual level.) A master will, and can, go through hell if necessary to help another. Otherwise, who would there be to help those in hell?

Ivan was 14 years my senior. We first met as newspaper reporters when he was with the Sydney *Sun* and I with the opposition *Daily Mirror*. We had nothing in common and did not get much further than exchanging casual nods when we happened to meet on the job. That wasn't very often as Ivan was employed on courts and city politics and my main assignment was police rounds. The only distinct recollection I have of him in those days was an incident in a popular Sydney restaurant when he and a couple of other journalists wrecked the place in a drunken brawl. Ivan, a bachelor, played pretty hard.

A few years later, when I was acting news editor of the *Mirror*, Ivan came in for a job. For some reason I was prejudiced and turned him down. Being a highly respected and well known journalist, he went straight over me to the editor-in-chief who immediately appointed him to the reporting staff. He didn't seem to hold any animosity and we worked well enough together in an impersonal way. He was a man who could be depended on to get a story and that was all that concerned me.

A couple of years passed. I transferred to another department to learn the technical side of newspaper production as make-up sub-editor in the hot-metal composing room. The next I heard of Ivan he was in India, 'sitting on a mountain contemplating his navel' as a wag colleague described it. We all had a good laugh and forgot him. In 30 seconds flat I had again dismissed Ivan.

Four or five years later, around 1962, he once again entered my life. A journalist friend told me Ivan was back from India. He said he'd mentioned to Ivan some of the peculiar things I'd told him that had happened to me and Ivan had suggested a meeting. (Ivan says it was me who suggested a meeting and I'm not going to dispute this as I was intensely grateful to have him there.)

Ivan was the first man of God-realised Consciousness I had met. He came out of his Himalayan retreat at exactly the right time. I couldn't attempt to tell his story but apparently it was a fairly typical old-style conversion – wine, women, dissatisfaction, discontent, self-disgust, turning away from the world, devotion to the divine, pain (physical as well as mental in his case) and finally realisation at the age of 49.

Ivan had basically followed the teachings of the Buddha. But like all men of truth he saw the truth wherever it was and never tried to restrict it to any particular religion or belief. I remember him saying he was a Brahmachari – that is, he had given up sexual love.

Ivan and I were of totally different temperaments. Yet only one man I have met since seems to have possessed the same love of the divine. Perhaps that love is the common ground we shared and which drew him to me (or vice versa). Ivan frequently used to read me extracts from the diaries he kept for five years in India right up to his final realisation. They read like poetry.

In India, Ivan at first stayed around the western hill stations of Pauri, Lansdowne, Mussoorie and Simla. He lived the simple life of a sannyasin, doing everything for himself. He was not attracted by the group idea so popular among disciples from the West after the Beatles discovered India eight or nine years later. Ivan lived where and as he was led until finally he made his way east to Almora, another Himalayan hill station 300 miles north of Delhi. There he had his realisation in 1961 and three weeks later was back in Sydney, heading towards our meeting.

When I met Ivan in a Sydney hotel a few months after his return from India, he was endeavouring to cope with what he described as 'that wretched business of having to make a living again.' How can a realised man speak this way? Very easily. A great deal is said about the "bliss" that comes from realisation. But this bliss is not always experienced in relation to the external world, not for some time anyway. The change in consciousness is so great, so fundamentally disturbing and reorienting that it can take months, and even years, for the personal machinery to adjust.

Years later, at one of my meetings, a silent and serious man sitting near me in a faded orange robe, said, 'I know I am realised. I know. But I fear. I have to identify with something, even if it is only a name. I need something to hold on to.'

Could such a man be realised? Yes. Indeed. His words revealed it immediately. This was not the buoyant, confident claptrap about bliss one hears so often from those who are blissful in their ignorance and bliss-less in their knowledge. This man knew. But he was engaged in sorting himself out in relation to the persona, the apparatus that must respond to the competitive world – or else. Within, he was on the edge of nothing, face to face with neverlastingness. In his realisation of the truth he was staring at the fact that there is no continuity of himself or anything else, that every moment represents the death and creation of everything, that all is new moment to moment.

He was too vast to comprehend his self in that vastness – so instantaneously new each moment – that he required some sort of formal identity for a while to mirror his existence. What this man apprehended as fear, which is a negative state, was in reality uncertainty. And any realised man will tell you and be able to explain that uncertainty, massive total uncertainty, is the positive creative side of being... of being Being... of being Consciousness.

Not everyone who realises the ultimate is built to cope with the competitive, jackal Western world. Some have to retreat in silence and continuous meditation to gradually repair the huge rents that occur in the persona so that it can once again begin performing reasonably. I had no great problem in this regard but that was not my doing. It was because I am what I am. And there are individuals like Ivan – beautiful men who have seen the truth – who also, being what they are, find it difficult to cope with normal living for a while, until they are led (or lead themselves) into the niche they are to occupy, or the purpose which is to occupy them.

Most people cannot just drop out of the world. Those few who ever realise consciousness in the West are deep in the heart of a hostile culture until they can adjust. In India, it is a totally different atmosphere. There, the realised man (or the uncertain sannyasin) – even if he is a well-read imposter – is guaranteed a degree of respect, sympathy and understanding by 90% of the population. The Indian mind is a product of 6,000 years of socio-religious tradition and is conditioned to accept that God-realisation is the highest good and the striving for it the most noble and difficult of aspirations. There the begging bowl, with its earnest innocence, humility and self-inflicted poverty, is a symbol of hope and faith to ordinary people.

In the sterile, whiter than white, scientific West, the realised man is likely to be locked up or discarded as a useless object and a social misfit. Fortunately, society can only abuse and ill-treat his apparatus. The realised man is always untouchable within. But those who love him and feel for him are affronted. Everyone engaged in the spiritual life should try to remember that sometimes it takes time for the machinery and circumstances to catch up.

There is little difference within, fundamentally, between God-realised individuals. Each has realised "nothing"; for "nothing" (that which is beyond words and existence) is where knowledge of God begins. Only in the expression of that knowledge, and according to the depth of God-realisation, does any difference manifest. The hostility and fear in the Western mind represent the unconscious and ignorant forces which the realised ones in the West have overcome. The Indian gurus in their relatively sympathetic environment are protected from this.

There are umpteen realisations on the way to higher consciousness. Each time we become aware that either physically or psychologically we are no longer dependent on something or somebody formerly regarded as being indispensable, we enjoy the freedom (power) of realisation, partial though it may be. The "impartial" or ultimate realisation is to realise that although the body exists, now I do not exist; I am nothing so I need nothing. This realisation, being so complete, is accompanied by an intense surge of freedom (power).

However, all freedom, all power, is registered only in the apparatus, not in the Being. The Being is neither this nor that. It has no attributes. The existing thing is the apparatus. Even the realisation is in the apparatus. The Being cannot be realised; it cannot realise itself. Only the apparatus can be purified sufficiently to realise the Being. This means that all that is being worked on and changed in spiritual endeavour is the self, the machine, the mind plus the emotions. The Being at birth and at death remains exactly the same.

The individual apparatus is continuously being refined or decongested through experience. This is the purpose of existence. But very rarely indeed does someone realise God as an uninterrupted state of consciousness. Even so, when the apparatus has been made simple enough, realisation of the one consciousness/freedom/power must occur.

Ivan, when I talked with him in Sydney, was having a hard time of it externally, trying to do a full-time job. I was having a hard time inwardly. He gave me the intuition I needed and continued to do so for the next two years. I in turn was able, through my professional contacts, to put the right kind of part-time writing work his way – producing a health-food magazine from home. Ten years later he was still producing the magazine and owned a seaweed health-tablet firm in a beautiful place which he had once remarked to me 'would be a heavenly place to live.' Thus does the Lord work in mysterious ways its wonders to perform.

Ivan was vegetarian and very strict about his diet. He used to grind his own grain and make his own bread, using an iron chapatti dish as found in every Indian village household. I have never "gone" vegetarian. In fact, I have not given up anything so as to conform to concepts of what the spiritual life requires. However, for years I practised conscious self-denial, doing my best with increasing success not to indulge negative emotions and doing what I could for others without looking for thanks. This included mowing old peoples' lawns; I also went to Sydney Hospital and asked to speak with any patients who had no visitors.

What I have shed in the way of habit and identification has been taken by circumstances or rejected in moment to moment discrimination. I smoked cigarettes from the age of 15 to 34. I didn't give them up. I just stopped. In India, vegetarianism was forced on me. I couldn't stomach the goat meat – or the flies that were more numerous on the meat behind the butcher's flyscreen than outside it. So I stuck to vegetables, fruit, rice, ground-grain porridge and yoghurt, which I made myself. The same with sex: my woman left me at times when celibacy was essential.

As soon as that time had passed, woman came again. I'd drunk alcohol since my youth. In India I could only afford a bottle occasionally, so temperance was forced on me, although I didn't miss drinking. However, on the occasions when I required a great deal of power to teach, penetrate or withstand opposing energies, I either abruptly stopped drinking (for no conscious reason) or was denied the opportunity to continue. Eventually I gave up altogether, which is another story further on.

Ivan (if I understood him correctly) at the end of his process found nothing producing shadows. I found nothing producing purpose among shadows. Both are inadequate descriptions. But the difference is: I always knew there was purpose, though no aim. He could not even acknowledge purpose, which to me shows the sublimity of his realisation. I cannot dispute that realisation is "nothing" and that this "knowledge", despite its absolute negation, is enough.

Ivan and Betty did not get on very well. He lived about 15 miles away from us and we used to spend hours talking on the phone. Betty, of course, couldn't help identifying him with the influence that had changed our lives, even though he'd come along well after it began.

I must point out that in the late 1950s and early 1960s there was a great scarcity of spiritual teachers, unlike today when they seem to be everywhere. When there is no one with real knowledge to affirm what is happening spiritually, doubt inevitably arises. So my main question to Ivan was, 'Tell me it's true.' His main role was to affirm what was happening in me. This is the important task of all real teachers – to keep the aspirant from doubting his or her own inspiration.

Ivan was my teacher in the flesh. A living teacher is the most important. But I had many teachers through the written word; and the teaching that revealed itself naturally in me was very different from his. My teaching is confrontative, energetic, vocal. I communicate very much by the resonance of my voice; I am aware that even if I were to speak in a foreign language the person listening would still receive the truth he or she required. This has happened with people who don't speak English sitting through my seminars. Along with presence this is the power all teachers must have.

Ivan was a soft-spoken, deliberate man. I am not. There is much in my style of teaching – though not in my sometimes assertive manner – resembling J. Krishnamurti. This was there even before I heard of him. His writings had a profound influence on me; his words were like keys that opened door after door in my understanding. Krishnamurti was a man who spoke the highest truth, so high, so essentially incommunicable, that only those who are one with him in Consciousness can possibly comprehend its full significance. And of course, being so meaningful for these individuals, it is meaningless to the intellectual mind.

The Indian guru, Osho Rajneesh, is reported to have said, 'Krishnamurti speaks to himself.' Yes. At the same time, however, Krishnamurti's words of truth, so abstract in one sense, contain a passionately creative energy (like the voice of the master) which works regeneratively in any mind that hears or reads them.

# CHAPTER 6

# BHAGAVATI,
# BHAGAVAT

I f God created woman, it was my insane God-love that created the divine illusion of Ann, the woman I was to fall in love with. Without knowing it at the time, I was to be taken the tantric way – the way of divine sexual love – a socially dubious aspect of my spiritual life which seldom seems to be encountered or, anyway, recorded.

Tantric love utilises man's vital sexual energy to unite him with the Beloved, the divine or God, in the form of woman. Fundamentally, woman is God or the divine Being in female form, and man is that in male form. In the absence of any knowledge in the West of such realities, I found the words for such a man and woman in a Hindu translation: *Bhagavat* (man as God) and *Bhagavati* (woman as God). Later, in an old book in a library in India, I discovered the only meaningful statement I can remember reading about tantric love. The gist of it was, "Every Bhagavat is provided with a Bhagavati so that the divine energy may personalise itself daily through their physical union."

I have not studied the Tantric religion (which is an offshoot of Hinduism) for the simple reason I've not found a description of it in English that was meaningful. Neither have I met another who came to the realisation of the divine in existence through tantra, although these individuals must of course exist. I have read all sorts of allusions to it, heard many people speak of it, but no one seems to have experienced it in all its ecstatic, terrifying and illuminating power.

This song I wrote at the time illustrates the point:

Bhagavati... Bhagavati...

Planted together by the eternal giver
Two willow trees
Dipped and sipped at the river of life.

Bhagavati... Bhagavati...

Neither in the shadow of the other
And yet
Both intermingled like wind that has met
Each one alone
Though eternally bound
By the ground.

Bhagavati... Bhagavati...

When death the compassionate giver arrives
Both fall in
And die.

Bhagavati... Bhagavati...


I first met Ann in 1963. She was 24. I was 36. I was then the Sydney manager of a Melbourne-based public relations company. I had accepted the job (involving a drop in salary) a couple of months before the 1962 state elections. Win or lose, I'd decided to finish with politics. I knew that if we won office and I stayed on, mine would be a very cushy and prestigious position as head of the Premier's press department. But other considerations were more important (and besides, unknown to me, the Bhagavati was waiting elsewhere). Politics were too slow and creatively undemanding for me. Anyway, we lost, and with the rest of the rats I handed Askin my notice the next day. Still, he was a realist and we parted on good terms. Three years later, after the next elections, he was Premier.

Before going to my new job in public relations in March 1962 I took a three week holiday with Betty and the children at Narooma. This was the "perfect" last holiday I spoke of earlier that we had together before the storm broke and washed me to other shores.

Ann did not appeal to me even slightly as a woman the first time I met her. In fact, I thought she was rather plain. This was not true, only my impression. The point seems to be that the Bhagavati may appear in a woman (and the Bhagavat in a man) 'fortuitously', where no original sexual desire or special personal interest exists. Suddenly, unbelievably, she is there.

About six months elapsed before I became conscious of an attraction. The first intimation of it was, strangely, when I glimpsed the back of her hair; I seemed to recognise something about it which made me feel terribly aware of her. This effect never diminished. We fell in love like most people do. There was nothing unusual about that. I knew I was imperilling my marriage and, like countless lovers before me, shrugged it off for the delight (and, for me, the extraordinary truth) of this new love.

I'm not going to attempt to justify my love for Ann by making excuses of spiritual necessity. No excuses can exist concerning the truth; what is done is part of the whole for all who are affected. However, for the breaking up of the home and the great suffering inflicted on Betty and the children through my love of this woman, I take full responsibility. I deceived Betty. By any ethic or standard of social morality and decency I behaved outrageously. I am as guilty as any man or woman who has done this thing. Nevertheless, the outcome is the only guide.

I recognised Ann as the Beloved on the second occasion we made love. She was as amazed as I. All she said was, 'It is so right.' Then came the ecstasy, the divine passion and the never-ending newness of our union. Now I had two loves – the divine formless and the divine form.

Separation from this woman was literally physical agony. When I was away from her a continuous pain gnawed at my solar plexus. At the same time, the emotional anguish and torment at being separated from the invisible divine still continued to wrack my body. In Ann's presence this disappeared and my only desire then was to teach the truth and to discover more. Otherwise, my consuming passion was to be united with the divine – in both forms.

The double life I was living – plus the certainty that what I was doing was right for me even though I didn't understand it all – brought my emotional fixation to needle-point intensity. I recognised the torturing, formless God-love of the previous two years as the same irresistible passion I now held for Ann. There was no difference: I knew it was holy; I knew it was divine. I knew that irrespective of any criticism or penalty I or anyone might have to endure, it was right. I knew... but that is not enough; I had not realised it. That is the subtlety of the spiritual process. Knowing must be realised. While there is knowing alone there is also the danger of not knowing. And that is the genesis of doubt. I did not doubt that my love of Ann and the divine was one and the same. But I hadn't "seen" it as one, hadn't realised its intrinsic unity.

This happened in the front garden one Sunday morning. I used to mow the lawn and work around the garden in a continuous daze of one-pointed contemplation. I couldn't separate Ann from the divine yet I still apprehended them as a duality. I was permanently "absent", fixed on this love within. It must have been wretched beyond belief for Betty. One day I even left our new garbage bin filled with garden refuse at the local tip, forgetting to empty it and put it back in the car!

On this particular Sunday the truth was revealed in a vision in my head. In the vision Ann walked towards me. Something intangible "dropped away" from her and I exclaimed (in my head) with instantaneous recognition, 'It is the Lord!' And the vision of Ann answered, 'Of course it is I. There is no Ann. But I will not reveal this to anyone else in the world; nor will you be able to tell anyone. In this way I will have my way. But I promise you I will unite you with this love.'

Her appearance hadn't changed at all. But something about her had vanished – the thin veil of self and illusion, Maya. I said in rapture, 'Please let me look once more upon your beautiful face.' And again Ann appeared as the divine.

This was indeed a remarkable point for me. Yet the knowledge that Ann was more than just a woman to me, and of divine significance, had been continuous from the start. The impersonal or universal character of my passion kept repeating itself in my poems. Earlier I had written this song:

> Ann ——, O mystic love, O Soul that's knit with mine
> You're everywhere Ann ——.

The sky, the fulsome clouds, the breeze that cools the day,
You're everywhere, Ann ——.

Wordsworth and his daffodils, I and my beloved – and all the other poets and lovers who glimpse the mystical union of man and beauty eternal – draw this inspiration from the same source. Again, I wrote:

Sweet death, where the beginning lies
I see you in the blackness of my Beloved's eyes.
Still, silent you look out at me,
End of becoming
O sweet eternity.

Poems flashed into my head, sometimes ending in mid-verse:

Within this hulk of creaking flesh a throne of light I've seen
And in it sits my own true self with my beloved queen.
Though seeming two we are but one as the petal is the rose...

But the song that seemed to express it all was Bhagavati, the one at the start of this chapter.

One of the most remarkable things I discovered about my love for Ann was its absence of selfishness. I could now give totally. Apparently, every other love I'd had to that time contained an element of holding back. I only became aware of this subtle reservation when it had disappeared, having been consumed in this new divine experience. I am not saying I was not selfish to others in my one-pointedness, just that my love for the first time was not self-centred. The spiritual life is a way of supreme selfishness as far as others are concerned. In truth there can be only one love. And it cannot be personal. The 'personality' of love – its selfish attachment – dissolves in the realisation that you are the vessel of love, that you are love's container, and not the love. To Ann I wrote:

I can't give you anything.
Every gift I give is the gift of Him
Whose gift of love we share

Whose gift of love so very rare
Takes all the world can give,
Its love and
Even the will to live,
And yet loses in the exchange.
This love beyond world, space and time
Whispers in the heart
Though unpossessed
You are forever mine.

As can be imagined, the pressure at home between Betty and me was appalling. She did not know about Ann. I abhorred the situation; so did Ann. Yet I could do nothing. How could a man who professed to love God, who claimed to speak the truth, behave in such an ignoble way? I don't know. Yes, I do know. But I can't justify it. The fact is, I did love God and I spoke the truth. What is this paradox?

Betty knew me, but didn't really know me. She'd heard the truth from me so often but couldn't remember it; even in the midst of her certainty that I was deluded she knew at a deeper level that I wasn't – as events were to show. Perhaps the answer to the paradox is in this song I wrote for Betty, as though she were singing it:

O LORD SAVE ME FROM MYSELF

I knew him well or was he a stranger?
O Lord save me from myself.
A thing from hell or a straw from the manger?
O Lord save me from myself.
A devil says the world and I have to agree
And then I recall the things he said to me
And my whole being cries 'Stop this heresy.'
O Lord save me from my self.
O Lord save me from my self.
The words that he spoke I can no longer remember.
O Lord save me from myself.
But they sounded a hope with a new kind of splendour.
O Lord save me from myself.

> I didn't hear a word with these ears of mine
> And I still would have seen had I been born blind.
> He raised me beyond the world of my mind.
> O Lord save me from my self.


In November 1963, 12 months before I left Australia, I was weeding the lawn in a deep state of contemplation when a voice spoke inside my head. 'You are going away,' it said. I knew this meant I was to leave my home and family.

I was astonished. Even though I had frequently looked at the possibility, I'd dismissed it each time as impossible. I remember as I crouched there in the garden looking up at the front of our modern cream-brick bungalow with its large expanse of plate-glass, sandstone patio, sandstone island fireplace and other small touches of luxury, replying, 'It's impossible. It would take £40 a week to run this place.' (Australian £s, a fair sum in those days.) 'And Betty,' I added, 'she would never understand.'

The voice replied, 'I will provide all, even the understanding.'

For two years Betty and I had continued to destroy each other psychologically and emotionally. I had watched every emotion in myself that I thought I was capable of. The worst memory, even today as I write this, is the dreadful pain I caused this woman who would weep open-faced before me, unable to comprehend the causes that were destroying her world. Had she known there was another woman she would have been able to handle it, to cope, to understand, to rise to her towering natural dignity and cease to acknowledge me as her husband. But her husband was not telling; he was hiding behind his lie. He denied her the strength and escape of outraged dignity and compelled her to suffer in love what she would never have consented to tolerate in knowing. Betty was betrayed and did not know it; I had passed to a higher love. Both of us were in the same boat, in a way. Love is never betrayed; love is never higher than at its lowest.

'But we love you,' she protested one day, her head held high while tears streamed down her cheeks as I tried to tell her that her love was not love. 'We love you. The three of us love you.'

Love, she did. She stuck it through. We did a great job on each other. Then, abruptly, it was over. She could not touch me any more. My children could not touch me any more. No claims of the past, its love, its sentiments, its traditions, its memories could ensnare me. I knew I was free. Something had happened inside.

I went to the office as usual next morning. The phone rang as I arrived. It was Betty.

'Barry,' she exclaimed. 'God is!'

Yes, we had both done a wonderful job on each other. She had been given understanding. I had been given freedom, though I didn't know yet in what way. From that day on Betty began asking me questions about the spiritual process and avidly reading every book on truth I possessed. We both walked together again down to the park, each with our books under our arms, or sat reading together on the lawn or in the house. Nothing had changed yet everything was different. She had found her own Lord, her own centre, her own inner space to which she had surrendered. She accepted what is. No longer did she demand to know the future. Betty was on the way.

Around March 1964, Ann moved with her family several hundred miles away to another state. We both knew it was right but inevitably the separation started up another cathartic wave for me. This is what emotion is and the "technique" of spiritual "advancement" lies in holding the emotional wave consciously with the attention and not allowing the discomforting energy to be dissipated in unconscious thought, physical action or talk. The pain and loneliness was intense. It was Kierkegaard who said 'suffering is the way' and there is no greater truth until both suffering and the way are left behind. On the strength of this energy I experienced an extraordinary realisation.

I was walking up the steps from the garage after having arrived home from work. Stepping into the house I was aware of being my own individual God, my own Lord – because I knew myself. The experience was not just a case of knowing or "seeing" but of actual participation – of being this I, this Lord. The state lasted for at least an hour. I kept describing it to Betty but the most significant point I can remember saying while in the state was, 'I love working in these lovable little bodies.'

I have in front of me a letter I wrote to Ann the following morning describing the incident. It is dated the 10th of September 1964.

> Beloved,
>
> It happened last night – the first vision of myself, what I am. It was you, or your absence, that did it.
>
> All day I'd had the dreadful pull within, the drag of old. The day before I'd wept for two hours with loneliness, even walked down under the Bridge [Sydney Harbour Bridge] because I couldn't find a place in this dreadful city to weep alone. Yesterday the weeping had stopped and only the terrible longing drag remained. I thought you might have phoned. No letter, no phone call, no news. And on top of this Ivan had kept telling me that you and I as such would have to part. Oh, the agony.
>
> Ivan is wrong. I saw it. He's wrong because he's speaking outside his experience. I saw that it is God who loves you, who longs to be with you… I saw that my desire for you is the desire or will of God… that what he desires will be… has to be… must be. I saw this because I saw that I know my God and then I saw I know my God because I know myself… and that *I am my God* or *Lord* but I am an *individual* Lord (that was the great revelation) yet still part of the whole which is the master of creation, just as the part can't be separated from the whole.
>
> God, as Goldsmith [Joel Goldsmith, *The Infinite Way*] says, is *individual* consciousness – you and me purified. And (I saw) he (it) loves living in the world and he loves loving himself as you to me and me to you and nothing will stop him (it). You are, and your Lord is what you are, using the individual faculties and peculiarities of these funny little bodies, because without them it cannot act here.

Ivan of course knew all about my relationship with Ann. His response was mixed. My deceiving of Betty he accepted as my affair. By nature he was something of a puritan; by realisation broad and understanding. When I described my love of Ann as divine he understood; he knew that in the awakened analysis all is divine. But the sexual side of it never really rested easily in his mind. His reaction was one of somewhat disapproving bewilderment which he rounded off with the subsequent prediction (referred to in my letter above) that Ann would 'have to go' eventually.

He was right. She did go. But he was also not right because the Bhagavati (the part of Ann that I loved) came again in another woman's form. Truth, of course, is always like this, ever moving on to wider and finer significance without destroying the previous validity. Ivan had seen *lingams* and *yonis* (statues of the male and female sexual organs) scattered over various parts of north India where tantra used to be practised as a religion. As a Brahmachari, the idea of sex in a spiritual context was repugnant to him. And yet five years later Ivan evidently found his own Bhagavati in a most surprising twist of circumstances.

I had not realised at this time that the Bhagavati is not any one woman, although she does manifest in the body of a particular woman. The Bhagavati is *Woman*, the superb divine feminine essence. To me in those early days it was enough, a miracle, to have found her and loved her in a particular physical body. I imagined we would go forward together in truth and love, physically inseparable in this life and together always in eternity. I had "seen" that we were linked eternally; there was no possible doubt about that. But my mistake or ignorance – due to my still insufficiently purified mind – was to limit the Bhagavati to one body, to physical individuality.

In the 3,000 million bodies of women on earth there is only She. But in practically every case She is buried under deep layers of conditioning, emotions, memory and the ceaseless activity of the mind. The love of man or God is supposed to bring her to the surface, to consciousness in existence. But with all the wrong notions of love in the human animal, this is a very rare occurrence. It shouldn't be, but it is because everyone puts love of someone or something before the love of truth.

The Bhagavati may appear to one man in a sequence of women but not, in my experience, in two women at the same time. She is recognised in the first instance only by the Bhagavat. To others she will appear quite normal, though always with an intangible, attractive quality.

Because tantric love is an intense sexual expression and no straightforward accounts of it seem to exist for guidance, it is wide-open to corruption and misrepresentation. All sex involves tantric energies. But tantric love, the final stage of tantra, is distinguished by one unmistakable fact – the man or woman who is loved so completely is seen literally to be the ineffable divine. The love is not just felt to be divine, which is a common experience of lovers. But the individual loved actually reveals his or her essence as the Beloved, God. If any doubt remains, the experience is not true or real enough yet. The revelation of the embodiment of divinity is beyond all question ever again for the one who beholds it. To love such a one physically is ecstasy and rightness. The rightness is even more exquisite than the ecstasy.

CHAPTER 7

# LEAVING

M y intention to leave Betty and the children to go to India was announced at the breakfast table one Sunday. There was no tense moment of decision – just a simple unrehearsed statement delivered casually like a comment on the weather. The complete absence of drama surprised both Betty and me, though we both knew something had to happen to remove the vacuum in which we were now living. It was obvious to me we had to part and yet I was still not prepared to make a break simply to set up house with Ann.

'What will you do now?' Betty had asked.

'Go to India,' I replied. I had not entertained the idea before but obviously I was influenced by Ivan's experience. Now it seemed the only possible move to make. Betty nodded without comment.

I set about arranging for Ann to accompany me. It seems invariable to me that mystics or lovers of God are forced, as part of their spiritual process, to act contrary to society's moral expectations. Sometimes they may be wrongly accused and be unable to convince anyone of their innocence. It seems to depend on what experience the individual needs to engender surrender to God rather than to his (or her) own guilt or fear of what people will say.

My need, clearly, was to have no ground for self-justification which innocence may have offered. The lesson was for me to understand that self-judgment and feelings of guilt are among the last strongholds of personal vanity. Whichever way, the lessons come. Viewing one's life in a correct perspective is a question of impersonal scale, not personal; and this has to be understood sooner or later. The crucial question for the mystic at every step is: Why? What is my motivation for this or that? He strives to know or be conscious of every facet of his psyche. Was I, in this case, fleeing to be with the woman of my desire as countless men have done before? Or was my overriding objective the search for truth alone?

I had noted this emotional grey-spot in my consciousness – call it a complex – where my love of Ann and my love of the truth conjoined. Which had precedence? That was the question. Up to that time it had not been necessary for a distinction to be made, we can only go as fast as our understanding allows. But eventually we are all forced to discriminate. Every shadowy complex, no matter how subtle, must come under conscious scrutiny so that not one speck of duality remains in our consciousness. There can be only one aim and one end in the search for truth: psychological nakedness, which means no past attachment at any moment and no selfish projection at any time.

My first glimpse of what I desired most came as the time for our departure to India approached and Ann wavered for a few minutes about going. To her as a woman it was of course a move of daunting implications. I was married, twelve years older, father of two young children, taking her to an unfamiliar, undeveloped country where I had no chance of earning a living and, by the very nature of my spiritual aspirations, could make no promises or plans for the future. What if she got pregnant? What if I went back to my wife (always her most disturbing thought)? What if I abandoned her for another woman?

Those are very worldly fears. But knowing that does not eliminate them. Fear is eliminated by fearing and observing the experience objectively while undergoing it. This conscious introspective attention is the only extra weapon the mystic possesses for his psychological journeying. And Ann was a mystic. She did not like what she was doing. She loved me, not out of choice, but out of compulsion. We both knew this. Later, when my mother, out of naive and grateful concern, thanked her for loving me, she replied, 'I love him because I must.' The Bhagavati in woman knows no sentiment.

The moment that Ann wavered I glimpsed the integrity of my search. 'I'm going with or without you,' I declared. And I knew I meant it. The truth was my goal; the love I sensed was simply the enabling energy of the means, without the end.

The rightness of my aim alone seems to me to account for the extra-ordinary kindness, love and tolerance I have received from the people I have hurt most in my struggle to break the cloying bonds of attachment (me to my children and my home; them to their attachment to me). Betty, even after discovering my deception, never displayed enmity, although under the pressure of raising the children she would occasionally bitterly draw my mother's attention to my dereliction. Betty, before I left, was under the impression that I was going to India for spiritual reasons. This turned out to be the truth of it. It is why I say my personal immorality was incidental to the main theme. It is this way with all of us as we reach for the sky through the murk of our apparent ignorance and selfish inclinations.

The old cliché maintains that the means justifies the end but this is a partial view; the means is the end. If the means is love and truth, the end is love and truth. Life as living is the means of the human drama and it never changes; nor does Consciousness (of life behind living) which is the end. Only circumstances, which are always uniquely our own, change and as such represent our limited life-form activity. And like our transient life-forms they are left behind like footprints. We are permanent, but only in an impermanent sense.

It is our nature to identify our circumstances and transient objectives with life itself. Yet, the set of circumstances we call "ours" merely comprises a particular life-form at a particular time. But sooner or later the mystic, the true searcher, as an outrider of consciousness, must disperse this grey-spot which mistakes *my* life for *the* life.

The illusion is a universal complex, common to all men and women, because it has not been dispersed yet by sufficient self-knowledge. This will be done by more and more individuals distinguishing between the permanent and impermanent; by realising that what they are looking for is the real life – the end – and not the merry-go-round of circumstances in between, whether represented by child, gold, man or woman.

Betty and I decided to sell the house. It was worth about £12,000 and after discharging the mortgage would yield about £9,000 cash. I told her I required £1,000 of this. I insisted we got the arrangement drawn up by a solicitor who was also instructed to begin divorce proceedings after the legal separation period which was then five years. I put the car in Betty's name. The idea was she would move with the children to the other side of the Sydney harbour, over Rose Bay way, and rent a flat near the water at around £15 a week. She had enough capital for at least four years – and the rest was up to life. (As it turned out, Betty prudently bought a flat at Rose Bay, rented it as a means of income, and with the children moved to Narooma where she didn't have to pay rent.)

I arranged with Ann to meet up in Singapore. After paying her and my one-way fares I ended up with £300 or £400. With £1,000 to come when the house was sold we had enough without looking too far ahead.

Ivan could not understand why I was saddling myself with Ann. He had experienced the primitiveness of life outside the Indian cities, not to mention in the foothills of the Himalayas. 'She'll be a millstone around your neck,' he said.

On the 25th of November 1964 I flew out of Sydney on Air India leaving four lonely, weeping figures waving goodbye. Annette, aged 12, and Scott, aged ten, could not comprehend that this was forever, anymore than could Betty. I think she felt that when I had finished with India I would return. My mother knew that this was impossible and the weight of this knowledge was her secret grief. All four, whom I had once loved most, I now (and for a long time yet to come) hurt most.

My mother, then aged 63, was devastated by the break-up of our little family. Here is something of what she felt, which I later asked her to write down.

> I must tell you of one of the greatest experiences I think I ever had in my life. Even now it affects me when I think about it. It still makes me want to weep.
>
> Barry was married to Betty, living in a lovely home in Wahroonga with the two children. This was about the time the great spirit was trying to enter Barry's body. I could see the difference in him. He seemed to get quiet and liked to be alone and not talk as usual. I knew something different was happening to him and I was fretting about it.

I shall always remember the morning Barry informed me he
had decided to go to India, leaving his wife and the children and
of course me. It was about 9 am and I was sitting in a bus with a
girlfriend waiting to leave for a two week holiday in Surfers
Paradise, Queensland. Barry came to the bus to wish us farewell
and break this news to me. I felt very upset and while away kept
thinking it would not eventuate; that by the time I returned he
would have changed his mind. But no, the driving force was
behind him. The amazing part was that Betty seemed to agree
with the fact that he had to go, although she was happy and
loved him. There were, I believe, many signs which confirmed
their belief that he was going in some way with the help and
wish of the Lord.

When I realised that this change had taken place and he was
really preparing to go, it was then I started to really fret as I
could not understand it all and could not accept the fact he was
really leaving us all for somewhere in the Himalayas with little
money. He was leaving so much. Although I did not tell him, I
never seemed to stop crying; it was no use, I could not stop.
Without knowing I would find tears running down my face in
the street, in buses or shops and had no control over it.

During this period I went and stayed with him and the
children while Betty was at Narooma with her father who was ill.
One evening in the kitchen I said, 'Barry, please couldn't you
give this thing away and not go?' He put both his arms out
against the wall and said, 'Mother, I would rather be nailed here
than change my mind.' I knew then it was hopeless to stop him.
I knew it was inevitable, that what he was doing was the right
thing and he just had to do it.

Next morning I took the children, who were on holiday, to
the pictures at Crows Nest. My heart was breaking and once
again I could not stop the tears from flowing down my face. I felt
ashamed in front of people but it was no use, I could not do
anything about it.

We got on a train in a carriage where there were about six
people sitting on both sides and there on the floor was this thing
shining at me. I held it up and asked the people on the seats if it
belonged to them. They all said no. I held it in my hand and
looked. It was the most beautiful gold cross, with a ruby shining

in the centre. It was the greatest omen I had ever received. I know God put it there to help me and let me know all was well.

It was not long before we were out at Sydney Airport saying goodbye to Barry. What a sad, sad day. The plane flew off with the four of us crying and sad. The children were crying, particularly Scott (aged nine) who said, 'What am I going to tell the kids at school about my father?' Betty was about the bravest as she understood more, and said, 'It had to be, Mum.' I stayed with them for a couple of days. I was so sad, not only for myself but for the children, Betty, the whole thing, even the dog Clementine.

# CHAPTER 8

# INDIA

M adras (now Chennai), India, was like a hot, bad breath. We landed in the early hours of the morning, and when the aircraft door opened the stench of the city, ten miles away, rolled in on a torrid wave. Singapore was bad enough to the unaccustomed temperate-zone nose; but tropical Madras, a city of two million people on the Bay of Bengal and off the usual tourist routes in those days, had the added stink of hopeless squalor and poverty – in the midst of uncaring wealth.

On our first morning I walked down the road to a roundabout and watched the incredible pageant of human activity that makes Indian cities throb with bare-knuckled reality. Beggars, living, decaying, dying where they sat – philosophers and stoics all, in their cold-blooded acceptance of their lot. Thin, shiny, black-bodied men pulling groaning dray-loads of steel. Sweat, time and home-made conveyances were cheap here, among such poverty and toiling wiry workers who wore tough skins for suits. Honking, fuming diesel lorries with cursing drivers bullying a right of way. A donkey, legs grotesquely splayed, too thin and underfed to support its body plus the shafts of an overloaded cart of sugarcane. Velvet-eyed water buffalo and yoked, white hump-necked Brahmin bulls unhurried, imperturbable. Jostling, ambling, shoving, shouting pedestrians carrying briefcases. There were children, baskets of fruit and vegetables, caged red-beaked finches and fortune-telling mongooses, monkeys, flutes and little palettes of betel-nut laid out on fresh green leaves, all ready for chewing. Everything was working to breaking point and beyond – machines, animals, buildings, people; nothing redundant, nothing out-of-date or incongruous, the whole scene a superb absurdity.

Madras, like most Indian cities which the British left behind, had a psychological mouldiness about it. The long-dead splendour of imperial hauteur lived on there in the habits and thinking of the ruling class. The vibrant, indigenous culture reached only to the height where influence, quasi-western sophistication and wealth began. At this intensely self-centred level, appearances counted far more than performance.

So life was unique and rich only down and around the grassroots of the people where few visitors – and even fewer of their own boss-wallahs – ever managed to penetrate or desired to. Amidst the English-accented Indians we found a few stalwart perennial British still doing their shopping at Spencer's, the local "European" emporium. Here the atmosphere was forty years out-of-date; a quaint attempt at perpetuation of class distinction which was a joke, until you realised everyone involved was deadly serious.

The clash of cultures wherever the British had been in India had created a terribly insulated mentality among most of the better off Indians. In Madras, they built their fine two and three storey houses with high surrounding walls to protect their lovely gardens and trees – and tossed their garbage and menstrual rags over the top to lie on the grass beside the footpaths.

Where street pavements had been lifted to make repairs to the city, sewer pipes were left open for months exhaling their poisonous indifference among hurrying crowds of equally indifferent white-laundered businessmen and pukka city officials. And the workers, toilers and beggars in turn showed their indifference by shitting where they must because no public toilets were provided, and spitting everywhere on pavements that long ago had turned near red from the stain of well-chewed betel-nut. Even if there had been toilets they would still have fouled them into uselessness; this was an unconscious protest against a failed compromise culture which the Indian people, in their political agony, are still doing their best to reject or rectify.

We rented a fairly modern (for India) unfurnished flat for £7 a week from a *ranee*, the wife of a deceased raja, who owned several properties in the city. These former parochial rulers, dispossessed of their powers and privileges since independence from Britain in 1947, had a pretty hard time of it trying to cope with normal living. Our flat was far better than the ranee's accommodation; she couldn't sell her properties as most of the proceeds would have been taken in taxes; and many of the places were empty.

Our second floor flat was gigantic compared to our needs: three bed-rooms, lounge, dining room, kitchen, covered balcony and sewered bathroom, all with mosaic tiled floors. Our three suitcases together in one room with a packing box for a table and a hired convertible sofa to sleep on, looked rather silly. As one so often does in the unsettled life, we bought a collection of saucepans and other kitchen paraphernalia and then looked around for what we could cook and eat.

Every piece of meat and seafood in the market was black with flies. We decided to stick to fruit, rice and vegetables that could be peeled or boiled. We boiled our drinking water. We discovered we had to lock up the food in the kitchen because at night huge rats would climb up the two floors of downpipes outside and enter through the barred but unshuttered window.

Within eight weeks we were both crawling off to a local doctor with disturbing symptoms. He diagnosed protein deficiency and after giving us a course of injections recommended a malt-type drink, Akta-Vite, which cost £1 a bottle. We got through three or four of these a week which kept the deficiency at bay. We didn't know about pulses and it was six months before I discovered that yoghurt, which is sold on every second market stall in India, is a sufficient source of protein. I also learned that the yoghurt, which was scooped out of large and shallow earthenware basins, didn't seem to get contaminated despite the unwashed fingers and roadside dust that went into it.

We remained in Madras for three months waiting for a small £100 second-hand van, a Ford Thames, to arrive by ship from Australia. The van was a gift from Betty – another example of her extraordinary gen-erosity. She'd had it overhauled and arranged the permit for export.

The time spent absolutely alone with Ann was idyllic. We saw Christmas 1964 come and go without one person referring to it – a strange experience the first time – except for the canny vegetable man who asked me for his Christmas present! The letters from home were tragic. 'Come back, Barry, let's start again,' was Betty's heart-cry that I shall never be able to forget. 'Don't do it, Barry,' wrote her bewildered and aged grandfather. Ivan reported, 'They're saying you left with the company funds,' and added that the children were missing me terribly.

'If you think, then you must drink at the place of the sinking heart…' I refused to think.

A week after our arrival an Indian knocked on the door and introduced himself as Professor Naidu, a palmist. Would I like him to read my hand? He would give me a good and honest reading, he said. I complied and Ann set up the tape recorder. He got off to an amazing start considering that I had no job or work, was in a foreign country with no base to return to, and was without any prospects other than my knowledge of truth.

He said in broken English, 'Your future very bright. You will get so many lakhs (hundreds of thousands) of money in your future life… Very good heart-line, very pure heart. You got very good God inside; that God very good help. Others can't see, can't understand; not here (tapping forehead) any marks, not here any ornaments, nothing, only inside very good straightforward prayer. Your hand very good philosophy-psychology hand, means very good art, editor. Now in this present period you have no peace of mind… Your plans very big plans, so many lakhs…'

I interrupted, 'How would I get 100,000?'

He replied, 'You'll get it. Very good God factor. Money in the box, not ready yet. Future will come. So many trips you travel in future. This science I know.'

A few days later I saw an advertisement in the English language paper announcing that Pandit J. S. V. Sastry was visiting Madras to read palms. Here I reckoned was a chance to confirm or deny the professor's very encouraging but unlikely predictions. So off I went to a large tower block of one room rented apartments and presented my open palms to the pandit.

'What do you see?' I asked, giving no clue to my background or myself. After a fairly accurate outline of my past and material fortunes he added:

> 'This is a hand called *hubbula*, meaning second class person. *Hatma* means first class person – they are all saints, great people, mahatmas who live a pure life without interest in the material world. You are a second class person who is interested in the material world, who wants name and fame. Even kings and maharajas come under the same sign but they're a bit what we call crooked or selfish. In your work you are not going to live for yourself, you are going to live for others. That work is not for your children; you are not going to leave a big fortune for them. A big name you are going to leave. You will win the hearts of the general public. Your audience or people, your appreciators, will be all over the world.'
>
> 'You have what is called "fish sign" that makes you travel all over the world, not only a few countries but you may have to travel at least once the entire world. Your mount of Jupiter promises great name, fame or popularity through your writings and discoveries. It is almost like a scientist or research scholar. There is every indication you are working or scheming to do some big work in which you are going to be very successful. You are not very much particular about accumulating money. You care more for fame, honour, dignity and reputation. The last time, when I read a palm like this, in Darjeeling, he was an ordinary horseman looking after our horses. And that gentleman today is well known world name – Tenzing.' [The sherpa who conquered Everest with Sir Edmund Hillary in 1953.]

Again all this was as though the man was hallucinating, although I couldn't help but be impressed by his apparent expertise and sincerity. Here again was a prediction of a life ahead that I couldn't have designed better myself.

The pandit pointed to a star on my hand.

> 'This is a sign called *kamulla*. It means you will be very, very successful in whatever work you do, if it is for others. You get thanks but not much material return. It gives you name, fame but not money.'

His next observation was astonishing.

> 'This sign also tells that you have got a mark on your private
> part, means *amucha*, like a brown spot on the tip. You may be
> knowing that.' (I didn't but I confirmed it later.) 'Many people
> will mistake that you are a very rich man and some, the opposite
> sex, may take an interest and try to harm you, or break your
> relationship with the wife. For their own selfish motive they
> would like to entangle themselves with you. Whenever that spot
> is there, whether you dress up well or not, it is a sign of
> magnetism.'

And finally:

> 'I do not know what your work is but it is in fine art, like
> radio, fine things. You will find out something wonderful and
> give it to the world.'

While we waited in Madras for the van to arrive I was not allowed to
waste any time. Panditji (*ji* is an Indian suffix of respect) Sastry was also
an astrologer and he prepared my horoscope. I have the transcript
beside me now. It is quite an extraordinary document considering that
only a couple of weeks before I had left my home, family and just about
all my possessions in Australia.

'Venus in your chart stands for immovable property, general happi-
ness,' he said. 'He is in the 12th house – if you had property it must go. If
you had house and movable things, all that you gave up. Loss, anxiety,
worry – all that came.'

I have checked this planetary position and Venus is definitely there.
But the pandit was using the Hindu system, which at that time subtract-
ed nearly 24 degrees from each planetary position to allow for polar
rotation. He made several other points including, 'You will have to wander this forest of India till about the end of 1965. Then something tells
you: "Should I go home? Should I do something else?" And I expect you
will.' The pandit's prediction of my length of stay proved very close to
the mark.

He said, 'Saturn in the middle of your life gives lots of suffering, trouble, agony and success won't come easily. But later it is guaranteed you are going to be the top man. Saturn in the long run gives you *raja yoga*, which means the material benefit. It is Saturn that gives you practical knowledge of practical reality. I expect you are going to do something with an extraordinary power or sight, affecting the general public, when kings and important people will come to you – just for the pleasure, just to meet you which they think is worth it.'

Panditji would sometimes visit us at our flat and one evening he knocked on the door looking very serious. He was a short, roly-poly man, about 63. When he spoke earnestly, as he did now, his eyes widened almost to the size of the lenses in his old-fashioned spectacles.

'I have decided,' he declared, 'to teach you astrology and to tell you my secret. You must never divulge it to another. It was given to me by a pandit in my youth for a great service and a considerable sum of money.'

'Why? Why do you do this?'

'Because I must. I have been told I must.'

Twice a week for the next two months he instructed me in Hindu stellar astrology. This is different from the solar system used in the West. He gave me original old manuscripts to study and I also recorded our sessions on tape for future reference. It is most unusual for an Indian astrologer to divulge his technique; as a class they are guarding of their secrets which are usually handed down from father to son, generation to generation. It is one of the reasons why there are hardly any really good books on the Indian system which dates back to the pre-history beginnings of Hindu culture; the ones who know won't tell. A sincere astrologer in India – and there are some – regards his art as a heritage as well as a meal ticket and will not endanger the tradition.

Panditji was a *Brahmin*, the priestly and teaching caste of the Hindus. In the 1930s he had been official court astrologer to the Maharaja of Mysore who conferred on him the high title of *Ventakachala*. Like most Indians who love to impress, he carried around with him yellowed press clippings and photos of himself dressed in his magnificent court regalia. Panditji was a bit tricky from a lifetime of living on his wits and an intuition that sometimes failed to deliver. Still, he believed passionately in the essential truth of astrology and always acknowledged it was an incomplete science which he never ceased studying in his spare time. He made some truly extraordinary predictions, among them the assassination of President Kennedy.

Why did Panditji have to teach me astrology? What place could astrology have in the life of a mystic and spiritual teacher whose truth was the reality of the Now? Was he talking nonsense?

Five years later in London I was to begin a 14 year writing association and deep friendship with Richard N. Beim, a remarkable man whose genius for popularising astrology led me to write (anonymously) a world bestseller and several other astrology books published internationally.

Astrology is a study in self-knowledge. When seriously approached it opens the mind. A mind that condemns astrology without understanding the principles behind it is closed. Coming as I did from the very closed, materialistic, largely racist and therefore bigoted society which Australia was at that time, my mind as well as my emotions needed opening to the greater possibilities of life and the universe. Astrology helped to do this. I was never interested in the predictive side of it, but through my astrology books I was able to introduce millions of ordinary people to spiritual ideas that otherwise they may never have encountered.

So, was Panditji right? Did he have to teach me astrology? Who or what ordained it, or knew what was to be? For me, it was Life. Life is all and knows all. Life is its own solution. Panditji, as part of that Life, had to do it. The remarkable thing is that he knew he had to. The subsequent events of my life continually confirmed his predictions.

Panditji's English was relatively good but his pronunciation did make us smile at times. Once he ended a sentence with 'and choss will devil up.' We just could not work it out. He had to repeat the phrase three times before I realised he was saying 'and chaos will develop.'

My plan, as soon as the van arrived, was to visit Meher Baba, the Sufi sage at his ashram at Ahmadnagar, about 500 miles north-west of Madras. From there we would make our way north to the Himalayas. Meher Baba was one of the five Indian teachers whose works had helped me. (His *Discourses*, if you can get them, are extremely good.) The others were Aurobindo, Ramana Maharshi, Sivananda and, as I mentioned, J. Krishnamurti.

Aurobindo's ashram was in Pondicherry, about 100 miles south of Madras, but he had died some years before and I was not interested in meeting his followers. That grand old man, Ramana Maharshi, of Arunachala, not far from Madras, was also dead.

I met Krishnamurti privately in Madras, as well as attending one of his open-air lectures. We sat opposite each other in silence for 15 minutes. There was nothing to say. He had already said it all.

When I phoned Krishnamurti's personal assistant to make the appointment, I said, 'I want to introduce myself. I am Barry Long from Australia, Krishnamurti's successor.'

She was both astonished and indignant, 'Krishnamurti doesn't have a successor!'

Many years later, in 1986 a couple of days after Krishnamurti died, a man who was with his teaching and knew of me knocked on the door of my home, apologised for disturbing me but said he'd had a dream that concerned me and seemed very important. He said in his dream he had walked into a room in which three men were seated at a table. He knew these were the successors to Krishnamurti. The table was in shadow and he could only make out one of the men. It was Barry Long.

When the van did eventually arrive in the middle of March it was already getting fiercely hot. We decided to by-pass Ahmadnagar and head straight for the Himalayas via Bombay and New Delhi, a good 1,500 miles across the centre of India and the heat and dust of the plains. Not only had Betty paid for the van and organised the shipping of it but she also arranged for a large iron trunk to be lightly welded to the floor and filled it with tins of food and powdered milk. When I boarded the ship to pick up the van I found the back door lock had been smashed, the padlocked trunk forced open, and every item of food stolen.

# CHAPTER 9

# TO THE HIMALAYAS

W e left Madras and headed for Bombay (now Mumbai). The trip, with a stopover at Panditji's home in Bangalore (now Bengaluru), took about eight days. It was hellishly hot. We drove only in the morning and late afternoon. The van was eight years old and I couldn't afford to push it in the heat and risk trouble. The four-bladed radiator fan just wasn't up to the job. Later I had another blade – a piece of an old shovel – welded onto it up in the hills by an ingenious Indian roadside mechanic. When Indians possess a flair they can be amazingly inventive and adaptive. When they don't they are terrifying. Whenever I pulled up for petrol I'd jump straight out and put my hand over the filler cap to prevent any enthusiastic helpers filling the tank with water in mistake for the radiator.

I solved the overheating problem by letting the partly opened bonnet, which in this model lifted up at the windscreen end, rest on a sun helmet I'd bought in Spencer's in Madras. I drove about 5,000 miles around India with the helmet perched under the bonnet in this way. It was so colonial looking and redolent of the British Raj, that I called it my "sahib hat" and wrote a silly little song about it.

I drove across India in a Ford
Me and my old sahib hat.

> I climbed the Himalayas to find the Lord
> Me and my old sahib hat.
> I sat in the winter sun and wrote a book
> And the natives all laughed when they took a look
> But how could I tell them I was still half-cooked
> Even in my old sahib hat.

When not driving it was essential to wear the helmet for protection against sunstroke. The Indian women oil their own and their children's hair; it is considered to be correct and attractive grooming but no doubt originates from a need to protect them from the sun's rays. Ann with her rather delicate complexion used a wide-brimmed straw hat which she wore with self-conscious resignation. For a touch of feminine reassurance she added a coloured ribbon which also acted as a chin-strap for those occasions when sudden gusts of wind would have sent the hat pirouetting across the Indian plains. She hated the chin-strap but hated even more having to cope with hordes of Indian men, women and children who would suddenly appear from nowhere in the centre of virtually uninhabitable desert to give chase after her hat and gleefully romp back with it for an agonisingly ceremonious handover. In those days every visitor to India was a film star as soon as he or she stepped off the beaten track. Within minutes of stopping we would be surrounded by a silent staring circle. Even going to the toilet was seldom a private affair for long.

When we reached the edge of the plateau of the Indian Deccan, some 1,200 feet above sea level, we looked down on a magnificent vista comprising the Arabian Sea, the coastal strip and the city of Bombay. We drove down out of the dry heat and dust into soaking humidity. My mother had motored from Europe to Bombay five years before. She had given me the address of a Christian church out on the harbour point in a fine residential area where she and her friend had been allowed to park their vehicle in the grounds and use the bathing and other facilities there. Ann and I drove up hot, exhausted and prepared to give anything for a bath or a shower. They turned us down flat. I should have guessed that something was about to happen but it's not often you can think positively in those situations.

We turned round and headed down to the seafront. Stuff it, I thought. We'll sit. We'll make it happen. I won't move, even if we've got to sit in one place for a week. I pulled up facing the sea. It was late afternoon, about six o'clock. Bombay faces west and the red Indian sun, immense like some comic strip drawing, mocked us through the windscreen while we sweated in shadeless, breezeless discomfort. I reached round the seat and pulled out a bottle of beer. We had no more boiled water left and I was in no mood for making any on the Primus. I poured the beer and we sat sipping it. An Indian came up to my window.

'Good evening,' he said.

'Oh, go away,' I retorted and wound up the window. It was hot but I couldn't bear the alternative of a silly chat.

'Excuse me,' he said, signalling through the glass. He was an older man, about 60, with light, fine skin. He was wearing Western-style trousers, shirt and tie. I wound down the window.

'I'm sorry to trouble you,' he said, 'but perhaps I can be of some assistance. I am the owner of the house behind you. Perhaps you and your lady would care to come inside and rest.'

I opened the door and looked back. The house was a mansion.

We parked the van in his grounds, unpacked and stayed for three days. We had every conceivable comfort. Mr Vakil was an industrialist. He loved gardens and music. His home and the grounds of his factory abounded in beautiful ornamental shrubs, fruit trees and plants. He had the best of hi-fi equipment and hundreds of classical recordings that he listened to for hours. Well rested, we left the Vakils and headed for New Delhi, 900 miles to the north.

We were fully self-contained in the van although it was difficult to sleep in. There wasn't enough headroom to stand up, and to lie down we had to transfer most of the cases and cooking equipment onto the roof-rack. We soon discovered the effort just wasn't worth it; and besides, the cabin with mosquito nets draped across the open rear doors was far too stuffy and hot. I used to chain and lock all the luggage to the roof rack as we had been warned against theft. The only item stolen while we slept was a pair of rubber thongs (flip-flop sandals). We had parked in a town behind some buildings and as Ann crawled into the back of the van to go to bed she left the thongs on the ground. During the night I heard a herd of goats around us but went back to sleep. In the morning the thongs had vanished. It was enough to demonstrate the risks we were running, possibly of physical attack, sleeping out in such exposed conditions. I was told it was a trick of thieves to drive animals around a vehicle or a hut to drown any noises they might make.

From then on we made a point of stopping at Dak bungalows. These were usually very well appointed and sometimes very luxurious villas – another hangover from the British Raj days. The buildings were kept in readiness to accommodate travelling government officials. India is such a vast country (with a first class network of roads) that surveyors and public works chiefs would often take two or three weeks to cover their inspectorate; and these gentlemen would see that the Dak bungalows were kept in good order.

A *chowkidar*, or watchman, was employed full-time at government expense. The chowkidars were invariably lazy and turned anyone (except officials) away if they could, although the Dak bungalow system was supposed to be available to tourists at a very cheap official rate. However, it didn't take long once in India to learn the way to a chowkidar's heart – few of them could resist a handful of rupees (say, £1 or $2) plus the official fee, which, if they felt you were trustworthy enough not to ask to sign the register, they would also pocket. By charging also for hot water, electricity, errands and fly spray (to kill the clouds of flies that shouldn't have been inside anyway) they had a nice little number going. Sometimes they would offer to cook for you but it would be a seasoned or intrepid European who accepted. To the traveller who had braved the day's dust and heat, not to mention the unbelievable numbers of human beings who crowded the roads and made driving a horn-blowing cacophonous nightmare, the price of a night in a Dak bungalow was cheap. The ones used by the British officials were small palaces; most had been commandeered for extra VIP usage. Once I stayed in one – a five room suite with all marble and tiled interior, 12 foot ceilings, sumptuous bathroom – in echoing, solitary splendour. Not at all bad for a mystic.

In New Delhi we rested for a few days in a pretty sleazy hotel, deciding to save our money for what might lie ahead in the Himalayas, now only 300 miles away. In true Indian style, a boy of about 12 slept outside our door, ostensibly to be available should we require him, but actually to collect a tip in the mornings. Life was incredibly hard for these young people and in these ways they managed to get by without resorting to begging.

I used to have something of a hang-up about hygiene and food. I still have it to a degree, although I'm much more resilient than I used to be, thanks to India. My problem in the third rate hotel in Delhi was to secure a breakfast (included in the tariff) which had not been handled, mishandled or otherwise tampered with by little fingers before it got to the room. You've got to think these things out strategically. My brilliant solution was to order boiled eggs. Very, very cunning. But you soon learn in India that they have an inexplicable way of beating you at your own game, although you keep trying again and again. The eggs arrived without their shells.

To have to live in India for 15 months was a fine bit of poetic (or divine) justice. The normal Indian idea of hygiene when observed at first hand through Western eyes was a pretty terrifying spectacle. Many of the population suffered from continuous diarrhea believing it to be the natural state. They didn't seem to comprehend the connection between transmitted bacteria and infectious diseases. They washed for holy or social reasons or personal comfort – they may have been very "clean" people – but they didn't see that the point was to prevent the spread of infection which was rampant in its most lethal forms all around them. It was easier to get sick in India because the potential of every contributing factor was greater. The diseases were all there, prevalent, virulent and waiting to spawn.

On one occasion we rented a timber cottage with earth floors on a small hill overlooking a village near Ranikhet, a Himalayan hillstation. It was quite an attractive spot and we wondered why the house was vacant. The next morning we found out. Hundreds of men and women from the village used the hill as a latrine. They spread out over the hill carrying little vase-like brass containers of water with which they washed themselves. Toilet paper was used only by Westernised Indians and the villagers regarded it as an unclean practice. Then we couldn't understand why the hill was so free from pollution, until the local swineherd arrived mid-morning on his daily round, driving 50 or 60 pigs which soon cleaned up the area. The pigs of course were raised to sell for human consumption.

Outside the towns it was not unusual for human excreta to be used as manure for crops. It was difficult for the authorities to impress on poor farmers and householders who couldn't afford fertilisers (or animal fodder) that human faeces were the host of most of man's worst diseases which may be very easily transmitted on onions, lettuce, tomatoes, fruits and the like. Vegetables had to be well boiled, fruit peeled, tomatoes, onions and lettuce soaked in "pink water" (permanganate of potash). Tomatoes I used to wash with soap, and then rinse. Onions – raw – and not previously a great favourite I used to eat just about every day, having found they seemed to keep me well. Also, when I couldn't boil my own water, I used to drink Coca Cola.

The only time I got sick was months later when I relaxed and ate a bit of salad with a buffalo steak in a hotel in Kathmandu, in neighbouring Nepal. Nepal is not India but its standard of hygiene was, if anything, far worse. I hadn't eaten a piece of steak in ten months. Also it was the first hotel I'd stayed in at that time and the few European guests seemed healthy enough. The price of a very cautious nibble at the side salad was a devastating dose of amoebic dysentery.

With this hygiene hang-up of mine, I was continuously running into situations which caused me intense discomfort. One night I dined with a wealthy Indian family in Agra, the Taj Mahal city. Their cook was a boy of 12 who had had the job for four years. He had a wonderful flair for it and was a professional by any standard. He was an orphan and had worked for the family as a domestic since he was six – in return for his keep. As I've mentioned, the unprivileged young Indian must grow up very quickly to survive. He confided to me that he loved his job and would never voluntarily leave it. His master, he said, used to beat him when he deserved it and he had no complaints about that; the last beating was for getting drunk on the boss's whisky. The alternative to living in this big comfortable house and working seven days a week with plenty of food as a sort of third class member of the family, was to go back to his grandfather's one room tin lean-to and subsist on what he could scrounge among the refuse at the local market.

This night he had prepared a wonderful array of dishes including a large central bowl of rice. One of my weaknesses is that I don't like to see food being handled and of course most Indians eat with their fingers and dip into the communal bowls as required. Fascinated, I watched the grandmother of the family, a fat grey-haired lady, dipping her hands into the bowl, scooping up palmfuls of rice and very deliberately (with much handling) squeezing the rice into a ball which she pushed into her mouth before going back for another dig.

Suddenly, she caught my eye. I'm sure my quick watery smile disclosed pain or disapproval as I did my best to acknowledge her happy brown-eyed chomping grin. She reached into the bowl once more and, still chomping, proceeded with palms and fingers to knead another sticky, soggy well-fingerprinted ball, all the time holding my gaze with a look of motherly good humour. Nervously, I laughed acknowledgment and with one movement she leant across and plopped the skin-warmed rice ball into my mouth. I froze. I chewed. I smiled, doing my best to swallow while trying not to vomit. Bit by bit I got it down.

Delhi is hot, very hot. It sprawls on a plateau-plain at the top-centre of India. Except for a brief three month winter when the temperature plunges into the 40s °F (4–9 °C), Delhi throbs day in and night out at well over 100 °F (38 °C). Many of the population sleep on little wood and webbing cots on the footpaths, not just because of the heat but because they have no other accommodation. Every year when the cold winter winds sweep across the plain many of them die. It's no one's fault. As far as I could see no political party in the foreseeable future would be able to put it right. India in many ways is a benign country to starve and die in. Most of the time the weather is warm and a frail, under-nourished body can burn the candle of life a little longer – for what reason, God knows. When it's cold, and the mind is made alert and man can be tempted to dwell too closely on his sorrows, they die quickly. The wick won't burn without fat.

We left Delhi and drove north 250 miles to Haldwani where the Himalayan foothills begin. Slowly we climbed off the plains. The temperature began to drop dramatically, deliciously. When we reached Nainital – a resort town nestled round a lake in a valley 6,500 feet (2,000 metres) above sea level – we were pulling on pullovers. By evening at Ranikhet, about 6,000 feet, it was gloriously chilly, almost cold. We allowed ourselves the luxury of a room with a bath, and to cap it, lit a wood fire in the fireplace. The contrast to the heat of Delhi and the plains of yesterday was incredible. The date was the 21st of March, the beginning of a brand new year in the Hindu calendar.

Next morning, driving along a ridge we caught our first glimpse of the Himalayan snow range. It is 120 miles long in this region and extends across the whole arc of vision. It is a magnificent, indescribable sight and an experience that seldom fails to stir a sense of awe and beauty. We dipped up and down through the valleys towards Almora, 20 miles away.

At the bottom of one hill was a parked car. This was unusual. Apart from lorries supplying the towns, and dusty, spartan-seated, jam-packed buses, very few private vehicles appeared on these roads. A man standing beside the car gingerly waved us down. He was in his late 20s and smartly dressed in a suit with the distinctive high-buttoned Indian-style collar which obviates a neck-tie.

'I have run out of petrol.' His English was impeccable. 'Do you have some I may borrow, please?'

I handed him a two gallon can which he emptied into his tank.

'Where are you heading?' he said.

'Almora.'

'Do you have a place to stay?'

'No.'

'It is very difficult there to find accommodation suitable for Europeans, especially ladies. The hotels are basic and I don't think you would be comfortable. Unless you are very accustomed to our country, the food would also be a problem.'

I told him we would look around for a place to rent. Did he know of one?

'I have such a place,' he declared. 'You are welcome to it as my guests. I am the District Cantonment Officer. I am responsible for maintaining the roads, buildings and civilian facilities in the Indian Army cantonment area there. I have a flat in the administration bungalow. It is fully furnished with its own kitchen and bathroom and is in very beautiful surroundings. You may have it for as long as you like. It is maintained for my use but when I visit each month I stay elsewhere with friends.'

We thanked him. The three of us couldn't help remarking on the coincidence of our meeting.

'Is it all right for us to stay in a military area?' I asked.

'Oh yes. There has been no trouble since the Chinese border warfare two years ago. The civilians who work for the army live in the cantonment area. The army camps of course are out of bounds. But there are no fences or guards around the cantonment. It is just a defined area – and much cleaner than the town, too.'

We then got around to introducing ourselves. His name was Yash Kapoor. His base and home were in Poona, the old British army town way down near Bombay, a thousand miles south. He drove off, leaving us directions and saying he would make the necessary arrangements with his administrative officer as soon as he arrived. We meandered along after him with the growing feeling that somehow our presence in the Himalayas was not unexpected.

The flat turned out to be everything he had described, and more. It was in a building erected by the British in the previous century. It was single storey, solid stone, roomy and (as usual) occupying a magnificent site. The British Raj always made a point of appropriating the dress circle of local real estate. The building was surrounded by beautiful gardens, the pride of two full-time gardeners. Our flat led onto a wide, covered verandah. This overlooked the tops of cone-laden pine trees growing among the tidy, well kept crisscross of roads below.

Our van only just made it up the steep hill to the flat. Unknown to me at the time, two pistons in the engine had broken rings and were scoring the cylinders. We had insufficient power and started to roll backwards. I stood on the brake and the horn and yelled for help to a group of bystanders watching with much amused expectation. They ran across. With me revving and them pushing, we made it. The van had had it. I wasn't sorry to park it on the back verandah and forget about it for a couple of weeks. We were here. Now what?

Almora was a nice town. It straddled a ridge that was not unlike a lizard's back. Down the residential and market end it was a bit rough and smelly but basically fairly clean. The sweepers, who were responsible for keeping the near mile long, 15 foot wide, market passage clean, worked in a continuous dust cloud as they flogged their way along the cobblestones using clusters of switches for brooms. The passage was lined with hundreds of little bazaar-like shops of every description — tailors, barbers, brass and copper mongers, grocers, watch repairers, boot repairers, tea rooms, confectioners, greengrocers, grain sellers, drapers, apothecaries – and dust, like the unstrained quality of mercy, settled gently over all.

Very few of the shopkeepers bothered to wear shoes. Some of them went unshaven on Tuesdays because that's the day ruled by Mars, the planet of bloodspilling – and who wanted to risk that just for a shave? The children, who lived with their mothers and fathers, grandparents and uncles and aunts above the shops, played happily in the market passage. Some of the toddlers, with enormous soulful eyes heavily out-lined in a black dye to protect them from the glare of the sun, looked weirdly, sophisticatedly beautiful. There wasn't so much indiscriminate spitting here. No adults fouled the footpaths. There was a sense of com-munity. A lot of the people were poor; but no one seemed to go hungry. Almora was a pretty self-respecting, well managed town.

I wrote to Ivan telling him we had arrived in Almora and he wrote me this letter from Australia:

> Dear Barry,
>
> I got your notice from 'dirty, but dear old Almora' as I used to call it when I was there. At first glance – and even after many days there – one would not realise just how much of the mysterious, or at least the very unusual, there is hidden in Almora. Don't leave it in a hurry – if you have to leave. Have you been out to see the Lama Li Gotama or Sunyata Sorenson out at Kalimath where Ivan found his Calvary and died on the Cross? If so, did you ask Sorenson to let you have a look at the little cottage where Ivan lived? Is the admonition (or was it a name?) SILENCE still on the wall? Have you visited Snow View out on the ridge, with its unbroken view of the Himalayas from one horizon to the other?
>
> Have no doubt that if you are destined for crucifixion your Calvary will be waiting for you – wherever it may be. You will be led without your realising it. It may be Almora – it may not be. Where can you go on – either east, west or south again into the heat? To the east directly, you have Nepal and you can't go in there. You must have a visa and when I was there it was hard to get more than a couple of weeks' residential permit. It is of course a fascinating and unusual place (even more so than India) but very, very primitive. To the west lie the other Himalayan hill stations – Mussoorie, Simla etc. If you find yourself near Mussoorie, you should visit Dehra Doon, and Rishikesh.
>
> The details, as you can see, of what your Lord's intentions are with you are not revealed to this mind… But what a glorious experience you are having! Do not forget what lies waiting for you when you return here. It will be all that wretched business over again. Count every hour of freedom that you are blessed with as precious. They will go all too soon. All too soon you will be faced with the problem of making a living again.

In Almora village, I ran into Sunyata Sorenson of Kalimath while he was doing some shopping. Although wearing Indian clothes he was unmistakably European. Sorenson, who was in his 70s at this time (1965), had come to Almora from Europe as a young man. He was himself a mystic who, the story goes, had been "recognised" in England by Rabindranath Tagore, the Indian philosopher-mystic-poet, who invited him to India in 1929. Ramana Maharshi was also supposed to have seen something in Sorenson and gave him the name Sunyata. Later, in the 1970s, he was taken up by some of Alan Watt's followers and went to California where he gave weekly darshan from a houseboat in Sausalito. When I bumped into him Sorenson remembered Ivan very well. 'He poisoned my dog!' exclaimed the old man with a touch of indignation. 'He was sick while he was staying here. He threw out some porridge with medicine in it and my dog ate it and died.'

And the word "SILENCE" on the wall of the hut where Ivan had lived? Later I discovered that it was still there, but now it was on the gate that led to the room where he had suffered so much. I posted him a photograph of it.

Lama Li Gotama lived in a secluded cottage on a hill with dozens of prayer flags fluttering in the constant breeze. We went up to see him but were turned away by his lady or housekeeper, who from reports kept him pretty much incommunicado.

At the cantonment flat we cooked our own meals. At the market we were able to choose from a wide assortment of fresh vegetables and fruit. We had our own shower, flush toilet, bedroom, sitting room, private entrance and a superb garden filled with sweet peas in which to walk. A plaque fixed to the verandah wall announced that Tagore had once lived here.

A couple of mornings after we moved in, a man selling bread knocked at the door. He wore the traditional Indian *dhoti* (a long white loincloth), loosely fitting white shirt and sandals. Would we like some bread? Yes please. Would I like to learn how to read palms? Yes please.

For the next six weeks he arrived every day at 7am and gave me an hour's lesson. So in addition to astrology, I was now having added to my repertoire of occult studies another branch of self-knowledge, the principles of hand reading. I do not read hands as a social, predictive pastime. I am interested in the psychological factors and tendencies of character which the lines in the hand clearly define. One has to read as many hands as possible for practice and it can be embarrassing as well as amusing when you don't know anything about the person. Later on in Almora I was reading the hands of a group of Indians that my teacher had brought along for me to practise on. The sign on one fellow's hand was obvious.

'You will have to be very careful,' I said cautiously. 'You could be extremely violent if you lose your temper and possibly injure someone.'

'Wonderful!' cried my teacher while the others laughed and the poor fellow whose hand I was studying looked sheepish. 'He's just this week come out of jail for attempted murder.'

My palm reading tutor was a Brahmin, a Bachelor of Arts and qualified school master. His bakery round was an attempt to break away into the commercial world. I'm afraid the only lasting results that came out of the venture were that he did teach me the philosophy of palmistry and became my very dear friend. Bhagwan Swaroop Vasishth, "Master Sahib" as the very respectful locals used to call him, later went back to teaching as the principal of a small school at Haldwani.

At 6am, about six weeks after our arrival at the flat, there was an urgent knock on the door. It was the administration officer himself. We had become quite friendly. He was agitated.

'I'm sorry, but you have to leave immediately. The Army has given orders that all foreigners living in the cantonment area [us] must vacate forthwith.'

'Why? What's happened?'

'I don't know officially. But it's some kind of spy scare. Two Europeans, Germans I think, have been found up in the Himalayan border passes, a strictly forbidden area. It is unfortunate. But you realise we also have this problem with Pakistan. The military are edgy.'

For some weeks there had been spasmodic fighting between Indian and Pakistani forces on the Kashmir border several hundred miles away to the north-west. But this was a new development, closer to the passes north of Almora forming the natural mountain barrier between Tibet (occupied by China) and India. The Indian Army would never forget the fearful lessons learnt on similar mountain passes when Chinese troops poured across the Indian version of the disputed border in 1962.

During our stay in the cantonment area, we were often invited to tea by the regular Indian Army officers, some of whom had fought the

Chinese. They were an impressive lot, smart, professional, dedicated – every bit in the tradition of the British Army which had trained their predecessors for 200 years. The story they told us about the Chinese invasion two years before was fascinating – and terrifying. They had come up against a new method of warfare which, as far as I am aware, was never reported in the newspapers.

To begin with, the battleground was probably the hardest and most difficult that men can be asked to fight on. In these mountain passes, 12,000 and 15,000 feet up, snow-choked and incredibly cold, troops often had to fight in oxygen masks. Ammunition, food and supplies all had to be transported by mule trains, and then manhandled up the last few thousand feet. Only limited supplies could be dropped by parachute; heavy ordnance buried itself irretrievably in the snow of the ravines or was lost among unreachable crags and crevices. But the diabolical side of this brief war at the top of the world lay in the alleged tactics employed by the Chinese Army. According to the Indian officers I spoke to, the Chinese sent in wave after wave of male civilians dressed like soldiers. The Indian troops killed them as fast as they came. They fired until their guns were too hot to touch. And still the Chinese kept coming. The piles of Chinese dead mounted and mounted, jamming the defiles. Those behind climbed over the dead, fell and advanced inexorably in a flow of corpses. The Indians were forced to fall back. They began running out of ammunition. In these conditions, no back up resource could supply sufficient tonnage of lead to keep the guns firing. When the Indian guns had gone silent the Chinese sent in their regular troops. These halted when they reached what the Chinese regarded as the border.

'How can you fight an enemy like that?' they asked.

Having heard these tales, it wasn't surprising to us that the Indians were restless. And that we had to move on. Where to? Fortunately, I'd had the van repaired. I'd located one of those wonderfully ingenious Indian mechanics whose "garage" was a corrugated iron lean-to on the roadside in Almora village. The job entailed taking out the entire engine (which he did with an improvised crane) having the cylinders re-bored, and reassembling the whole thing with what appeared to me to be the most rudimentary tool kit. This was the man who earlier had turned a piece of a rusty old shovel into a highly effective fifth blade on the radiator fan.

We packed up the van and within an hour were on our way. We decided to try to get further into the foothills, away from civilisation, deeper into this Himalayan vastness that seems to have always attracted seekers after the intangible. Yet no matter how far you penetrate there is nothing there – of course. We pushed in, and in, beyond outposts like Binsar, Kosi, Kausani, Bageshwar, Gwaldam, virtually to the end of the road where there are not even Indians, only jungle (as they call it) and snow-coned Trisul in the background.

India, and particularly the Himalayas, contains an energy, something like a presence, which activates a certain part of the subconscious in receptive individuals. These people seem to find their way there from all parts of the world. Whereas the energy of the West seems to affirm the feeling of individuality, India awakens a personal sense of universality.

After three weeks of wandering, we returned to Almora and headed up the winding, dusty road to Kalimath, four miles away and 1,500 feet higher. It seemed to us we had tried everywhere and there was just nowhere else to go. And Kalimath? Two dilapidated teashops on a bend between two hills. I took our two enamel mugs over and brought them back filled with hot, sweet, black tea. (It wasn't wise to risk the milk in the teashops; and the sugar helped in the heat.) We sat silent and sipping. Obviously, there was nowhere to stay here.

'Hello!' An Indian lady with very well groomed hair and wearing a fine, colourful sari, was standing beside Ann's open window.

'Would you like to come and have tea with us, my husband and I? It would be much more comfortable.'

We looked around quizzically.

'Our bungalow is at the top of that hill,' she said. 'Up that narrow drive beside our garage there.'

The garage was almost obscured by growth at the bottom of a steep unmade drive which disappeared into the trees. The lady looked to be in her early 40s and spoke excellent English. We accepted her invitation gratefully.

In low gear, we started up the drive. After about 30 yards we passed a high hedge and then a little wooden gate in the middle of it. On the gate was that word "SILENCE". I could have reached out and touched it as we crawled past. It was the entrance to Sunyata Sorenson's place where Ivan had lived. I couldn't remember him ever mentioning a bungalow at the top of the hill. We continued up the drive which was now becoming steeper and very rough. In the midst of a cluster of shrubs and trees we stopped. The van could climb no further. We got out, walked a couple of yards and stepped onto the most panoramic residential site I have ever seen; the view of the Himalayas was breathtaking.

The whole top of the hill had been cut away leaving a flat half acre circle overlooking everything. Ornamental shrubs, fruit trees and huge deodar cedars (Sanskrit: timber of the gods) dotted the perimeter with an abundance of flower gardens in between. Below to the south was Almora village; to the east, valley after valley of jungle; to the west, the driveway down to the teashops and more jungle; and to the north, the Himalayan snow range, the finest view of it I have ever had. The centre-piece was a large stone bungalow, again built by the British in their heyday, and now a little dilapidated and inside uncomfortably old fashioned. To emphasise the building's faded nostalgia was a disused and forlorn-looking croquet court in the grounds at the back.

Major Chowdhry (Indian Army, retired) and his wife and children spent the summers here to escape the heat of their home in Lucknow on the plains.

'Are you travelling through?' asked Chowdhry. We were sitting in garden chairs around an outdoor table under the pines while his wife prepared tea.

'Not really,' I said and explained about our stay at the cantonment. 'We're hoping to find somewhere else.'

'Look no further,' he declared, pointing just beyond the pines to where the roof of a small building jutted up from a terrace in the side of the hill. 'We recently built it for my grandmother. She died just as it was being finished and never moved in. The place is small, but everything you need is there. And as you see, it has a beautiful unencumbered view of the snow range. You are welcome to stay there as long as you wish.'

We stayed seven weeks. Four of these were spent alone in magnificent isolation in our little mountain top hut after the Chowdhry's had returned to Lucknow. The monsoon arrived. It deluged off and on for several weeks but was never continuous for more than a day. Bright, warming sunlight kept any damp at bay. The rain washed the air crystal clear and dissolved the clouds from around the Himalayas. Unless these giants are seen during the monsoon season they can't really be fully appreciated. We woke with them and went to sleep with them – under an incredible starry sky.

And again we were apparently following in good footsteps... Chowdhry mentioned that an Indian yogi saint had lived and meditated on the spot where our hut was located. (Such reports don't seem unusual in India.)

The garden contained several fruit trees. We watched the bounty ripen. But before we could get to the fruit a horde of chattering monkeys descended and cleaned up the lot, ripe and unripe.

Much of our time was spent in meditation and contemplation. I knew that inner change was occurring. This was affirmed by a most significant event for me. Throughout our journey across India, and while in Australia, I would often gaze at the clouds on the horizon far away and feel a pang of distance and separation from the beauty. On this particular day from our mountain top I was looking again at the distant clouds and suddenly realised I was no longer separate from the beauty of them. It was now inside me. I knew that my old self, which had created the distance, was beginning to drop away. I put it this way in a song:

> Goodbye, old friend
> This is the end
> For you and me the path splits here.
> You must know it's time to go
> Old friend
> My fiercest foe, farewell.
> It once was fun to think we'd done
> To win and lose, reject and choose.
> But as the youth discards the toy
> Dearest possession of the boy
> We're through.

# CHAPTER 10

# GOODBYE ANN

A nd what was happening to Ann, and in Ann, all this idyllic time we were together? I really don't know. I remember very little. It's as though most of my memories of her have been erased. Which is strange considering my great love of her at the time. As she once said, she only loved me because she must. Perhaps, when what that meant was done, there was little need for memories.

I remember small things. She would often sit down and scribble rhyming poetry about life and living. She'd write at great speed, notepage after notepage. One line I recall was in a poem about the nature of humanity and so apt was it that I have used it in my own writings. "We are a struggling pain to know..." it said.

I remember her having her palm read. The palmist said, looking at her mount of Venus under the thumb, 'You could have been a dancer.' That's all I can recall and although I taped my own readings, there's not a trace among my papers of any transcript of hers. But the reference to her dancing had an actual meaning which I have only just seen. She would sometimes dance for me. And I described it in a little song which I'd sing to her.

> Dance, dance, dance for me
> Swish your skirt, let your hair fall free

Stamp your heel and let me see
The dance of my beloved.

Clearly, I cannot do her justice for she was an extraordinary woman. That I do not remember. I just know it.

We were running short of money. Nine months in India, plus the van repairs, had cost more than I'd estimated. There was only one thing to do: Get Ann out while we still had her fare back to Australia. I could manage alone; a man can. Ann didn't want to go at first but then realised the logic of the situation. If it is not time for a person to leave India, they won't go, no matter how rational the argument may be. Ann went.

On the 2nd of August, the day after my 39th birthday, we said farewell to Kalimath and headed back to Delhi. There we would book her a berth on a ship to Australia. She would catch the air-conditioned train down to Bombay, while I would drive the van 1,200 miles in the opposite direction to Kathmandu, Nepal, and sell it. This, I estimated, would provide enough rupees for me to live on in India while Ann got a job in Australia and saved up some hard currency for us to plan the next move.

She obtained a berth on one of the P&O liners and on a beautiful, clear August morning, at Delhi railway station, we pledged our undying love and parted.

I had driven only one day from Delhi, as far as a town named Bareilly, when the pain of absence from Ann started up. I hadn't experienced it for nine months. There were now longer periods of peace, but when the emotion came it was like an axe-blow in my solar plexus. I wept. I held my arms across my body and doubled up. And wept and wept. The pain seemed worse than it had ever been. God, how I was missing her.

At times the pain seemed unbearable; but there was nothing I could do for relief. I just was the pain when it was there. The peace that came in between was as though nothing had happened; as though there was only now and what was happening at this moment. At these times I even enjoyed the rest of the 900 mile drive across India. It took about four days to reach the Indian/Nepalese border town of Raxaul.

On the way, there was a highly disturbing incident. The main roads in India are of bitumen and good, and I was travelling at about 30 miles per hour (50 km/h). A bus was parked off the road on the opposite side and a number of families were sitting on the dirt in front of it. Suddenly, a boy of about seven ran from around the back of the bus straight across my path. I stood on the brake, turning the wheel as much as I could away from him. In what seemed an interminably slow motion action, I watched the van slowing, the boy coming towards it and just as it was about to stop, him disappearing under the front. I jumped out, ran around to the boy and saw that he was just under the bonnet and between the wheels. I helped him up. He had a slight cut on his forehead but otherwise seemed okay. He ran off back to the bus. At the same time several of the men and women approached me in a rather hostile manner. Using gestures I explained how the boy had run across the road in front of me. They knew this to be the case but I wasn't sure they wanted to admit it. I could see an indeterminate situation developing if I stayed. The boy was okay. So I dug out a handful of rupee notes, handed them to the man making the most noise, jumped in the van and drove on.

The one road up to Kathmandu was a 70 mile, one track horror-stretch. It contorted backwards and forwards up the side of a mountain to a height of 8,000 feet. On crossing the border, and to reach this road, I had to traverse a small but fast-running stream. It was the rainy season; the stream was already 18 inches deep and obviously would rise before it fell. The force of a current of water like this on the side of a small vehicle is likely to sweep it downstream. I had covered several of these tragedies while reporting floods in Australia. So I opened both doors wide, jammed them in that position and with six or eight inches of water racing over the floor, chugged the 20 or 30 feet across the stony bed to the other side. How the electrics didn't short out I'll never know.

The road to Kathmandu was built in the 1950s as a gift to Nepal by the Indian government. Most of Nepal's imports went up the road in a constant stream of heavy diesel lorries. In wet weather the lorries carved tracks two feet deep. This meant driving the low-slung van a lot of the time with the right wheel on the centre line and the left wheel a foot or two from the edge of the road, mostly an unfenced 1,000 foot drop. People told me that an average of one lorry a week was lost over the side. If two vehicles were approaching one had to back up to a passing bay. Landslides were regular and shovels standard equipment. Once you started out there was no stopping till you got to the top.

In those days Kathmandu was chronically short of private vehicles. The country had no spare foreign currency to import them. The locals would buy just about anything that was mobile. Many Europeans visiting India were taking the overland route through Iran, selling their clapped-out vehicles in Kathmandu, and flying out to Delhi with a huge profit in rupees. Once in India, Nepalese rupees were fully convertible to local rupees. But the catch was getting the Nepalese rupees out; the export of the currency was forbidden and any notes seized were confiscated.

The sale of vehicles by foreigners was also illegal, strictly speaking; but the Nepalese government was prepared to turn a blind eye if the local purchaser paid a whacking 100% tax. In other words, he paid double. As I drove into the city scores of locals in their tight trousers and jaunty-angled skullcaps ran beside the van shouting, 'Four thousand'… 'Five thousand'… 'You sell to me!'

I eventually settled for 6,000 rupees (£300). Considering that the fellow who bought it had to pay another 6,000 in tax and that he would sell the van at a good profit, the final buyer would pay the price of a very nice new car outside Nepal.

The only problem remaining was how to smuggle out the loot. Could I outwit the Nepalese with more success than I usually managed with the Indians? Periodic searches were made of passengers at the airport. With most of the Europeans up there to sell their cars it wasn't difficult for the authorities to guess who was flying out with what. Everyone of course devised their secret methods and hiding places which I'm sure by then must have all been familiar to the officials, as well as to the local population. The authorities didn't want to end this lucrative traffic but they had to make a show. A chap who left the day before me lost half of his rupee roll when they searched his girlfriend and found it sewn into her bra.

My plan was hardly more original; but it really should have worked. I made four parcels of the rupees. Three I posted at the Kathmandu post office in separate envelopes: one to myself care of a New Delhi hotel, one to Almora and the other care of the Delhi post office. The fourth lot of notes (after paying accommodation and airfare to Delhi) I put in my money belt (worn next to the skin) and took my chances. The Nepalese didn't search my flight. But they still outmanoeuvred me. Only the letter to the hotel got through. Some alert brown fingers somehow pocketed the other £140. Still, after expenses, I had cleared the equivalent of £100. That would be enough to keep me for a few more months back in Almora.

I flew out of Kathmandu sick with stomach pains and diarrhea. By the time I'd checked into Narulan's Hotel in Delhi, I was nearly passing out. The doctor diagnosed amoebic dysentery and put me on a powerful new drug. This is something one has to be careful of in these places; the zealous use of new drugs may cure the immediate complaint but cause other damage. It pays the traveller to read the warnings on the drug packets, particularly the time specified as being safe to take the drug.

While I lay for eight days in absolute misery on my back in the hotel room, the Indian and Pakistani air forces fought it out overhead and Delhi's anti-aircraft defences boomed most of the night in a brief clash between the two hostile nations.

The wonder capsules did the trick. The doctor explained that amoebic dysentery had a habit of recurring nine months after the first attack. The treatment, he said, should be repeated then, even in the absence of symptoms. In London eight months later I reported to the School of Tropical Medicine where the Indian capsules were spirited away and I was given something else to take. Still, I'm certainly not knocking the treatment I received in Delhi; the London tests proved negative and I've never had a recurrence, despite another visit to India and Kathmandu.

On the 7th of September 1965, still a bit groggy and weak, I caught the train from Delhi to Kathgodam, the end of the line for Indian railways. I taxied to Haldwani at the edge of the plains and bussed it up to Almora, arriving three days later after an overnight stay at the Nainital Hotel. I headed straight for Chilkapita where Bhagwan, my tutor in palmistry, lived.

Chilkapita is the name of the large bungalow mentioned in the introduction to this book. It means "high-flying birds" and is about two miles from Almora village on the opposite side to Kalimath. The bungalow is isolated, with terraced gardens and vegetable plots cut into the side of the hill. Again, an Indian yogi saint is said to have lived in one of the outhouses for several years. Chilkapita is in a beautiful spot but it can only be reached through the pines by rough and rocky paths that drop 300 feet in less than half a mile. To climb down is to emulate a mountain goat.

I rounded the final bend to the gate of the bungalow, and froze. Standing quietly behind it, too quietly, as though he had been expecting me for some time, was a very large dog. He didn't bark or move. His silence and restraint were oddly sinister. I hadn't seen a breed like this before; greyish, curly hair, big head – and so quiet and still.

'Bhagwan,' I shouted. 'Bhagwan. It's Barry.'

Bhagwan, smiling hugely under his broad moustache, hurried forward to greet me. He was as usual dressed in dhoti, shirt and sandals. He threw open the gate and we shook hands.

'Welcome,' he said. 'Come.'

I hesitated, glancing at the dog still standing in motionless vigil behind the slats of the open gate.

'Don't worry. He won't harm *you*.'

I was going to ask why but the conversation moved on. We walked around the back of the house to the terraced lawn and sat on the edge of the verandah overlooking the valley.

'Ann has gone?'

'Yes.'

'You must stay here.'

'I have arranged with Chowdhry to go back to the hut at Kalimath.'

'It's too dangerous to live up there alone. You could be murdered. No one would know. Every European is a millionaire to the Indians. You know that. It would be foolhardy. Stay here.'

I looked across at the dog, now lying stretched out on his stomach with muzzle along the ground, watching me. 'He's new.'

'Yes. He's a Bhotia. No one will harm us while he's here. He's only a pup, nine months old. He'll grow twice as big.'

I decided to take Bhagwan's advice and stay with him at Chilkapita.

Over a cup of tea, Bhagwan told me the story of Bhotia hounds. The breed was developed by the shepherds of Bhutan, at the time a poor and mountainous little country on the northeast frontier, next to Nepal. The mountain tribes right up as far as Afghanistan used the dogs to protect their flocks from marauding leopards (actually cheetahs) and tigers. A good, fully grown male dog with a female partner could fight off a cheetah and three or four of them were often a match for a tiger. They worked instinctively in pairs or as a team.

Bhagwan, with fondness and enthusiasm, described the Bhotia's unusual characteristics. First, he said, he was a one-man dog. He regarded his master's property – the home and the family members – as his own. Whoever the master accepted as a friend, the dog accepted. Second, the Bhotia was mainly a night hound; his senses became extraordinarily keen after dusk. This is the time when the leopards came out to hunt and were most likely to attack the flock.

Bhagwan said he got his first Bhotia from a party of hillsmen who camped near the bungalow on the way down to sell their goats and sheep in the villages. They had four Bhotias with them, two dogs, two bitches, and a litter. The four dogs used to circle the animals like sentries, keeping them in a compact group while the shepherds slept. They never failed to sense a leopard nearby and to raise the alarm. Their presence as a pack usually deterred an attack. If a leopard did try to attack, three of the Bhotias would endeavour to deal with the intruder while the fourth stayed close to the flock as long as possible, in case the leopard had a mate.

I was surprised when Bhagwan announced that leopards were fairly prevalent around Chilkapita. Unlike tigers, he said, they didn't usually attack people; but dogs were their favourite meal. The leopard was an amazingly resourceful and silent hunter, he said, and any dog that wasn't locked up at night didn't last long.

I was even more surprised when he said a leopard had actually taken a fully grown Bhotia dog from his bedroom here in the bungalow while he (Bhagwan) was asleep on the bed! I must say it did sound a bit like an active imagination working overtime for the entertainment of a visitor. But Bhagwan was not the leg-pulling type. He was extremely serious when he described the incident and showed the genuine concern of the dog lover for the loss of his canine companion.

'It was a hot night, I should have known better,' he started. 'The dog was lying in the half open door leading onto the balcony there. There was an electrical storm; much lighting and thunder. I can only assume that this impaired his senses. Anyway, I was awakened by a sudden heavy thump. The leopard had grabbed the Bhotia at the back of the neck, snapping the vertebrae in the same bite so that no sound was emitted. This is the leopard's style of attack. It then raced off over the terrace here and down the hill with the carcass.

'Leopards have ferocious strength and agility – they can run at 60 miles an hour you know. I didn't see any of the attack. It was dark. But that's what happened. There were bloodstains to the edge of the terrace. The dog must have weighed 60 or 70 pounds. The leopard throws its prey across its back. The remains were found a few days later three quarters of a mile down there in the jungle.'

A couple of weeks later we heard that a tiger had taken an eight year old girl from a nearby village. The villagers tracked the animal down and killed it. As is not uncommon in an attack of this kind, the tiger was lame from old wounds, which would have reduced its ability to hunt its natural food. When prey is short in the hills a hungry and crippled tiger will attack human beings, especially children. But these days tigers are rare in the Himalayan foothills.

One October evening about a month after my arrival at Chilkapita, Bhagwan and I were returning home from a walk with the Bhotia dog on a lead. We were on the last turn in the path before the bungalow gate. On our right was the bank of the hill where the pine trees grow, and on our left a very steep incline down to a gully about 40 feet below. As we had only ten yards or so to go, Bhagwan let the dog off the lead. It was just about dark. The dog padded off ahead around the bend and out of sight. We were just rounding the bend when there was a "flash" of sound across the path, the choked beginning of some sort of cry and the pounding of two or three heavy landings down the incline. Then silence.

The Bhotia had been taken. The attack occurred less than 12 feet in front of us. The leopard had obviously had the dog marked out for some time, waiting for an opportunity. It was customary for us to go for a walk most evenings about this time but Bhagwan had not unleashed the dog before. The leopard evidently had waited on the bank above, sprung, killed the dog in flight with one terrible bite, and in two or three bounds was down the gully and out of earshot with its victim.

I was dumbfounded. Bhagwan was almost in tears, blaming himself for his negligence. I must say that for quite a few nights afterwards I used to contemplate the fragile mosquito wirescreen across the open window just above my bed.

The bungalow was roomy with stone floors, the architecture staidly Indian Victorian. Bhagwan lived in one side so I moved into the other. In between was a very large lounge and dining room and at my end a kitchen, both of which we shared. Each of us had his own bathroom, that is, a bare and empty room with a central drain where one could pour water over himself Indian style, after carting it from a spring ten yards away in the garden.

The spring water came straight out of the side of the hill through a one inch pipe someone had driven into the rocks. It ran perpetually at about a gallon every six or seven minutes. This is the only water I risked drinking without boiling in India; it was sweet, cool and crystal clear – and too darned cold in the winter to use unwarmed for bathing. Heating meant burning hard-to-get paraffin oil in the Primus so I decided to introduce a system used in outback Australia where water is in short supply and a daily shower a therapeutic necessity. This involved acquiring an empty four gallon paraffin tin, cutting it in half, affixing a wire handle and punching twenty or thirty small nail holes in the bottom to make a shower rose. A saucepan of cold water and then one of near boiling are poured in, the tin hoisted to hang by its handle from a nail or fixing overhead, and a refreshing shower, as warm as you want and lasting six or seven minutes, can be enjoyed at very little cost in money or effort. (You must of course be stripped and ready when you hoist the tin!)

Bhagwan was away most of the day on his bread round. He soon taught me that yoghurt was the simplest and cheapest source of protein. I used to eat about a pound a day, taking it with bananas and sugar, with rice and nuts. In the winter I bought it from a little roadside stall where the milk was boiled in a large open clay vessel – and the dust from passing trucks and even stray hairs from passing bodies found their way into the bowl, and stayed there. But the yoghurt culture seems to devour harmful bacteria and for this reason it is often a cure when taken alone for diarrhea. In the summer I used to make my own yoghurt by leaving the little wooden container in the sun on the verandah, a process that in other climes usually requires the use of a warm oven.

During my six month stay at Chilkapita I was vegetarian by compulsion, as well as celibate.

# CHAPTER 11

# IMMORTALITY

*You will be alone when you discover the secret of death.*
*And you will be alone when you discover the secret of life.*

T he loneliness, the confusion, the pain of psychological isolation that precedes the realisation of immortality is appalling. I can only describe the way it happened to me. Circumstances may differ. But the reality of the experience itself, even though it is subjective, has to be the same for all those who have it. Immortality is immortality. It is not a concept. It is a state of being. It is not survival since it reveals there is nothing to survive. Yet it is far greater than any notion of survival. Immortality is the realisation that death is a myth. And in that realisation, freed of the primary human fear, I discover I am the life in all living things.

I know personally four other people who have had the experience. Three of us suffered a long period of psychological agony beforehand. The other, a woman, had no pain, initially. She had one single realisation that embodied immortality plus something even greater. So circumstances vary but the knowledge does not. All I can say is my realisations of both immortality and later, transcendence, were preceded by tremendous mental suffering and a kind of emotional disintegration. In my experience, unless there is the intervention of a master and the realisation is instantaneous, agony is the only way to these higher truths.

Many people have experienced flashes of immortality; some have spent hours in the state. But the realisation process as I am defining it, by making the person actually pass through death, permanently removes from the mind the very subtle dread of dying. Without "dying" first, the dread will remain when the experience has passed.

My separation from Ann was again the catalyst. The pain of this gradually purged me of the exclusive emotion of "my" love, "my" Ann, "my" Bhagavati, "my" pain. I seemed to have an inexhaustible supply of this personal, possessive emotion. After every paroxysmal wringing out it seeped again into my depths demanding further purgation. The pain of separation from Ann was now greater than it had ever been.

One day, as I stumbled through the pines to get where I could just lie down and die, a voice in my consciousness said, 'Let it run.' In that moment I realised that the thing that was suffering, running, sobbing, was not I; it was what was being purged, it was the possessive concept of "my" and "mine".

Next, I knew I was going to die. In such devastating pain of loss there was no way that I could continue. I knew I was going to die physically. I was quite healthy but that was irrelevant. I knew I was going to die. I wrote a sort of will leaving Bhagwan my typewriter and a few possessions at Chilkapita, and requesting him to send a couple of things back to Ann. I wrote as obliquely as I could to my mother in Australia telling her what to do 'should anything ever happen to me while I was in India.' I think I also informed Ann and told her to keep anything she had of mine, including a rather expensive tape recorder.

The sense of imminent death, fear, hopelessness and being deserted, as well as the inner emotional spasms, continued for eight weeks. Once as I lay in a clearing looking up at the sky, a high flying aeroplane came into view and I cried out pathetically, 'Please, please don't leave me behind.'

Then followed three days of astonishing confusion and uncertainty. I was adrift. I had no will. I could not make the simplest decision. I could not even decide when to get up in the mornings – as though a decision was necessary. Two paths led up to the village from the bungalow; I stood for 20 minutes trying to decide which one to take, as if it mattered. On the third day I realised I was dead.

Shortly after, I realised immortality. Death was a condition of the mind but it was not a fact. I had somehow passed through that condition. And now I was exultant, filled with the joy and knowledge that I was actually one with the life in nature, with every creature and living thing. I was forever, as life was. I was at peace. I was in no hurry to do anything, or not to do anything. I was choiceless. I was free.

Then, as I stood on the verandah of the bungalow looking up at the pine trees, the second verse of the song quoted in the introduction came to me.

> I must go where the four winds blow
> Where the spirit speaks to its own,
> For now I am free like the wind I must be
> And help the others home.

The job was done. I had been made eternally free as the first verse had predicted. (Eternally free is a spiritual dimension and it means to be uninterruptedly everlasting, like nature. Absolutely free is something else: the final God-given state marked by the absence of desire or suffering. For that blessing I had to wait three years.)

A few hours later in the same spot on the verandah another spiritual experience overtook me. An inner voice said, 'Do you love the Bhagavati?'

I replied, 'I do.'

'Do you honour her, cherish her, serve her – and forsaking any other, keep yourself forever wholly unto her?'

'I do.'

'Then I unite you as you always have been, as you always will be and as you always are.'

When the voice mentioned the Bhagavati, I identified her with Ann's form. This, as I've said, I had yet to learn was the error of my love.


It was now early November 1965. I had been writing my first book for some time before my realisation and now with the new knowledge was able to expand on the finer points. I wrote sitting at a table on the grass outside the bungalow wearing "my old sahib hat". It was this setting, and a few well-meaning laughs from a couple of Bhagwan's friends, that prompted the song about the hat. Although it was winter, it was hot –

hot, hot! So hot that unbeknown to me the heat dried the oil out of my little Hermes portable typewriter and by the time I'd finished the book, the machine was literally clapped out.

In between writing I took time to walk up to Kalimath where, about a kilometre past the teashops, I'd seen a vacant property that took my fancy. For some time I'd been thinking about living in India and this property of about ten acres seemed just right. It was called Deena Pani, meaning shallow water, after the spring that rose from an underground stream close to the surface.

Some of the foundations of the original British built house were still there but most had been carted away by the locals. Anyway, my fantasy, and I don't think I'd ever had one like this before, had even reached the stage where I'd drawn a plan of the type of residence I envisioned; an oblong building of two storeys around a large courtyard onto which every room opened. I also noted that there was just enough room for me to land a light aircraft – even though I couldn't fly! So serious was I that I applied (unsuccessfully) in the local magistrate's court for permission as a foreigner to buy the land, if necessary in partnership with a local Indian. That was the stumbling block, as foreigners were not allowed to directly own Indian land, it had to be arranged unofficially in the name of an Indian national and I couldn't find one with enough money.

Was I thinking that my book was going to make me a millionaire? Had the predictions of earning huge sums of money in the future convinced me subconsciously that I could do all this? Really, the motivation for my fantasy was altruistic. I had developed a deep affection for the ordinary Indian people. And I was aware of the numbers of young Indian men and women graduates who never, and would never, have the opportunity to follow their chosen career. There were too many of them for the country's lack of commercial and industrial development, particularly in the hills. My plan was to turn Deena Pani into a farm for the benefit of all who worked on it. I wanted to run it with graduates in agriculture, animal husbandry, etc. The only condition was that each one must love the land and their own particular calling.

It was a dream, and I'm not really a dreamer. I suspect that someone, somewhere, sometime will live out that dream, just as with our lives we are all living out someone's past dream that never got lived. Anyway, I was seized enough by the dream of Deena Pani to write this song:

Deena Pani, shallow water.
Deena Pani, water of life.
Fated to be mine since time began
To hold for a few of those who love the land.
Deena Pani, shallow water,
Deena Pani, giver of life.

Ann had been gone four months. Her letters contained ominous sounds of change. She was having second thoughts. Things were different back in the harsh clear light of Australia. It was all right for me on my Himalayan mountain top, she wrote, but for her having to cope with two jobs and trying to save, it was hard and rough. And besides, she had heard I intended to return to my wife. (Where that report came from I don't know and it was utterly false; I had no such intention.) One of Ann's last letters contained this not so cryptic statement, 'I think I'll go on the Pill.'

I was not free of Ann but no longer bound by her. I shall never be free of the Bhagavati. As I am eternally free so I am eternally bound, not to her, but with her, to God. The Bhagavati now is within me realised, as the anima is the polarisation of my animus. Those Jungian insights constitute the impulse of life, the love of God from which I am absolutely inseparable.

My realisation had removed the urgency of physical separation from Ann. I was not yet one with her, as such, but I now possessed a new knowledge of purpose. I was able to wait without fretting, even though the letters from her physical self continued to expand the theme of her disillusionment. She was going. I knew it. It was over. But how could that be possible? Hadn't I "seen" that we were forever linked? Couldn't I see it now within me at any moment I wished to? I knew it as a spiritual truth, as certain as I knew anything. And yet the relationship was finished. At that time, as I have said, I had not realised that the Bhagavati is the one *Woman*, the female principle, who is not limited to any one form. I was mystified by the contradiction of events, but could not for one single moment doubt that the woman I loved, the Bhagavati, was coming back to me.

Just after my realisation I had a vision of a fluffy little brown chicken asleep in the shell of a partly opened egg while another chicken out of its shell pecked at the ground nearby. I knew the one curled up in the egg was the woman I loved, waiting to awake.

One beautiful, clear starry night I was out walking when I saw a vision of a very beautiful flower opening out from a bud. I had in fact watched this same flower gradually bloom over a period of a week or so in the cantonment garden months before. As the flower opened in the vision, a voice said, 'She is coming. You cannot hold back the birth or the bloom.'

Again I knew that despite the external evidence of Ann's letters to the contrary, she was coming.


I waited and continued writing the book. When it was finished, just after Christmas, I wrote to several publishers in England asking if I could send them the manuscript to read. None was interested.

Quite out of the blue, my mother wrote saying a cheque had arrived for me from the Taxation Department in Australia. It was a rebate of the tax I had paid in the year I left. It was exactly the amount I needed for my fare to England. I decided to take the manuscript over myself. (Fares out of India had to be paid in external currency, which is why I hadn't even considered leaving before. I possessed only Indian rupees.) I decided to go as soon as a berth in a ship could be arranged. Ann secured one for me in a P&O Orient Line ship sailing from Sydney and arriving Bombay in the first week in March.

Ann's last letter could not have made the position plainer about our relationship. 'I have now got you out of India,' she wrote, 'I don't want to see or hear from you again.'

The liner berthed for half a day in Naples, Italy, and I took the opportunity to visit the ruins of Pompeii, the Roman city of instant death which in AD 79 was drowned under 20 feet of volcanic ash when Vesuvius exploded one August morning. So immediate was the devastation that a couple making love were engulfed, and a natural cast of their entwined bodies was preserved, allowing plaster models to be made after excavations. Meals were still on tables. It is really like that for all of us. Dying might take time – but death is instantaneous.

On the 22nd of March 1966 I arrived in London and wrote to Ann saying, 'I know you are coming. I don't care what you say. I have been told you are coming.' The letter was returned to me unopened from Australia, marked "return to sender". I never saw her again.

What now?

The realisation of immortality had entrenched in me an unshakeable knowledge of formless everlasting life as my own being. How did immortality work for me in my day-to-day life? I was only 39 and there was a lot more life ahead to live.

Every truth realised, and any knowledge of a spiritual nature that anyone has, or professes to have, is tested and grounded in the events and circumstances of the ongoing life. This creates the troubling (testing) situations. All spiritual knowledge, whether great or small, provides a certain detachment from events. This means not identifying with the pressure of what is happening. Thus, according to the depth of our spiritual knowledge, we are troubled less and suffer less.

Inwardly, what had happened to me (although I didn't know it then) was that my consciousness was now one with the intelligence that as I ran desolate up the hill in Almora had said, 'Let it run.' Of course it was my body that ran. And what I called the apparatus in those days I know now to be my self – mind and emotions – the troublesome suffering desolation that so often drives and distresses the body with its ignorance.

Uninterrupted immortality brings spiritual equilibrium and freedom from suffering. There can be no more fear, no more emotional ups and downs. Fear and emotional instability are basically caused by the fear of death, and immortality is the knowledge that there is no death. The realisation itself determines the events that will have to be faced. I did not know this at the time. I knew only that I had this extraordinary inner equilibrium which had not left me since the realisation, in spite of the pressure of Ann's letters and her leaving me.

My inner state was due to a climacteric, a fundamental opening deep inside. And it included the strange ceremony back at Chilkapita of being united forever with the Bhagavati 'as you always have been, as you always will be and as you always are.' This is a classic tautology, a seeming needless repetition. But really it's not. The statement emphasises so well that the love or fulfilment we all search for in our lives is already there, within, behind the searching. Even so, this knowledge of woman and love also remained to be tested.

Barry on the running board of Uncle Perce's Oakland with Aunt Elvie and cousin Jill, Bective, NSW, c. 1930.

Barry and his mother, Kathleen (Gar).

Above: Barry and Kathleen out shopping, c. 1937.

Right: "Mum and Dad".

Barry, the reporter (third from left), covering a story about two boys trapped on a cliff ledge at MacKenzies Point, Sydney.

With driver Gus Gimelli returning from Katoomba, Blue Mountains, at 11 pm after a search for two lost girls.

Taking part for the *Sunday Mirror* in the Redex Trial, 1954. Photos taken at Camooweal, 900 miles from Darwin.

Above and top right: Barry and Betty.　　Barry and Gar, 1964.

Above: The family – Annette, Scott,
Barry and Betty, the day Barry left
Australia for India, 25 November 1964.

Right: At Sydney Airport, 25 November
1964.

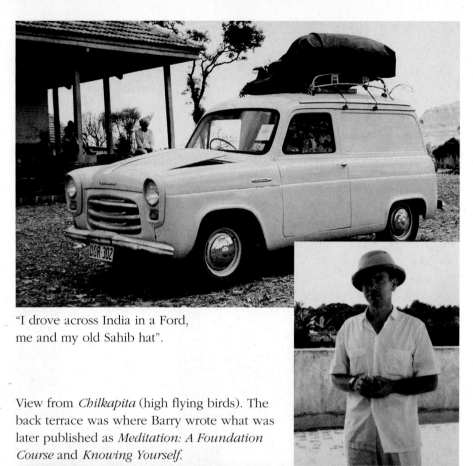

"I drove across India in a Ford,
me and my old Sahib hat".

View from *Chilkapita* (high flying birds). The
back terrace was where Barry wrote what was
later published as *Meditation: A Foundation
Course* and *Knowing Yourself.*

# CHAPTER 12

# HELLO JULIE

O n arrival in England I headed straight for bedsit land, Bayswater, in central London and rented a tiny room handy to the Underground. The manuscript I confidently distributed among a number of publishers – and stood by to accept the best offer. I waited. And waited. None of them wanted it. I was astounded.

I'd never had any great desire to travel. And of all the places visualised, England had the least appeal. I had come here solely to give the world my knowledge through my book. I was not interested in seeing any of the sights of London or in visiting the famous countryside. One thing I was not, was a tourist. People used to ask why I didn't live in Earls Court, the Australian enclave in London. To begin with, I am far from gregarious, and secondly, the average Aussie expatriate to me is like a hot poultice – good for you only while you need it.

I found London as I had imagined – grubby, grey, grimy, wearied, dark and depressing, but in this late spring not so cold. The people, I liked. After six weeks of hawking the manuscript around I realised that the chances of having it accepted were negligible. My money was running out; I could last at the most two weeks. As I had not desired to come to this country, I certainly wasn't going to work to earn money to live here. So, once again, I decided to sit and make it happen.

A week or so later I had a great idea. I decided to learn to fly. I had always wanted to fly. I'd joined the Royal Australian Air Force at 18 as a trainee pilot but the war ended before my course reached Flying School. And, of course, at the back of my mind was still Deena Pani and that strip I'd selected to land on!

I sat down and wrote letters to four or five newspapers offering my services as a sub-editor. The London *Evening News*, the paper with the largest afternoon sales in the world, was the first to reply and on the following Monday I was sitting at the sub-editors' table as a summer holiday relief. My engagement was for three months. I stayed four years.

I now had ample money and spent most of it on flying lessons at the Blackbushe Aero Club, Camberley, Surrey, a pleasant 40 minute train ride from London. Four months later I had my private pilot's licence and a splendid suntan from hours of exposure under perspex 2,000 feet above the haze.

At this point I'd like to mention something about my work, and the amazing way life tends to prepare us all for what we have to do in the future. At the *Evening News* the practice was that each of the 14 sub-editors had to take a one day turn as make-up man – a job despised by all. It meant descending from the relative quiet of the editorial floor into the non-stop noisy (from Latin *nausea*) clamour of the composing room to ensure a smooth transition of the written stories into pages of metal type.

For seven hours there was the ceaseless clatter and commotion of 40 Linotype machines casting molten metal into slugs of type, and compositors belting the stuff down into the steel page-frames ready for casting into plates for the high speed printing presses. This was repeated in great haste for every edition, five times a day, five days a week – with the added possibility of the make-up man getting his clothes smeared with printer's ink.

Back in Australia 13 years earlier, while I was chief of staff of the Sydney *Daily Mirror*, the millionaire proprietor Ezra Norton had called me down to his city office and said he wanted his editorial executives to have a complete experience of newspaper production. I was assigned to the composing room full time to learn the make-up sub-editor's job. When I returned to the editorial department 18 months later, I was pretty expert. In particular, I'd enjoyed working with the tradesmen, the compositors. So, not surprisingly, at the *Evening News* I volunteered for the make-up job immediately and to the delight of the other sub-editors worked in the composing room for those four years.

Again I got on particularly well with the compositors, many of whom were Cockneys, natives of the East End of London, and in character not unlike the no-nonsense typical Australian. They talk "funny" (to the rest of the world), often in slang, are sharply intelligent, natural comedians and they eat jellied eels. Jellied eels! Certainly not my Aussie idea of a good feed. But then these were my fond working friends and my winning of their good humoured acceptance was marked by an invitation to join them in a lunch of jellied eels. In such good company, of course, my prejudice disappeared.

The fact that I was a bit strange, they laughed off with enjoyment – not getting the point at all. I chided them for hanging up Christmas decorations and for not putting them up in the middle of the year. 'Go home you Aussie git,' would be the response, to which I would reply something like, 'You pommy bastards never learn.' In those days my hair was dense and black. With unforgettable camaraderie, when they required me at their particular page, they'd shout, 'Hey, Wiggy!'


About three months after joining the *Evening News*, I met Julie. She was 24 (I was 39) and very happily married to Ken, 29, a fellow sub-editor. They had two sons, Mark, aged five, and Jonathan, 14 months. They lived in a small semi-detached house in a pleasant suburb just outside Brighton, 50 miles south of London. I was invited to their home for the weekend.

Strange things had been happening to the young wife before my arrival. Later she described them to me, saying, 'I started lying on the bed every day and for some unknown reason really crying and weeping for a teacher. I didn't understand that, and neither did Ken. I remember him standing at the door and looking at me as I was saying, "I need a teacher, I need a teacher" and looking at me so sad and helpless with real tears. I realised it was nothing to do with Ken; it was something lacking in myself. Then I tried to love him more, and do more, and get over it.'

She continued, 'As a child I used to visualise that one day someone with dark hair was going to knock on my door and take me away and he

MY LIFE OF LOVE AND TRUTH

was the father, my real father. Then we went to the library one day. I was rejecting all the books that Ken brought over, the sort of books I'd really embraced before. I remember saying, "I don't want those books – I hate those books. There is something in this library that I know I can understand and I need it desperately." I was crying and Ken was getting very annoyed because of me lying on the bed and crying and then going to the library and causing this big scene of tears and passion about books I knew were there but didn't know where... He thought I was dramatising.

'Soon after the library incident Ken and I were out walking and he said, "I've met this man on the *Evening News* who went to India and he was in such a state of meditation that he experienced himself as being God." I remember my whole heart leaping and I said, "That's it! That's it!" It was the first time I'd heard that man is God or could experience being God and I said to Ken, "That is wonderful and yet at school you are not supposed to understand this until you die." Ken started to get worried and said he thought I was going to grasp this too quickly and spoil it for us both and that I was not going to be able to hold it and was going too fast. But I understood.'

Well, the man with black hair did knock on her door. It was Ken's enthusiasm, and the desire to share the excitement he felt with his young wife, that led him to invite me to their home. I talked most of the time about self-knowledge and the things in my book. I had often spoken in this vein to Ken, who was keenly receptive. His wife listened quietly the whole time but in the end didn't seem to have grasped much of what had been said. Oddly, however, she did seem to understand two ideas which are usually the most difficult to comprehend: that we are "nothing", and that in India I had "seen" or experienced "being God".

This did not prevent her from judging me harshly to herself for my having left two young children and a wife. By the time she went to bed on the Sunday night she believed I was mad, and was a little afraid. She told Ken she didn't think he ought to invite me to the house again.

During the night she had a mighty realisation. It continued for two days. She was completely changed, an entirely different individual.

First thing on the Monday morning Ken and I left the house together for work and she had no opportunity to tell him what had occurred. Nor did I see her. The next day he told me something wonderful had hap-

pened to her on the Sunday night. She would tell me about it when I
came again. She had written something down that morning after we'd
left, to describe what she was feeling. He handed me a piece of notepa-
per. It read:

> The wonder fills my heart. Oh, beauty, such beauty.
> It fills, spills over, always leaving room for more.
> Last night I was aware of an ache, a pain. I asked, 'What do you
> want of me?'
> No answer came. It grew and grew like burning rays of sun. It
> filled my body. My throat was dry. My arms were wrapped
> around me like chains. I could not move.
> I asked again, 'What do you want of me?'
> It slowly went and the sleep I thought would come never came.
> Answer: 'My will *shall* be done.'
> Darkness will come. I must not be afraid. All is beyond my
> power.
> I am nothing. I cannot hide. No one can give me peace.
> I clutched to a child [her eldest] to share its warmth. But still I
> was cold.
> Answer: 'Out of this darkness will come light. This shall be so.'
> I ache. Why do I ache? Is my body tired?
> Answer: 'It is me. I am aware.'
> Me? What is me?
> Answer: 'Nothing.'
> I have always known. It matters no longer. Wise men are fools.
> Humble people are ignorant. Thank you, God. Thank you for
> making me nothing. I do not have to know myself. There is
> nothing to know. Nothing. I shall ask nothing. What is – is. Only
> then shall I walk hand in hand with God.

The next day he handed me another note she'd written:

> Yesterday I was nothing
> Today I am.
> I go unending as the breeze.
> I comb my hair with fern.
> I bathe in streams.
> I laugh with the sun.

> I sing in verse.
> I am thunder, lightning, rain
> And yet the rainbow, too.
> I am darkness, light.
> And the joy of pain.
> I am lasting, lasting life.
> I am you.

She was I. She had come. The Bhagavati was here.

Five weeks later Julie left her husband and two children and, with one battered old suitcase, came to live with me.

After her realisation Julie was in a state of inner exaltation and peace. Ken was very happy for her but mystified by some of the effects. She did not seem to be anxious, as she used to be. She did her housework and looked after the family as before – but the urgency, the trying, was missing. She was placid. She was flowing, more contained. She seemed preoccupied, happy, but absorbed. She was in another world, which to him was a little too exclusive and unreachable for comfort. He was extremely understanding and helped all he could around the house when she had to be alone.

In her diary, Julie described what had happened to her:

> Soul experience or the realisation of immortality is different to God-realisation. God-realisation is to completely surrender the individual will. One experiences death. After three days of death I experienced immortality. It is such a vital, clear state that colour changes. I walked into the garden and looked at a rose. I knew that in all my 24 years I had never seen a rose before. It was so unbelievably beautiful. I felt a strange feeling like being a goddess. I heard a voice say, 'It is I.' The trees were blowing quite fiercely all around me. They all seemed to be saying, 'It is I.' I wrote a poem and the last line said, 'I am lasting, lasting life.' I had experienced death, immortality and rebirth.

Julie's first name was not Julie before I met her. The urge for me to change it came a few days after her realisation. The old name didn't "fit"; she was not that person any more. I kept forgetting her name in conversation and noticed I was trying to substitute another – Julian, a boy's name! Then I realised I was trying to say Julie Anne. This became Julie. She loved the name as soon as she heard it and from then on would shrink inside if addressed by her old first name.

I was now visiting them during the week and at weekends. Julie understood all that I had been saying and found any topic other than the truth irrelevant. She was reading the scriptures with riveting insight and understanding philosophic thought far beyond the comprehension of the girl she had been. She was also studying life, people, events, and her own responses with a fine, new, discrimination and wisdom. Julie now looked more and more towards me as a source of truth and inspiration. There was no one else around who understood. And as good and understanding as her husband was, and as much as she loved and respected him, he did not possess the sense-transcending knowledge that was now hers.

Julie knew the truth. She knew I knew. But that made only two of us. In a diary entry some time later, she wrote:

> Such an experience changes totally the old life. It is a death to all that was. Ken and the children were no longer more important than the children in the street. Me and mine was no longer. Attachments just did not exist. This was very painful for Ken. He mistook it for not loving. I did love, yet the quality of love was God orientated. Barry was the only person I could speak to.
>
> Ken sometimes understood. Then he would become frightened and confused. For the first time in our life together he would hit me. I would just sit there hardly feeling the blows. They were nothing except a sign the house was no longer my home. My little boy Mark would kick me and say, 'I am doing it for you Daddy.'
>
> Ken had once thought himself a good man or a kind man. To his horror he saw himself. Barry wrote him a poem:

THE PIGMY

Just spill one drop from his twisted tin cup
And watch the filthy mess erupt.
The pacifist he turns to war.
What for? There is no war.
Yes there is my friend you see
Every war begins in me
The pigmy.

This was terrible suffering for any man. He had all the worldly
right to anger. Yet in the spirit he had none. Sometimes when the
pain and anger were at their greatest he would suddenly laugh
and give up in some kind of sweet joy. He was strong. He held
on to his children and rebuilt his life.

By now Julie and I had declared our deep love for each other. We both
knew that she had to leave and come and live with me. It was impossible for us to be apart. But we both knew she could only come when the
time was right. So we waited. Before we made love she meditated on the
rightness of it and the silent voice inside her, which she knew to be her
God, said, 'Love one another for it is I.'

As soon as we'd made love, she told Ken. He was not surprised. But
at times, when he thought about it, he was distraught.

Ken was also having wonderful spiritual experiences and insights. I
was continually talking to him and doing all in my power to get him to
realisation. Repeatedly I told him, 'I'm going to get you there.' But I did-
n't. Realisation is not the gift of prophets or the product of trying. It
occurs when it occurs – by grace, by divine will.

Julie was special, not as a person but as the immortal vital energy she
had realised. Her continued existential development in the influence of
the spirit was paramount. Much in the future depended on her being
with me and my being with her. There were others unmet to be taught
and inspired, as well as unconsciousness to be dissolved in both of us
through the fusion of our tantric energies.

One of the threesome, Ken, had to stay behind; someone had to retain
sufficient worldly values to be able to devote themselves to bringing up

the children. Realisation would largely destroy this capability in a normal domestic environment; for all children, not just "mine", are the dependents of the realised consciousness. The greater purpose, when realised, must be served. This is the cruel but so-bright light of truth.

One evening I'd just left the house to return to London. The house was in a short cul-de-sac and all the middle class neighbours knew each other. But none so far knew of the break up and the three of us made a point of doing nothing that would cause gossip. I was 20 yards down the street when I looked back and saw Julie running towards me. With her long hair streaming behind her she threw herself breathless into my outstretched arms and we embraced with the joy and fullness that only true lovers can.

Her action in throwing social caution to the wind inspired me to write the epic poem *Wild Wild Life*. It began:

> Wild, wild Julie
> Wild streaming hair
> Wild breathlessness
> Wild girl
> Wild deathlessness
> End of compromise
> End of all that dies
> Birth of wild wild purpose
> And wild wild life.

In the house there was an electrifying intensity of energy. About three weeks before Julie left, Ken was sitting in a chair opposite me when I saw from his face that something significant had happened. For a brief moment he had realised the divine energy.

Not once did this man Ken, despite all my provocation, show hatred. His misery and wretchedness of feeling must have been ghastly. He despised what I had done, was outraged by it as well as by his own helplessness to change events. He slated me, ignored me, suffered me, and even gave me a half-hearted punch on the ear as I walked past him in the office one day. But he was too strong for hate or pettiness. Once he described me as nothing more than a constant irritation. I have not forgotten this because it made me – probably the most destructive and cruel influence in his life – insignificant in his loftier perspective. He wasn't fooled by the sub-drama like those who hate are; he was big enough to play the part of loser.

# CHAPTER 13

# THE BROOM THAT SWEPT BY ITSELF

Weird psychic happenings added to the general air of confusion and unreality at the little house in Brighton. One night Ken, Julie and her girlfriend Anne were sitting talking in the dining room. Without warning, a long-handled broom standing in the corner lifted off the floor and swept slowly backwards and forwards.

Anne, not quite believing her eyes, turned to the others. 'Did you see that broom move?'

Indeed they had. They were just as stunned and amazed. As they all looked back towards the broom it rose once more into the air and gave another two sweeps.

Over a period of several weeks the two women were repeatedly splashed on the forehead with drops of water in different rooms although there were no leaking pipes or other people in the house.

One morning, Ken decided to repair the radiator bracket in the lounge room where one of the children had pulled it away from the wall. He inspected the damage. It needed plugging and re-screwing. He went into the kitchen where Julie was working, collected a screwdriver and some rawl plugs and returned to the radiator. A second later he was back in the kitchen white and shaken.

'It's been done!' he exclaimed. 'While I was out here. The thing's as solid as a rock. I didn't put the screwdriver near it.'

Another morning Ken received a nastier shock.

Long before I came on the scene, Julie had been hearing children laughing and playing on the lawn in the middle of the night. When she got up and looked out no one, of course, was ever there. Ken used to call her imaginative. Julie also used to hear children's footsteps running across the upstairs landing (which I subsequently also heard) followed by very heavy, sensuous adult breathing. Whenever she investigated, their two boys were always sound asleep and there was no sign of anyone else. Again, Ken dismissed it as her imagination.

On this particular morning at about five o'clock it was still dark and Ken was down in the kitchen preparing his breakfast before catching the train for an early start in Fleet Street. Suddenly, he heard the sound of children running across the landing just above his head. He knew his own were fast asleep. And then the heavy breathing started, so clearly that he expected whatever it was to appear at any moment on the staircase a few feet away. For an instant his eyes were riveted to the gloom. Then in terror he turned and ran out of the back door, leaving his breakfast untouched, and made for the railway station. Only when he was halfway there did it occur to him that he had run out and left the family sleeping in the house. He confided later to Julie that he'd felt quite guilty at that moment, although of course there was nothing he could have done. But now he realised they had been living with the phenomenon for a long time.

Ken was a solid, though sensitive, logical type of person. As a newspaperman he'd had plenty of experience of observing people's reactions to odd situations and was sceptical of any form of emotionalism. Despite his frequent, firsthand experiences of psychic phenomena he kept disputing these and usually ended up appearing to convince himself that he had imagined them (even though there were other witnesses). However, as the incidents piled up, particularly after Julie's realisation, he became increasingly alarmed. He was running out of excuses and rational explanations. Ken had always felt that Julie in some way was the cause of the psychic happenings, although there was evidence to suggest that the previous tenants had experienced similar disturbances and may even have sold the place rather cheaply to get out quickly.

Often in the mornings Ken and Julie found the baby's toys had been thrown out of the cot to the far side of the room, an impossible feat for the infant. Later when the child was able to talk, he repeatedly said he thought his toys came to life at night. Sometimes the older boy, Mark, would wake the house screaming and his mother would find him out of bed in his sleep and twirling around in the middle of the floor. When Anne slept in the same room, she also screamed and was found twirling on her feet still asleep.

After his wife's realisation and inexplicable change of personality, Ken became more and more unnerved at seeing her still and silent in meditation around the home. In another diary entry, Julie wrote:

> All changed. I felt strangely different. I meditated a great deal.
> I saw my children and husband without emotional attachment.
> My head was empty. I kept looking inside my head which was
> free from all thought. I whispered as if my vocal cords had run
> down. At night, little Mark would open our bedroom door to
> come to our bed. Each time I saw him completely white,
> illuminated. I would hold him to feel warmth but it was like
> holding nothing. My husband was respectively confused and
> intrigued but was also using the situation to come home late. The
> only one who could understand the strange state I had entered
> was Barry. I phoned him. He stayed with us. He taught me. Ken
> and Mark were becoming more violent in trying to restore our
> old way of life. I became very much like a seer. Also a psychic
> force entered the house which Ken had no chance of refuting.

By the time she left, the whole thing was getting a bit too much for Ken. Her departure, although a time of sorrow, was also something of a relief. The psychic disturbances ceased, as far as I know, as soon as she moved out, although there was one reported to me which I'll describe in its place. Julie herself felt that the intensity of psychic phenomena at this time was to show Ken in his own undeniable experience that incredible things do happen, and that realisations which change people overnight were not that much more fantastic.

The extraordinary circumstances which allowed Julie to walk out of the house five weeks after our first meeting were no less fantastic. She

MY LIFE OF LOVE AND TRUTH

was walking down to the shops with Mark, contemplating the disintegration of the home and family and wondering what the solution could
possibly be. Her attention was drawn to the sky. She looked up and saw
an image of the face of her closest girlfriend, Anne.

Julie phoned me immediately. 'I'll be coming to you in three weeks,'
she said. 'I've been shown that Anne is going to live with Ken and look
after the children.'

'It's too easy,' I said. 'It doesn't happen like that.'

'It will,' she replied. 'You wait and see. Three weeks.'

The following week Anne phoned Julie and asked if she could stay
with them for a few days while the builders came in to treat her flat for
dry rot. She came, and apart from a period of some months later on,
never left. Two weeks later Julie came to live with me in my Bayswater
bedsit, just as she had predicted.

Anne and Ken were married three years later, about the time that I
married Julie. It was also about the time that Betty remarried. She wed
Ivan, my first spiritual teacher. And at about the same time, man landed
on the moon.

Julie described her leaving in her diary:

> I left the house after laying my 16 month old child, Jonathan,
> in his cot. I remember his eyes, blue, awake, staring into mine,
> quiet and still. I kissed him. I spoke to Mark as if he had become
> wise and understanding. He told me he loved his Daddy most,
> but when he was older he would love me. In the safe-keeping of
> Anne, my best friend, I left them as a family. I had one suitcase
> and not enough for the fare. No expectation, just a sense of
> purpose. I did not see my children for six months. I felt deep
> pain but could not cry. A voice kept saying, 'Be still and know
> that I am God.'

I met Julie off the train at London Bridge Station and paid the fare.
The old suitcase containing all her belongings had a strap around it and
as I lifted the case onto the platform the strap broke and out spilled half
the contents. A sad and shoddy beginning, perhaps. But I loved her, and
I loved her even more at that moment.

Julie, despite her realisation and entry into the Bhagavati state of consciousness, came to me as a student. It has to be that way. Consciousness realised does not conglomerate. Where two realised people live together, one is the student, one is the teacher.

How can a realised man or woman be taught anything?

It is the existential apparatus that has to be taught, disciplined and given the necessary experience for the significance of the life to be extracted as individual consciousness. Universal or cosmic consciousness itself is perfect, self-sufficient, needs nothing except, one could say, more consciousness, more of itself. This is another way of saying that consciousness through its pressure on the individual apparatus – the mind, body and emotions of each person – is continuously eliminating unconsciousness. We all know this to be a fact of experience. We grow older, become wiser, more conscious of what is meaningful in personal terms. Even the child who yesterday unconsciously was absorbed in certain games, today consciously rejects them and turns unconsciously (or consciously) to something else which he or she will subsequently consciously modify. It is called progress, advancement, evolution, living.

Realisation is a kind of ultimate view of significance. But the individual viewer cannot reach the state of enlightenment while there are still unconscious parts in him or her to be made conscious. So Buddhi – the universal viewer – returns, with its detached intelligence, to help the vast global movement towards more consciousness. Buddhi, the realised part in the individual, must continue to illuminate the experience of the other parts – the body, emotions, feelings, impressions, even the food consumed and the air breathed. Every next moment of experience must be informed. No body escapes this process. For every one of us alive represents the presence of some form of unconsciousness still waiting to be rooted out!

In another diary entry, Julie wrote briefly about our early days together in the Bayswater bedsit:

> I walked in Hyde Park while Barry worked. It was very
> strange. Barry drank rather a lot of sherry at night. I prepared the
> meals with love, expecting to experience the gratitude and

pleasure that Ken had shown. Instead, Barry seemed displeased. He felt the food would complicate his life. He burnt his tongue because it was too hot. He gave me little housekeeping. It was cold and the first thing he did when he walked in was to see how much gas I had used. So I would sit in bed with no fire to keep warm. I was confused.

With Ken, we had always been free and easy over heating, eating and in general living. Ken was unrestrictive to the point of being sloppy, spoiling and indulging the children and the dog. I had a great need for discipline so I gladly suffered the horror of it. Barry was also a great lover of movies. The only time we went out was to see a terrible film. All American trash. I told him so. He said he was not sure I was right but he would look at it.

Barry was also a superb lover. I felt as I lay beside him a beauty and white cleanness of sex. We were very compatible. To make love was a joy I'd never before experienced. Perfect, ecstasy. This, like realisation, was as if Barry had opened parts of my body that were dormant. I knew I could not make love with an ordinary man again.

# CHAPTER 14

# THE STAR

J ulie's spiritual impact on me was tremendous. I have not known anyone before or since who loved the divine as yieldingly as she did. I was her teacher. But she was my inspiration. Living with her was physical perfection; the tantric harmony of our bodies was unimaginably sweet, swift and powerfully provocative of strange energies. It was almost impossible to get enough of her.

Her will she surrendered completely to the divine. Her instinctive self, her mind and her body, she gave to me. Her emotional self she kept and it was my constant endeavour to eliminate this. I took absolute responsibility for her as teacher and provider – the total commitment of love. It was not easy for either of us. But it was productive.

No longer did the term Bhagavati seem enough to describe the innate purity which I saw in her. Incongruously, at my stand-up desk in the middle of the hectic and noisy hot-lead composing room of the *Evening News*, I wrote this sudden inner vision of her:

Julie
I have found the place you are.
Julie
How could I miss you
You are a star.

Foolish mind, cage of vision
Sees the light but not the star
Staggers at the beauty it imagines to be far.
Julie, You are a star.
No mind through glutton eye has ever seen a star
Just the light...
And many lights there are.
Then where is beauty?
In the star.
Where the star?
Where you are.
And where is that?
Glutton eye would see you as afar
Again the light
And not the star.
Julie, Where are you?
In the beholder
I
That's where you are.

Finally, only the stellar system is profound and vast enough to illustrate the possibilities of man and woman. The universe, in fact, is the symbol of their potential.

Running on from this simple poem I wrote (still in the composing room of the newspaper) a saga of poems describing the spiritual life and the mighty power and vast scheme behind existence. The first poem was *The Glutton Eye*, followed by *Wild Wild Life, The Way of Woman, Now* and *Man The Thinking Piece of Sand*, all published years later in audio tape and book form.

Julie knew my love for her was inspired by the divine. She would not have come to me otherwise. Even in the chaotic weeks before leaving her husband, when she pondered on our physical relationship, she was told inwardly, 'Love one another; it is I.' Even so, love is not a raft to sleep and drift on. It was my job to teach her, to align her existential apparatus as much as possible with the divine Being she had realised. Her job was to be taught, to willingly give up the entrenched mindsets and attitudes of all her yesterdays. The power for her to do this was my great love of her.

I was tough and hard. Whatever I insisted on was usually the opposite to her conditioning and habitual inclinations. Julie had been the darling of a wealthy county family, the pretty, angelic-looking youngest child. She was compassionate and loving of the hired help while they and her doting mother made sure she never had to do any unpleasant or menial chores. She seemed genuinely willing to try to do the chores but no one ever really took her seriously; and besides, she didn't have the will to persist or insist. So she danced off guiltlessly indulged, singing her little songs around the spacious gardens, talking to God, and generally bewitching everyone with her unselfconscious innocence.

As she grew older she learnt here and there that the outside world was a pretty sordid place. So she never looked in those directions. When inadvertently caught up in unpleasantness she charmed her way out, but if that failed or escape was impossible, she surrendered herself to her God within and performed automaton-like until the circumstances had passed. She knew how to die into her being.

In her teens she loved excitement, boys and being romantically pursued, but fled at the first sign of involvement or pressure. She hated responsibility of any kind. She loved physical contact. She was aware of the sexual power she had over boys; but as much as she sometimes wanted them to make love to her, she could not allow it – she felt God didn't want her to.

At 13 she was precocious in sex psychology. She had realised that as long as she never allowed herself to fall in love, no man would ever have power over her. She also learnt that if a man didn't love her absolutely, she didn't want him. And she knew that the only way she could ever hope to preserve a friendship or stimulating association with a man was never to go to bed with him.

Many other women also know these things. But usually in a mad or ecstatic moment they forget and betray their own intrinsic wisdom. But Julie never did. She didn't settle for second best. And she never gave any boy or man two chances. That was the inner, powerful woman, always subjectively alert, analysing and conscious; yet in her exterior life always looking for a psychologically safe and comfortable place to hide.

At 18, rather than continue having to cope with working as a trainee hairdresser, she married Ken, five years her senior. Fortunately she loved him. She discovered she loved him after confiding to him that she was acutely aware of death and very frightened of it. She informed him that whenever she tried to speak to others about this feeling they told her death was a morbid and unhealthy subject for anyone so young to be concerned with. Ken thought it showed an intelligent attitude. From that moment on she seemed to love him. She had found another comforter, a strong and understanding man in whom she could hide. But only for six years.

Julie came to me in London shy, retiring, over-sensitive and so inoffensive that in private I called her "Mrs Mouse". She looked 16 and incredibly "innocent". Every landlady loved her.

I pushed her out to work and made her continue when she pleaded to be allowed to stay home. Anything she wanted out of habit I denied her. She pined over her children daily but refused to weep for them. Each time I demanded to know if she wanted to go back she would look inside and say no – and pine some more.

She was forced to consider every desire, to make herself vividly conscious of the source of her reactions and impulses. Even when she asked for an ice cream on our first visit to the cinema, I replied, 'Do you really want it?' Obediently, she looked within, beyond the robot apparatus, and saw she didn't; it was habit. After a few months of this, nothing seemed simple or natural to her any more. She began to lose what she thought was her spontaneity. What she was actually shedding was her habitual background of expectations and dependence. She could depend on me – but only to show her the reality she had managed to sidestep.

We had no friends. No one was ever invited to visit. We lived entirely alone. I went to bed early. She was used to staying up till midnight. She just sat there or lay awake beside me. We walked a lot, in Hyde Park and around Bayswater. But otherwise, at weekends and even during my holidays, I tapped away all day at the typewriter in that one room, and she sat there. (I was writing hour-long drama scripts to try to break into English television.)

All her life Julie had depended on others for her psychological security – first her mother, then her adoring boyfriends, and then her loving husband, her children and her little home. Now, all the crutches were gone, torn away. And I alone remained, loving, protective, but relentless in my instruction – her love, her lover and her jailer. As the past she had avoided gradually shifted back onto her, where it belonged, she became more and more confused, uncertain – and conscious.

This abstract gap between the self – consisting of all the emotions of the past – and the physical body of the present has to be "bridged" in all of us before the divine unity can be enjoyed. Julie, as I have mentioned, had always had the gift of consciously scrutinising her own motives, as well as her relationships. When she came to me she was profound in self-knowledge. But she still had not bridged the gap. She could not cope with her emotional self. Her impulse was either to let it run "in freedom" which would have ended in chaos and destruction (for inwardly she knew that nothing matters), or to allow it to hide in the dark-minded obscurity of isolation, guilt, self-judgment and fear.

Her personal concept of "freedom" was a way to despair because she was projecting her self-consciousness into the world instead of containing it in the body. Self-consciousness is an awkward, ungainly and even insane thing when it appears in a person. We have all experienced the stinging embarrassment and discomfort it occasions. Self-consciousness cannot cope with the external world for the simple reason it has no place there. It naturally wants to hide. It was this that made her duck for cover – like many people are inclined to do; only in Julie's case, through her realisation, she was far more conscious of her self than most. By the power of truth, which insists on greater responsibility where there is greater knowledge, she was not allowed to get away with it any longer.

Over the next two or so years Julie was gradually transformed. We lived in various bedsits in Bayswater and then moved to a more comfortable place in grotty Shepherds Bush. I was now sending a third of my take-home pay to Betty and the children in Australia. We had enough to live on but none to spare.

For the last ten months of those years, Julie returned to the home in Brighton. Ken had not been able to free himself of his attachment to her. He still imagined she was the same woman he had married. At his request, and with my blessing, she agreed to return. She wanted him to realise for himself that they were finished and this time to let her go without regrets. She wanted no karma, no residue of unlived-out past, left behind there. Anne also understood and moved out; she loved Ken and like Julie wanted him to accept the new, for she truly believed he loved her.

The parting from Julie was a terrible wrench for me, even though I knew that what she was doing had to be done. We knew our love for each other was untouchable and that this was merely a necessary interlude. We had said our goodbyes. Nevertheless, I was pathetic as she walked out of the front door behind Ken and the two children. My face screwed up and I wept. She turned to me sharply, and with wonderful emotionless clarity, said, 'Stop it! Be the man you are.' And walked on.

Back with Ken, Julie performed her household duties consciously and conscientiously. Unlike in the old days when she used to be able to give up and lie down, out of feelings of physical weakness or depression, she persevered. She concentrated on completing each task, resisting the old familiar urge to break off and start something new each time she was tired or bored. The self-discipline of the last 14 months was now her strength.

She enjoyed looking after her children, receiving intense satisfaction from sending her oldest son, Mark, now six, spick and span off to school. Her youngest, Jonathan, two, was as placid by nature as she was now, and he delighted her. She was happy to be out of the bedsit environment and to have a home again, but not happy with the situation. She could not show Ken the warmth and love he had known. She was dutiful and resigned. She intended to stay without complaint for as long as it took her husband to face the fact and let her go.


Julie and I were in regular touch by phone, although I did not visit her. After six months in Brighton, she phoned and said Ken had told her she could go. This was indeed good news for us both. But the spiritual life dissolves the usual need to look forward to things; so although I was pleased I had no expectations. And just as well. When I drove up in a rental car Julie was waiting for me outside the house. Ken had changed his mind, she said. She could not come. It was not finished yet. But she would make sure, she said, that there would be no more false alarms. Ken would have to demonstrate that he really meant her to go.

One morning in September 1968 Julie was looking out the kitchen window at the beauty of the day when she 'smelled spring flowers'. This had always been a sign to her that something extraordinary was about to happen. She phoned Anne immediately and said she believed this meant

Ken had broken the attachment. Ten minutes later he phoned Julie and suggested they get a divorce. Within days, Julie moved out and Anne moved back.

# CHAPTER 15

# WHO WILL TEACH
# THE TEACHER?

O nce more Julie and I were united. But back again in our
Shepherds Bush bedsit, she yearned for respite from the isolation and severity of the past. We had both certainly earned
some sort of relief or change. I was gradually withering, not physically,
but somewhere within. I was becoming the stern, austere, authoritarian
who'd had to impose an unbending discipline on another for too long,
and who finally could no longer dis-identify with the role. I was beginning to be corrupted by my own intransigence and fixity of purpose. A
surface rift was developing between us, although it never interfered with
our love for each other.

Julie had always felt she could "will" events. One day she picked up
the Bible, opened it randomly, and saw a "message" – a line from the
Book of Samuel, 'Send me your son David, who is with the sheep.' She
phoned her girlfriend and said 'A man named David is coming.'

The following week a young man Julie's age joined the sub-editors'
desk at the *Evening News*. His name was David White. Under his arm he
had a copy of the biography of the 19th century Indian master,
Ramakrishna. We talked about philosophy. He said he was a poet as well
as a journalist. I told him I'd also written some poetry and he asked to

read it. After that we met and talked nearly every lunch hour for a couple of weeks. Finally I took him home to meet Julie.

David turned out to be an angel in disguise. He took us everywhere. He was a devotee of classical music, a gourmet who did not eat a great deal and a wine lover who seldom drank much at all. He wrote fine poetry and possessed an uncanny intuition. He owned a car, was unmarried, and was extraordinarily generous and kind. He floated into our bedsitter regimen like a fine ray of sunlight.

Julie loved him like a brother and he loved us both. To me, he was a dear son. He took us regularly to the Proms at the Albert Hall, to concerts, musical evenings in Wigmore Street and plays in the West End; to restaurants, museums, galleries, exhibitions, castles, stately homes – wherever there was cultural or artistic appeal. For the first time together, Julie and I began absorbing something outside the intensity of our own joint development. David White was searching for the truth and apparently had discovered in us what he wanted. While he engendered in us, particularly in me, a finer appreciation of music and things cultural, which he understood, I introduced him to my philosophy and the universal culture of self-knowledge.

He began bringing friends, pals from his student days, along to our bedsit to hear my teaching. They in turn introduced their friends and there was seldom a night that someone didn't arrive. One of David's friends was John Hart. John was 26 and had no regular job. He wore a "Che Guevara" beret, like the revolutionary, and a green twill windbreaker, and he wanted to make the world a better place for everyone to live in. He had once been a journalist but gave that up, along with a youthful marriage, in order to wander in search of himself. Once in North Africa he had thrown his haversack with all his possessions into the sea because he didn't want to feel he had anything to depend on.

John was looking for the moment. When we met him he had got a bit lost. He was mistaking the moment for the momentum of political ideals. He desperately needed something and he didn't know what it was. We talked. He came four or five times. Then he hitchhiked up to Scotland to camp on his own in the mountains for a week. He returned and we talked some more.

One night John phoned, extremely agitated. Extraordinary things were happening to him, he said. He muttered something about the fist, a mighty fist of power that was smashing him to pieces... He had been told he must get to me... Would I stay there?... He was coming.

Twenty minutes later he arrived and breathing heavily, slumped onto the settee. He sat in silence and gradually calmed down. When he opened his eyes I asked him about his experience. He was a different man from the John we had known. By his answers I could tell he had gone far beyond me, not beyond what I could experience but beyond what I had experienced. He had had a mighty realisation – and was still going through it. Talking to him was like groping for a light-cord in the dark.

During the previous few weeks, in my certainty and arrogant disdain, I had often made statements like, 'Who will teach the teacher?' and 'Show me a man who knows more than I.'

Here he was. John himself didn't seem to be aware of any difference. He talked of having been told he must get to me wherever I was. Why, he didn't know and he didn't care. He was here. He told me what had happened. He talked of energies on which his perception had entered realms of consciousness impossible of description, except to say that there was an ascending series of heavens. And then he left.

Over the next few weeks I gave five public lectures arranged by David in a preview cinema in Wardour Street, central London. He paid the expenses including advertising. Most of those who turned up were people who had been coming along to the bedsit. John dropped in a couple of times but didn't stay long. He was a loner now, self-sufficient in his realisation but oddly still "around".

I remember answering a question at one of the lectures about pain being the energy of loss. I must have caught the emotion of the audience for when I concluded with the statement 'What has I AM got to lose?' they clapped enthusiastically. It was an ominous portent. I would soon find out its meaning.

The lectures were recorded and subsequently I transcribed them into a book, *Wisdom and Where to Find It*, which David published for private sale and distribution to the group. The lectures seemed to mark the end of a phase for me. Between my first book written in India (still not published at that time), my epic poems and the lectures, I had said just about everything I knew. In a way, I was played out.

131

For four years I'd been experiencing the tantric love energies. Through two Bhagavatis, Ann and now Julie, I had penetrated deeper and deeper into this extraordinary dynamic field. The conjunction of our particular male and female energies appeared to release a fundamental power. This did not seem at times to be all that "good" and benign, either. But undeniably, the power was connected with some kind of spiritual or uncommonly specific state of consciousness. Our lovemaking was certainly the making of love. Any man who has had a physical connection with a Bhagavati woman, or a woman with a Bhagavat man, knows this beyond doubt. The love produced is impersonal. And impersonal love is the precise opposite to normal love which is personal and problematical. The power of impersonal love, on the other hand, forces problems to be faced, and dissolves them.

To me, love made with the Bhagavati was a positive, creative thing, productive of the power to understand life and love more deeply; it was not just a beautiful sensation that ended with the doing. I knew I could and did communicate self-knowledge and a finer love of God to woman through lovemaking. But this was possible (or knowable) only after my capacity to love woman became "selfless". And that happened through the Bhagavati as I became increasingly "absent" from the act; in other words, as my lovemaking was depersonalised I became more selfless and more unselfish. Unselfish simply means absence of self-consideration in action or intention. And this inevitably means a deepening knowledge that there is something greater than myself behind the appearance of things. Selflessness, as I mean it, can be understood through the lines quoted earlier in my poem to the first Bhagavati, Ann:

> I can't give you anything
> Every gift I give is the gift of Him [God or It!]
> Whose gift of love we share...

Selflessness is depersonalisation, the absence of the vanity of believing you can give anyone anything, particularly love. Whenever lovers love selflessly the Bhagavat and Bhagavati are the action – and the ecstasy (meaning pleasure and beauty) is divine, as anyone knows who has experienced these usually rare occasions. In our society we use the word "love" to describe many attachments. There is love of parents, children, animals, partner. But only the love that man and woman make together is galvanising enough, electrifying, tempestuous and irresponsible enough to override all other considerations, all other loves irrespective of personal consequences.

As a young man, and before I met the first Bhagavati, I had made love to about a dozen women. None of them, nor I, could generate the depersonalised field of love (which I speak of now as tantric love) so that it could be realised. With one older woman it was repeatedly approached – to my amazement. But overall there was too much selfishness and ignorance, too much self and sexuality between the women and me. The magnetic field produced by our male and female poles was distorted and incapable (at least in me) of registering in our consciousness the presence of the divine lovemaker.

Conversely, it would appear that the intense kind of divine lovemaking that Julie and I experienced can produce an excitation of the tantric field which may have weird, inexplicable and terrifying results.

# CHAPTER 16

# THE BLACK ENERGY

*There is no shortage of experts who can advise about madness; but there's a great shortage of experts who have been mad and can talk sanely about it.*

About midnight in October 1968 Julie and I were asleep. We had made our usual rapturous love earlier in the night. I was lying on my side towards Julie, my head on the pillow facing away from the window on the other side of the room. Suddenly, without opening my eyes and apparently while still asleep, I was aware of something streaking across the room from the open window and hovering above my face between the two of us. It was black and square, about the size of a tea-towel, and it vibrated with immense energy. I opened my eyes. It was still there, exactly as I had perceived it with my eyes closed. Then it "entered" me.

Julie, also still asleep and facing the other way, had "seen" the thing streaking through her consciousness (the room?) towards her. She gave out a terrified but, I recall, beautiful, melodious scream. She jack-knifed up into a sitting position, shaking and petrified with fear, while the black energy streaked back across the room and disappeared in the direction from which it had come.

As I sat up, Julie was fumbling for the switch on the standard lamp beside the bed.

'Don't,' I said. 'Let's see what it is.'

My voice! It was weird. It was several tones deeper and unnaturally drawling like a tape being played at the wrong speed. Julie swung round towards me. In terror she grabbed my hands and held them down as if to stop me touching her. Both our hands were sweating. She backed away, trying to scramble off the bed.

'Keep your head,' I drawled. The grotesquely lengthened tones of my voice only helped to increase her panic and fear.

'Keep away from me,' she pleaded.

She got her feet on the floor, stood up and switched on the light.

Her face was dead white and pinched with terror. From the look of her I could tell something was wrong with my appearance. She kept repeating, 'Stay there. Don't move. Please don't move.'

I was calm although I knew something uncanny and very disturbing had happened. To observe an event inwardly and externally at the same instant, and to share it with another person without any normal communication between you, is an astonishing experience. I have a scientific turn of mind and my impulse from the first moment was to observe everything that was happening in the greatest possible detail. For that reason, I asked Julie not to switch on the light; I wanted to look into the gloom and see if any phenomena remained. As soon as I spoke I realised I didn't have to look far.

My first caution was to avoid upsetting Julie further. It was obvious she was very close to hysteria. Only instinctive cunning was keeping her rational; she believed that while she could converse with me in a fairly unemotional way, there was a better chance of getting me to do as she said. Again, in the dreadful spooky voice I said, 'Don't worry. I won't move. I won't touch you or come near you.'

'Your voice...'

'I know. Don't worry. What else?'

'Look in the mirror.'

The mirror was fixed to the wardrobe door beside her. I leaned forward slowly and looked into it. My features were weirdly distorted. It was me but not me. The muscles were pulled into an unfamiliar mask, not ugly but strangely primitive, disturbing, compelling – and extremely intense. Then I noticed the eyes. They were smiling, goading, mocking with a "knowing" craftiness that demanded I continue looking into the mirror.

I then realised that I was looking at the animal, the ape, that the spirit of man had entered at the beginning of time. This was that. Only I was

136

man; I was the spirit of man, the creative self-reflection in man's animal body. The cunning and shame I was seeing was what happens when the self-consciousness of man reflects on the animal's natural unconscious sexual instinct. Fortunately, self-consciousness occurs only in the man animal; but even there it is responsible for all the wars and sexual violence that afflict the earth.

As I continued to gaze at the reflection of my eyes in the mirror I became aware of something else. An energy was rising from my solar plexus. It grew stronger and began spiralling towards my head. I wrenched my gaze away. The energy pulsed inside my chest and throat, struggling to get to my head. Any emotive thought at all I knew would provide it with a bridge of access.

I looked across at Julie and had to lower my eyes. I felt shame. There was a shiftiness in the energy; an awareness for me of some sort of guilt. The lowering of the eyes (strangely, the traditional gesture of humility) combined with absence of thinking, seemed the only device that would give me control.

How we got through those next few weeks I do not know. Lovemaking was impossible. Julie and I meditated on our predicament and both simultaneously announced: no sex. Whenever an erotic situation occurred, the energy would rise with tremendous gusto. I did not apprehend actual violence or physical danger from it; it just seemed literally to electrify the psychic and physical space around me.

On the night it happened I tried to placate Julie but my drawling voice and contorted features made this almost impossible. Finally she got me to dress. We walked to a public phone and rang David. It was about 2 am. David was living in a rented mews house, 20 minutes away in Portman Close, in the West End. He drove across, spent the night on the settee and stayed most nights for two weeks.

One evening I showed him the energy. By now I had managed to get some control over it. My voice and face had returned to normal in a couple of days, although I was never to look as young again. I knew exactly how to arouse the energy. I told David to stand opposite me in the darkened room. With my head away from him I excited the energy. I waited until it was spiralling powerfully and abruptly faced him, catching his eyes. I saw a flash of light between us and heard its crackle.

'My God,' he gasped and staggered back. He saw nothing tangible.

David was the only person other than Julie to see the energy. My concern was to not display it and to find a way to absorb and dissolve it. Looking in mirrors was dangerous. As soon as I caught the reflection of my eyes – and of course mirrors were the energy's compulsive focal point – it would zip towards the top of my head as if to invade my brain. The same effect would occur when I happened to look into Julie's eyes. This energy definitely wanted a springboard into the world.

What would have happened had it reached the top of my head I do not know. All I understood was that I had to stop it ever getting that far. The first precaution was to deny it excitation through the senses, especially sight and imagination. As my mind had ceased discursive thinking years before, the last precaution was not difficult.

For a few days I felt I was doomed. I could not see how I could possibly go on holding and containing the energy. It was like living with a rebellious entity in the same body, a deplorably depressing existence. I considered who on earth I could turn to for help; and saw that there was no one who in all my vast reading had ever reported such a thing happening to them. There is no shortage of experts who can advise about madness; but there's a great shortage of experts who have been mad and can talk sanely about it. It was something like that for me now. Also, there was the spiritual dilemma. My knowledge of experience was that whatever happened to me was for my eventual advancement. How could this latest eventuality be equated with my faith in life? The pressure of the energy seemed imminently to threaten my being. I was very close to the ultimate despair of hopelessness.

And then, like the dawning of a new day, the solution was offered from within my own consciousness. It involved employing another energy – really a power – which I did not know existed in me. This energy, I discovered, occupies a very shallow hemisphere at the top of the skull. Although quantitatively small, qualitatively it was finer and more powerful than the black energy. Over the next few weeks this tiny buttress of spirit met and held the insurgent energy. Gradually the power worked down, absorbing and transforming the other into a quality evidently similar to its own.

As can be imagined, my conflict with the black energy was tremendously productive of self-knowledge and knowledge beyond my self. As I absorbed the energy into my existential being it yielded the knowledge of itself. This enables me to describe exactly what it is and where it comes from.

The black energy is the fundamental energy of sex and death (these two being obversely inseparable in consciousness). It is seated deep in the collective unconscious, that is, in the intermediate world between spirit and existence. To me it is the earth *daimon*. The word daimon derives from ancient Greek mythology and denotes a supernatural power, akin to spirit.

I have not read or heard of anyone who has been entered by the earth daimon or who has given a consistent and rational account of the event and the means of transmuting the energy. No doubt many of the psychic and emotional possessions reported down through the centuries, as well as in our own time, and the hysteria surrounding them, are due to the influence of the earth daimon. The Roman and subsequent Christian worlds, which were far more ignorant of truth than the ancient Greeks, branded the daimon a "demon", an evil spirit. But the daimon is apparently only "evil" to the "victim" and to those observing the victim's behaviour. This is due to the lack of spiritual understanding in both, and because the truth of the phenomenon has not been explained. I will now do this – since the daimon is fundamental to everybody's life and existence, not just to those possessed by it.

The daimon or black energy comes from what to us is the "dark" world of the unconscious. But in truth that is the world of radiant light; and the daimon there is fully conscious, an aspect of God as the spirit of pure love. This spiritual aspect of God and love is (like God) forever endeavouring to rise out of the unconscious into the awareness of man and woman. But when it enters the density of the human brain and emotions, it loses consciousness and becomes a blind compulsive drive. From being love it turns into sex.

The sexual daimon is what keeps the whole world moving. It is responsible for the instinctive reproductive urge of the species; and it is behind every argument, every violent action, all excitement and all disruption of harmony and love.

Before entering the physical world the daimon is one with divine love. The influence of this love, radiating continuously from the unconscious, creates all union in the physical world – the union that holds a tree together, an animal together, a house together, an organisation together. But it is the aberrant energy of the daimon in existence that causes the break up or death of these unified objects. And in that break up a release of force inevitably occurs. In death, although we may not know it, there is a release of pure vital force; and in the splitting of the unity of the atom, an enormous explosion of force – both demonstrations in and out of existence of the power of the earth daimon to destroy and convert objects to pure energy.

Pure love is not energetic. Pure love is power, doesn't have force and manifests in existence as tantric love. Tantric love is the rarest form of love on earth and it was my tantric presence that gave Julie her initial realisation without making physical love. However, such a realisation has to be affirmed or consummated physically with the pure love of the initiating master, which is what happened. Tantric love is synonymous with the transmuting power of the love of God. Tantric love is the closest quality to the non-existent invisible world from which the daimon comes.

On earth it is the task of man and woman to make the daimon conscious and so start to restore harmony between them and in their lives. It must be converted back from blind sex into love. This is the spiritual task. As we all can see from observing the dominance of sex in man's world, it is an awesome undertaking. But the good thing is that the world doesn't have to be changed; only the blind and unconscious effects of sex in the individual.

A man's cursory glance at himself may satisfy him that there's not that much sex in him. But the truth is that while a man masturbates or fantasises about woman (or vice versa), he is sexually possessed. If he resorts to sexual devices from the sex shop, uses pornographic videos or magazines, he has much work to do to break this obsession. The drive of sex between man and woman is limitless in its selfish striving for enhanced excitement, indulgence and satisfaction. Then there are the effects of sex: frustration, moods, depressions, resentment, anger, fear, self-doubt, etc., all of which are dissolved by love.

But what is love? Love has two real aspects. The first is the love of God within. This love is negation, which means it has no effect in existence, except to dissolve the individual's attachment to existence. The second aspect is the love between man and woman. The first is love out of existence; the second is love in existence. All other loves come out of the second for without it no one would exist. And if it is thought that man and woman can produce babies without love, the answer is that real love is beyond such rational thought. The reproduction of the species is controlled by God, or the daimon state of consciousness behind existence. Human love or sexual love is too shallow and change-able for this.

For man, the love that overcomes and transmutes sex is the pure love of woman. Man has so many other loves that he overlooks this love which is basic to his nature and existence. He thinks more about woman and her parts than anything else in his life. But still he goes on loving all his distractions ahead of her; and in doing so loses the power to change himself and to realise love – the daimon or God in the invisible world within him.

Woman does not have the same distractions from love as man. She in her natural state puts love first. But her difficulty since time began has been to find a man who really loves her. In the absence of this man she has surrendered her God-given knowledge of love and accepted man's substitute for love – sexual satisfaction and excitement. In her inner being she senses the substitute is not true. But since she has not been shown the difference between sex and love she finds she can cope with her lovelife by engaging as much as possible in the momentum of sexu-al excitation, despite its inevitable bouts of depression and self-doubt. Or she simply gives up loving man. But in the latter case her thoughts soon turn to her natural need of love and she is likely to eventually try again with similar results.

With man not available to really love her she will sometimes turn to the seemingly easier alternative of loving woman physically. With man becoming increasingly sexual due to the society and the media, more and more women will exercise the lesbian alternative. Man, finding it too difficult to love woman, because of her emotions, sometimes turns to loving man physically. And the impressionable, parentally love-starved youth of both genders, attracted by the homosexual propaganda of free-dom and revolution, give the exciting alternative a try and frequently get hooked.

The increasing homosexual activity in both men and women compounds permanently in the commonly shared psyche. Because the inclination to homosexuality is in the psyche, the slightest exposure to sexual abuse in infancy may trigger a preference for the same gender in the vulnerable or impressionable. Very, very few are born with the entrenched psychic inclination towards homosexuality. But it does happen, which accounts for the distinctly male physical appearance and mannerisms in some women; and conversely in men.

Each day, in our global society of distractions and alternatives, the love between man and woman, which gives real freedom, is made more and more redundant.

# CHAPTER 17

# TEACH ME!

The coming of the black energy widened the surface rift between Julie and me. I was getting weaker; Julie was getting stronger or rather, more independent in a worldly way. My power was diminishing as I fought day and night to convert the black energy into a stable and manageable form. I was still teaching and lecturing.

Although I had recovered from the physical effects of the energy, Julie could not forget what it had done to my face and voice. She was frightened of me. She was constantly glancing at me to reassure herself that it had not affected me again. Her doubting penetrated me and caused a self-consciousness that should not have been there. She could not sleep at night. She felt the black energy kept coming out of me and menacing her. We often had to sleep with the light on. She was terrified she would wake and see me as I had been that night.

I was losing my authority over Julie and in many ways deserved to. This would have been all right had she been growing more self-sufficient in truth and not just independence. She was working in a Knightsbridge boutique. She was getting hooked on clothes and fashion and never had enough of the latest. She was using excessive make-up and was preoccupied with her image in the mirror. She was unhappy. She told me she often walked home to our bedsit, where I would sometimes have the evening meal prepared, with joyless steps.

We decided to move to better accommodation, away from the reminders of the black energy and what was happening to us. We moved to Putney, south London, into a newly renovated place with a modern kitchen, nicely furnished bedroom and a luxury bathroom which we shared with two or three others. Still, it was a step up. We thought things would be different. They were not, of course. I continued to wither (though I had the energy under control). Julie was now applying eyeliner and feeling naked without it as she settled deeper into the mask of independent sophistication.

Somehow, my flexibility had gone. I was steeped in my own philosophic habit. Despite our love, the black energy and the rigours of the past stood between us. We were diverging. But love was converging.


John Hart was staying with David at the mews house in Portman Close and they called in at Putney one night about two weeks before Christmas. We sat around talking and in the middle of the conversation Julie pointed at John and said, 'Look at him...'

David exclaimed, 'He's getting smaller!'

With amazement they both described how John continued to shrink in their perception to almost a pin-point before gradually resuming his "normal" size. I witnessed nothing unusual but recalled having read about this happening to people in India in the presence of certain yogis.

John had grown tremendously in presence and inner strength. He was very serious about teaching. He said that everything was teaching and that his teaching would be different from mine. He found words limiting. Nonetheless we discussed the energies he was experiencing and he asked me to describe the levels of consciousness as far as I could. This I did. John, as a poet and a user of right words, never discredited the power of language but was intolerant of concepts. In my teaching I used finer concepts to destroy concepts – and conceptual thinking. John used love and his way of life. About this time he wrote:

> I despise myself for writing of love. I agree I only attempt to
> describe fragments, half-moments of it, and never attempt

definition. But even this is debasing, defiling, conceptualising, destroying. I think that I will pledge myself not to repeat the pillage of the temple, but I know that I will try again, and having tried, feel base, shoddy, unworthy. Why in the name of love must I write this crap – and even keep it? Not only love but the whole beautiful world I defile – why?

(Not that he kept anything he wrote. The extract is from a letter he wrote to Julie and me.)

David kept a rough personal diary of events over the next five weeks and I will quote from it from time to time. He had left the *Evening News* and was now working as a sub-editor at the BBC. About the "shrinking" incident, he wrote:

> We, the four of us, were sitting in the Putney bedsit when the light started to change; it became greener and an echo came into the room. Then John physically shrunk in size as he sat by the bed. We were astonished and thought it was some power of Julie's. But now we realise it was John's power.

Again David wrote:

> I had the day off. John Hart and I talked and he told me a number of strange things. The black energy had visited him, he said – that thing that had terrified and nearly destroyed Barry and Julie. Next day when I returned from work John told me he had been in Hyde Park in the rain. He said he had been dying to emotion. Gradually I noticed a change in him. Great strength. For a number of days before all this he had told me of visions, devils, etc. which had happened to him, and strangely perhaps, I believed him – partly because of the strange things that had happened to me at Barry's previously. (I remember on two occasions feeling a heat build-up inside after talking or while talking with Barry.) John says that in the last two days he has experienced the astral body, and a journey through the creation and beyond the universe. He says the energy needed to take the

black energy (he called it the Death Body) has to be released outside our solar system and his astral trips have continued to destroy the energy absorbed from Barry and Julie. He said there are seven heavens outside the universe.

The night after the "shrinking" incident, John phoned me from David's. He said he could take the black thing from Julie. Would I let her come to him the next evening after she had finished work?

I knew John had great spiritual power. I knew that if anyone could help us he could. I said yes, she could go to him if she wished. Julie's response was she would only go if I said she should. I told her it was best.

The following morning she left for work as usual with the intention of visiting John for a few hours afterwards and then returning home. About ten o'clock that night she phoned. She said John wanted her to stay with him. Would I agree?

For how long? She did not know, as long as it took to get rid of the black energy. I agreed.

That was the end of Julie.

David's diary entry for the 10th of December says:

> John said Julie was going to come and stay with him for a
> little while because he had to "suck out" the black thing from
> her. She could then reach a state of pure consciousness, as
> opposed to the impure state that all other people are in to some
> degree.

The next entry says:

> Julie came to stay and has been at Portman Close since. The
> first night she says she did not sleep (the third day and night
> without sleep) for fear that the black energy would return. John
> ate little and clearly had enormous power and understanding –
> more so than Barry. He explained many things to me and said he
> knew now that Jesus Christ was the Son but he (John) was the

Father and the Son. I said nothing and suspended judgment –
there are too many nuts around – but I was deeply impressed by
the change in him day after day as he sat by the fire. He ate little
or nothing and still eats very little. Julie has changed. Barry came
to visit twice and accepted John as his teacher. He said he would
obey John if he would teach him.


After Julie phoned me about staying over with John I did not hear from
her. Three days passed. On the fourth day I went to Portman Close to
ask her to return. She opened the door. I was astounded. Her face was
alight, "open", smiling without the aid of lips. And around her eyes,
especially in the corners near the nose, were little "freckles" which had
not been there before. These freckles I knew then are seen in a face that
has been made new by the spirit (but I would not make a rule of this).

My own face felt dark, "black", rigid, compared with the sight of hers.
She was sparkling new. I walked in. John was sitting on the floor beside
the small electric wall-fire. I sat down and faced him, cross-legged.

'Teach me,' I said. 'Teach me and I'll obey you absolutely.'

Each day I would go to Portman Close and be with John and Julie.
They had no money and I used to bring food. None of us was eating
very much anyway but we did drink innumerable cups of tea. John said
tea was uniting; coffee separated by feeding the independence.

John taught me with his words, his presence and his love. He knew
exactly what I needed to know and he handed it to me piece by piece so
that at the end of each day I could leave him and go home to Putney and
work on it within in the isolation of my room.


A most distressing, and therefore valuable experience for me, was when
I arrived at Portman Close the first morning after I had asked John to
teach me. I walked in and there was Julie lying beside John in their
makeshift bed on the floor. Naively, it had not occurred to me on the
night he had asked Julie to stay that they would make love. The thought
probably was too painful for me to allow it to rise in my awareness. I
was very possessive, jealous and guarding of Julie sexually. It was right –
and always has been – that I should guard the Bhagavati from sexual

contact with other men; it is my power as the Bhagavat to do this to keep her pure. Bhagavati's task in the same way is to protect the man she loves by keeping the claw of the world – sex – out of him. Nothing contaminates the developing spiritual consciousness as much as intercourse with wrong (meaning ordinary, emotional and sexual) man or woman. But within my possessiveness was a flaw – wrong emotional attachment, and I knew it. It had to be got rid of. Julie was not mine for myself; Julie was mine only to protect and husband for the spirit, and that only while the spirit and she allowed it.

I had seen some time before that I would have to go through the pain of her making love with another man. The message came from reading John Fowles's book *The Magus*. In one scene, the man whose consciousness is being raised is forced to sit and watch the woman he loved, and imagined was exclusively his, making love in front of him to a black man – and with great relish. It hurt me deeply, and the image and pain kept recurring in my mind. It was a loveless weakness. I knew it had to happen – because I needed it. If I don't need anything, nothing happens.

Julie said later that when John suggested they go to bed together, she asked him to put his hands on her head. She would know from his touch whether it was right. When I arrived that first morning, I knocked. The door was unlatched and I walked in. There, as I've said, right in front of me they were still asleep in bed together: my first lesson. Gulp. Second lesson: Julie, naked, stepped out of bed over John's naked torso to make a cup of tea. Gulp. Gulp. But it was all right. Gulp. Gulp. Gulp.

I loved her and I wanted what was best for her.

Julie obeyed John absolutely. On the first night she went to him she said she looked into his eyes and saw the purity of the Christ. She did not see it again in another person, although she "read" eyes and saw much purity and beauty (as well as greed and cruelty) in others.

John's first shock for Julie was to suggest she no longer wore make-up of any description. The second was to suggest she did not return to work the next day. He seldom told her to do anything. She was with him to obey of her own volition, and implicit in that state of surrender is "knowing" what is required. This power of communication is inherent in every genuine master/student combination. John would say, 'It is right to suggest, but it is not right to persuade.'

Next morning Julie went in to the boutique and told them she was leaving without notice. Although sorely tempted to, she offered no excuses and gave no explanations – that would have been a compromise and she had left that world now (at least for a few precious weeks). Her employers were understanding and gave her the week's wages owing, about £12.

She went back to John with the money. It was very near Christmas. She wanted to give her children a present each – for the younger, a three-wheeler bike, his first. But she thought she had better save the money as she and John were otherwise penniless and John refused to think about eating or living in the next moment. When Julie mentioned the children's Christmas presents to him he said, 'Always do what is the biggest yes in you.' I contributed £5 and she bought the gifts.

One of John's friends called in and mentioned that he badly needed money.

'How much?' said John.

'A fiver would do.'

John reached over to where the balance of Julie's money was on the table and handed the man a £5 note, 'It's yours.'

Julie winced, but understood. John was not giving away her money. It was not in his character to rob or exploit anyone. To him it was simply the moment asking, and the moment responding.

The two of them went out to eat. Julie thought they would have a cheap snack like a hamburger or egg and chips. John swept into a good restaurant and ordered salmon trout. He enjoyed good food (as well as cooking) when it was available. When it wasn't, he ate what was provided or went without. The meal left them broke again.

On another occasion they were walking past a high class restaurant in Kensington and a chef was taking some air outside the kitchen door in the basement area. John got talking to him about cooking a particular sauce. The chef invited him in to make some. John did, with the result that he and Julie were invited to sit down and enjoy a spanking great three course meal with a bottle of wine to boot!

Julie loved John profoundly. They were linked by a spiritual bond. For much of the time they communicated wordlessly. Nevertheless, she used to say she was not in love with John – and that was what would make it impossible for her to stay with him any longer than was necessary.

'I love you and being with you, Barry,' she would say. 'You are my home. I will never leave you. I will always find you.' We both longed for the day when we would be united again. But we would and could do nothing about it. We both loved the Blessed John, the Master.

John was indeed now the Master. And the blessed one, blessed by the grace of that which I could only call God. He had the power of the spirit which he demonstrated in so many ways every day. I was at my nadir. My Bhagavati had left me because it was right. I was miserably weak. I was being reduced in power every day. At times I felt she despised me for my weakness – for the Bhagavati loves only the divine energy in man. But I could do nothing about it. I was literally insignificant.

Even when I spoke, others seemed not to hear. When we went walking most days in Hyde Park I followed behind either John or David. It was a repeat all over again of the bewildering uncertainty and ineffectualness of my days at Chilkapita in India before my "death". No one followed me; why should they? I was just there seemingly redundant and directionless – truly being humbled in the face of the Lord.

# CHAPTER 18

# AND HIS TEARS WERE
# OF JOY NOT SORROW

The surrendering of my "authority" – or the act symbolising that
surrender – occurred a couple of nights after John started to
teach me. The lectures in Wardour Street had finished and I had
begun giving private talks to groups of students in different homes. The
week that I went to John the talk was to be at Portman Close.

John, Julie, David and I were waiting for the first of the group to
arrive. They were seated at one end of the room and I was down the
other, meditating. Suddenly, I became aware that John wished me to
leave. I got to my feet and said, 'You want me to go. I go.'

Julie and David were astonished. It was ten minutes before the meeting. I put on my anorak and walked out. Heading back to Putney I
realised that yet another prop had been taken – first my woman, then my
independence, and now my students. What else can I AM lose? I was
getting the answer. There is always something to lose until there is nothing to lose.

David's diary described the incident:

> John said – by a clearly telepathic order as he clearly can
> manipulate things now – that Barry should not speak at the
> second of our informal meetings, but should go away. John took

the meeting. About fifteen people piled into the little room. They could not understand why Barry was not there – I knew because I was told by John earlier that he could teach by presence – there was no need of words. Four or five walked out when they heard this. We sat and meditated for perhaps 45 minutes. Then John Horridge asked me a few questions – there was great peace in the room – and I referred to John for answers as he sat quietly on the floor by the fire. Others then spoke and were answered and all left about 10pm apparently happy and satisfied.

David's diary then goes on to describe an incident that happened immediately after the meeting:

Just after they [the group] had left, Barry rang and I answered. There was great urgency in his tone and he asked for John. John listened in silence and gradually a few tears came down his face and he kept quite still. I felt that Barry had died because the strain had been too much for him. But I went upstairs and then came down and thought he had not. Julie put her head in her arms and wept and I found a few tears in my own eyes. A few minutes later John said Barry had told him, 'You are the living God. You are the living God.' – and his tears were of joy not sorrow.

I had made that phone call from Putney after seeing an extraordinary vision of John and Julie together. I'd returned, after leaving the meeting to John, and was lying on the bed in the dark. Julie appeared impeccably pure, so immaculate that I heard a "heavenly choir" singing in adoration of her essential being and describing her in a very strange religious term. The tune, the metre, and the words that were sung are still in my head:

Julie is the Lamb of God
Lamb of God, Lamb of God.
Julie is the Lamb of God.
Julie is the Lamb of God.

The choir chanted the song over and over for the whole time Julie's image was before me; probably for two minutes. The Lamb of God, of course, brings to mind the sacrifice of the lamb, the innocent one, in the devotions of the Old Testament; and in Christian liturgy refers to the mythologised sacrifice of Jesus on the cross as the Lamb of God. In Julie's case it was both descriptive and prophetic.

In the vision I then observed that the Julie I had known no longer occupied her body; it had been taken over by the unspeakably pure energy of John, who now appeared beside her holding her hand. They were absolutely transparent and transfigured, linked by the sublime quality of John's spiritual essence. There was nothing in either figure but translucent purity. I was overwhelmed by love and joy. Such a vision is beyond imagining. I went straight out to the payphone in the hall and called John.

David's diary continues:

> The next day I went to see Barry and he told me some strange
> things. He was in a very odd state. I felt great love for him but
> also great tension as he spoke. He told me that an "operation"
> had been performed on his head by a team of (spirit energy)
> surgeons who had put a small white box in his forehead. I was
> highly dubious of this but he was changed and I remember
> Lobsang Rampa (author of *The Third Eye*) talking of similar
> things. As I myself had experienced so many odd things I again
> reserved judgment as I realised that this operation was a
> subjective one.

During the "operation" mentioned in David's diary, I was lying on the bed in the dark and seemed to be looking up as one would from an operating table while five or six figures bent over me in a circle. Their "faces" or heads were just luminous white images but I had the clear impression of surgeons. The box was a small cube, also luminous white. By luminous white I mean the opposite of a silhouette which is a dark figure against a bright background. These were intensely bright figures against a black background, and so intensely bright that no features were discernible.

The monologue during the operation went something like this: 'We are now going to place this box in your forehead. It won't hurt. Remain as still as you can. It won't take long.' I watched the box come down into my forehead. I was aware of pressure above and between the eyes but no pain. 'Don't move,' said the voice. The pressure was quite intense for a minute or so. Then, 'There. That is all.'

All this and the rest that followed in those remarkable weeks over Christmas and New Year 1968–9 seem to demand some sort of advance explanation or comment if only as a gesture to rationality. The fact is that the story in places is not going to make sense. It cannot make sense because I'm talking about preliminaries to the transcendental realisation that I was about to undergo. Transcendental simply means consciously transcending sense, or the data of the senses, as interpreted by reason. Reason alone is incapable of understanding such things; a stillness of mind and presence is required in which all judgment is suspended.

David's diary, continuing on from the above entry, gives some indication of what was to come:

> Barry also talked of a master who had been talking to him in his head, giving him instructions, all designed to break Barry's rigid dependence on reason not intuition – things like burning money (I saw the charred remains) and not using his mind to get home by Tube, just obeying instructions no matter what they said. I did not think he was nearly insane. He spoke of Julie coming physically into him and living through him, and how she had left him and then been returned "by the law" and that they could both live as a unity in him. He explained about the so called rings of consciousness at the very top of the head and I definitely felt a flat part, very sensitively tingling on top of my head.
>
> He said John (God) had taken over Julie's body – he called her Julia – but Julie had come back to him. Then we both wept because Julie, as I knew her, was dead. This in a way is true: both the old Barry and Julie are now gone and I was right to weep for the death of the old pair I loved.
>
> I went back to Portman Close and told John about it. He explained that Barry was practically insane because he had to break his desperately rigid strength of reason to destroy the black energy totally. Later John said Julie had nearly physically died at least twice to destroy the black energy – her love for Barry, great, great, love – but it was at last done. It all sounds so

preposterous in print and yet I feel completely content at the
house (Portman Close) – and learn and learn and learn.


I'll now endeavour to recount firsthand some of the things I experienced.
The first incident occurred at the end of the first day John began to teach
me. I'd returned to Putney and was sitting in meditation when a voice
spoke inside my head, 'What do you see?' I was looking at the wall.
Speaking silently in my own head, I described the wall. The voice said
again, 'What do you see?' I kept answering by describing everything in
greater detail. 'What do you see?' the voice persisted. I then noticed that
the room – that is, the space in it – had turned a distinct golden colour.

'The space around me is golden,' I said.

'That is consciousness. What do you hear?'

'Nothing.'

'What do you hear?'

'Nothing.'

'What do you hear?'

'I hear you.'

'Where am I?'

'In the top of my head.'

'Where?'

'Towards the front of the top of my head.'

'This is a part of the seat of consciousness. I am in your consciousness.'

The rest of that conversation I can't recall.

It was soon made evident to me that the voice giving instructions in
my consciousness was intelligent beyond my own conscious powers.
One could of course say it was my higher self. Or one might call it a spirit master or one of the gods. What it is called is really irrelevant when
one experiences this wonderful inner integrity. For there is no doubt it is
intelligent and vastly wise. The important thing is it is there, within each
of us, the individual.


One night, the voice said, 'Take your best suit out into the back garden
and throw it on the fire.' I had two very good suits. One had been made
for me when I was a director of the Men's Fashion Council of Australia

155

(part of my public relations function). The other had been a gift from the chairman of the Council when he visited London shortly before this. That suit was a little better than the other. I selected the older one.

'The best one,' said the voice.

I took the suit from the wardrobe, unlocked the back door and stepped out into the garden. I looked around. It was winter and everything was wet and damp.

'There is no fire,' I said.

'No. Know that whenever you are required to do something the means will be there. Otherwise do not obey. Take the suit back inside and put it away.'

On another day the voice said, 'What money do you have?'

I produced two £1 notes, one ten shilling note and some silver. It was all I had. I was still sending money back to Australia and did not have much over each week. I had earmarked £1 for food to take to John and Julie.

'Keep the £1 for them, burn the rest.'

I dropped the notes in an ashtray, put a match to them and watched them shrink into ash. I can't recall what was said. But I got the message: I had the matches.

One other evening I was writing a note for the milkman.

'Take it straight out now and put it in the bottle,' said the voice.

I walked out to the front porch where the empty bottles were usually left. None was there. I returned to my room.

'Take the note out again.'

I returned to the porch. Someone had put out an empty bottle.

'The bottle came to the note,' said the voice. I understood.

When I went to work I used to get the train from Putney to Earls Court and change there for Temple, the closest station to the *Evening News*. This morning, at a station somewhere before Temple and just as the automatic doors were closing, the voice said, 'Quick, get out!'

I was deep in meditation. I darted for the doors and just managed to slip through onto the platform. I didn't know where I was and knew not to look.

A train drew in. The doors opened. I waited. They closed.

'The next one,' said the voice.

The boarding and alighting instructions, many of them at an instant's notice, went on for about half an hour until I had no idea where I was. When I finally knew the exercise was over the train had deposited me at Temple. Going home that night the same thing happened. Only, in the end, there was no voice: I just knew when to move and when not to.

I was made very much aware of the golden colour of consciousness. Sometimes it filled my room, sometimes it was in my head and once it became the colour of a new tone to sound.

The mornings were dark and I had to set the alarm for about 7 am to be at work at 8.30. Since the start of this period when I accepted John as my teacher, I'd kept the clock buried under clothing in the chest of drawers to deaden the tick and the alarm bell. These sounds had become extremely strident and irritating and even the muffling did not eliminate the harshness. On this particular morning, the alarm jangled with its usual raw effect. And then suddenly the tone of the noise "changed to gold", giving it an unobtrusive and "rounded" ring that has remained integral to my sense of hearing ever since. From that moment on, all traffic and other sounds have contained for me this muted though extra-dimensional golden quality. Noise certainly still affects me; but I know that it can never sound the same in its full forceful stridence as it did then. Perhaps "silence is golden", as the old saying goes.

It was around this time also that I had to "give up" my dependence on the clock. I knew my inner being would tell me when it was time to go to work. I deliberately did not wind the clock. I knew I must be self-reliant. I would get up in the morning and head for work when I felt it was time. I would not look at any timepieces on the way or endeavour to assess the time from events. I would just proceed, wait, proceed, wait, until I got there. I sometimes arrived at work two hours early and at other times just as late. The worldly consequences were mine to deal with. The essential thing was to go through the experience, to leave the effects to the effectual world, and to participate for a little time in the seeming insanity of causality.

It is an aberration of the mind to imagine that in the divine life circumstances have to "work out" to the satisfaction of reason. Life itself, which is totally divine, consists mainly of circumstances that seldom work out to anyone's satisfaction. What we call a satisfactory conclusion is always some sort of a compromise. Life is not a jigsaw puzzle because all the pieces are already in place to begin with. Late is late. Early is early. Failure is failure. Success is success. They are all there. Causality or the mystery of life is learned in participation, without the need for personal survival in conceptual or mind terms. If you are not prepared to risk your reputation, your job or your possessions for what you know to be the truth for you, you cannot expect to experience consciously the mysteries of the divine life. Causality only has to be participated in until the individual consciousness realises the unreality of the world of cause and effect. It is not a lifetime "sentence" or necessarily a way of everyday living, but just another phase in the amazing revelations of the spiritual life.

There are some interesting sidelines concerning the voice instructing me in my consciousness. The dialogue continued night and day for about two weeks. I frequently asked questions and received the impression that there were a number of these "masters" or intelligences "there", although I always seemed to be speaking to a particular one. I got the distinct impression that "they" were working at great speed in a situation that was fluid and constantly changing at an enormous rate. Nothing there was definite or predetermined; any move or possibility depended on streams of different factors operating at that precise moment. One could say that much of what was happening in the world was managed from "there".

On a couple of occasions I made specific requests. One reply was, 'Wait a minute while I see...' There was a pause. Then, 'Yes, that should be all right.' Another reply was, 'We are doing all we can... but I can't say.' And always there was the impression of extraordinary haste and speed.

CHAPTER 19

# JULIA

One evening while sitting in a chair in front of the electric fire at Putney, I was "visited" within by an extremely strong and severe female entity who said she was coming to "destroy" me in order to make me stronger. Without warning I received a tremendous blow inside the solar plexus. I doubled up in pain. I saw the image of a woman's face, identical to Julie's, but infinitely stronger, wilder and scornfully contemptuous of me, a she-cat who snarled, 'I'm going to destroy you...' I felt another blow which doubled me up again so that my head almost hit my knee. '... to smash you to pieces!' This time the effect in my body was like receiving an electric shock. Then she was gone. I was left breathless.

The fury of the woman verged on hate it seemed; and in her ruthless determination to afflict me personally in some way I sensed a viciousness not experienced before. And yet I got the impression that her motive was purely to make me strong. I asked the master energy inside me who was this woman and he replied, 'She is the woman who will phone you in one minute.'

A minute later the phone rang in the hall; I jumped out of the chair and answered it. It was Julie, now Julia.

Living the spiritual life, as I have already said in different ways, is a continuous "dying" of layers of the individual's self. With each significant "death" there is an advance in consciousness marked by a finer perception of spiritual truth and a distinct change in the persona. At the spiritual energy level the change is usually startlingly dramatic and is often referred to as a realisation. One example in this book was back in 1966 when my spiritual presence overnight changed the happily married mother of two young children into Julie. The married mother persona "died". As Julie put it in her poem describing her realisation, 'I am you.' In other words she became me. Two years later, in 1968, it was Julie's turn to "die". That sweet little God-loving personality, who for a while had become preoccupied with clothes and make-up, was being disposed of by John's superior spiritual presence. As Julie "left" I had the temporary experience of absorbing her, and becoming her.

In front of me now is the typewritten record of it, dated 12.30 am on the 15ᵗʰ of December 1968, written while I was adding to the text of *Wisdom and Where to Find It*. The note says, 'I am the air Julie breathes, the grass she walks upon, her movements, her fingers, her hair, her smile, her eyes, her tongue, her words and every experience her body and mind will ever have. I am Julie.'

That, as I said, was the end of Julie. Who then was the new woman beginning to appear in the same body under those quaint freckles? It was Julia – coming up, or in, from the deep unconscious. The deep unconscious is synonymous with cosmic or "outer" space. In outer space from where she visited my inner space she was not yet embodied. Without the deadening cocoon of the physical body she was wild and powerful and determined to make me, her love in existence, stronger.

So when I talk of the Julie whom I knew in the body I am talking about the formal embodied Julie. But when I talk of Julia (or of anybody's true being) I am talking of the real energy, the cosmic essence, behind Julie (or that person). Julia is Julie's true presence in the unconscious and that true presence (in everyone) is constantly endeavouring to enter more purely the formal body (or person) we are. The same thing had happened to the student John who became the uncompromising and selfless Blessed John.

In the spiritual life when you go deep enough into the unconscious within your body you eventually enter the reality of external space –

what we call outer space, or the space between the stars (astral space, from the Latin *astrum*, star). This is another world of supreme stillness and nothingness. Conversely, if man is ever able to actually travel deep enough into outer space (far beyond the influence of the solar system), he will end up in his own unconscious, the same other world of sublime stillness and nothingness. But unless he has been spiritually prepared, which is most unlikely, he won't perceive any great difference and will fill this space – as he fills his inner space – with the mundanity of his thinking and rationality. For finally "out there" or "in there" – the outer and the inner – merge to become the one consciousness.

But ultimately there is no "out there"; even "out there" vanishes to become "in there".

Julia was a female energy from outer space – an extraterrestrial being. The cosmos – the deep unconscious where outer and inner space merge – is filled with such extraterrestrial beings or intelligences. But they are too deep within or without – too spiritual or refined – to ordinarily be perceived by the human mind.

From deep outer/inner space, Julia was able to communicate with me in the physical through the medium of my love and my emotional attachment to her Julie body on earth. Julia, like all extraterrestrial beings – and like every individual's true being – was a very powerful causal energy. These beings are completely free and when coming into the confining body awareness of an earth person, can seem to be violent, reckless, irresponsible, wild, wilful, wanton and undisciplined – which of course they are not, except to our restricted perception.

The physical body that Julia was to enter had been raised and prepared for her from birth as Julie. Some of the later psychological and emotional preparations, coinciding with my entry into her life at the age of 24, I have already described. However, from the time of our meeting it took another seven years for Julia to "come in" to the halfway point. That achievement was accompanied by tremendous emotional upheaval which I will describe in its place. The stressful effects at the time appeared to be successfully held or contained by her physical apparatus.

From those days on Julie varied between being "nice and friendly Julie" (the refined residue of the old persona) and Julia, the wise, cold, uncompromising, pristinely beautiful, profoundly perceptive, inspirational cosmic spirit. The entry of such a being into a human body imposes tremendous strains on the physical apparatus. If the body is not up to it the result can be derangement or premature death.

Everyone's life is more or less reflective of the Julie/Julia experience. We change and are changed at various stages but because of the absence of teachings that extend to this depth, the events pass without a clear knowledge of the amazing causality behind them.


At the end of two weeks I noticed that a different inner voice was now instructing me. Also that the voice had moved to the top of my head, the centre of my consciousness. This voice was John's. At any time of the day or night I could contact him instantaneously. I would say in my head, 'John?' And immediately he would answer, 'Yes, Barry'. I would ask my question and he would reply.

# CHAPTER 20

# THE WORKING OF
# THE GREAT WILL

O n another night after being with John I was walking up to the
bedsit from Putney tube station, a distance of about half a
mile. It was cold and dark with few streetlights. Suddenly, in
my head I heard a scream and the wailing, 'I don't want to die...
please... let me live... please... please...', the last word gradually tailing
off into silence as though death had come. Cries to the same effect were
repeated six or seven times by different voices, with the same pathetic
result.

All this, as I say, happened inside me; I was simply the observer or lis-
tener. As tragic as it sounded there was no sense of pain or concern in
me. John explained that each was the death of a memory cell being
burned out by spiritual energy. Memory cells make up our sense of personal identity and I was in the process of losing my old identity.

My own knowledge now is that every spiritual realisation has a similar effect on the memory cells. The individual is relieved of some or most
of the old persona with the distinct sense of being "made" new.
Psychiatry attempted something similar with frontal lobotomy surgery in
which nerve fibres were severed by incision into the brain for the relief
of some mental disorders and tensions. I also know now that as a part of
evolution and in the great slowness of evolutionary time there is a natur-

al clearing out of the brain's old identities. For example, the identities of pre-dinosaur creatures were once in the brain but these have been superseded, making way for new identities which themselves will be exceeded in time.

At this point I had taken a couple of weeks off work and spent days in the bedsit between the chair in front of the fire and lying cold on the bed. Alternating heat and cold were very important to my intake of knowledge. I learned that heat – whether induced by the electric fire or inwardly – represented the period of ingestion or learning, and that cold, actual or subjective, was a time of digestion and "work". I ate virtually nothing and eventually settled on an egg-flip each morning. My sleeping was very shallow and "active". I was aware of vital energy working in me most of the time.

Being suddenly immobilised with considerable pain was frequent. While sitting or standing, my muscles would suddenly seem to "freeze". I would be forced to hold the position for up to an hour. This was not an imposed or unconscious condition: I was always aware that if I desired I could move – but I did not wish to. These periods helped to introduce me to an understanding of the Great Will, which is inviolable and implacable in all our lives. One of its agencies is the consistency of natural law.

On occasions I would be lying with my head back without a pillow and have to allow the saliva to run down my throat without swallowing. It requires tremendous conscious attention to withstand, without suppression, the instinctive urge to swallow. One has to get "around" instinct – itself an aspect of the Great Will – without denying it. The causes of greed and impatience must be discovered by self-experience. This discovery is made by intelligent penetration of the body without restriction or repression. Intelligence, which is the pure observation of what is (as distinct from what's going on – curiosity), is the instrument used.

Two of the most remarkable of the extraordinary experiences I had during this period – again a demonstration of the Great Will – were the stopping of my heartbeat and my breathing. It may be argued that this is a subjective experience. But as can be seen from the events I have described, it is extremely difficult, in fact impossible, to glibly draw a line between subjective and objective experience. As one proceeds deeper and deeper into the unconscious, it becomes evident that the inner and outer worlds are identical except that in the physical the individual exists in a formal sensory world, whereas in the internal reality all that exists is in consciousness, the one vital continuum. It is a question of perspective plus speed of perception and this is achieved by a reorientation of fundamental values.

My heart and breathing were stopped on two separate occasions while I lay on the bed. The object of this seems to be to eliminate the idea that life or perception is dependent on either of these vital functions. I wrote the following description at the time under the heading *The Transcendental Realisation*:

> In this realisation there seems a distinct possibility of physical death. At one point the perception watches the heartbeat and breathing cease and observes the body continuing to survive independent of both.
>
> The watching here is not from a separate entity looking down on the body from a spatial position as happens in out-of-the-body experiences. This perception I can only describe as integral consciousness – pure knowledge – in which there is no duality, no this and no that. In this state, physical death is irrelevant.

I mention the stopping of the heart and breathing – although only a part of this vast realisation – to illustrate the personal drama involved. The experiences are so abnormal, varied and continuous that to write of them probably tests the credulity of the most sympathetic reader.

I lost 20 pounds in weight in ten days and ate nothing substantial for six weeks. For six months the body was kept at about 20 pounds below average weight despite a large intake of starch-rich foods, normally a dietary "disaster" for me. Two people inquired if I was dying. The weight loss and emaciation were not caused by lack of food, but by the release of a new energy which causes a metamorphosis in the physical body and its inner system. During the critical period the energy itself substitutes for food and maintains a remarkable reservoir of vital strength, despite the body's starved and sick appearance.

David's diary says:

For nine days Barry ate virtually no food, a few bottles of milk, mostly just water for five days, and he says he is not hungry, will not eat, is unable to, and yet appears perfectly fit – in fact fitter than ever. Incredible. Yes, but less incredible than so many other things. It would perhaps have been better if I had kept a more detailed diary, but I am not writing to convince anyone else – these are notes for my own reference.

At another point, when there seemed to be a great battle going on inside me, I was walking in Hyde Park beside busy Park Lane. I stopped for no reason and looked up. Above me was the bronze sculpture of a gladiator fighting (I presume for his life) with sword and shield in hand. The symbolism had a great impact on me. I walked a few yards further and the voice in my consciousness spoke, 'Look!' All that was in my gaze was the traffic going towards Marble Arch. 'It is all symbolic, Barry.'

Symbolic of what? I didn't ask because I know the external formal world symbolises the inner fluid vital world; except that the senses "freeze" the vital reality into frames something like those that make up a movie film. The sensory frames, which are the slowest forms of manifestation possible, are then run in a continuum by the brain at great speed (similar to a movie projector); and this creates our sense of the moving physical world. From the symbol of the environment you can often assess your own inner state. I was once shown that every dot of light, from spark and headlamp to the twinkling of a star, is a symbol of consciousness. Consciousness lights the way for us all.

# CHAPTER 21

# THE CLIMAX

I t was just before Christmas. All day I had been lying on a bed in Portman Close, no thought, no mind. John was in meditation in the house. David had gone to visit his mother in Jersey in the Channel Islands. I knew something important was happening, but not what.

In the late afternoon, Julie switched on the vacuum cleaner. My attention became riveted on the sound. I was aware that My consciousness – *the* consciousness – was producing the "nothing" that prevented that sound from enveloping the entire world. Without My consciousness, without My "nothing", which I was producing, I realised that all phenomena would continue to expand infinitely and obliterate existence. My consciousness kept every thing in due proportion – even the hair on a dog's body. The hair could not grow longer than prescribed by the breed because I was keeping all that grew or manifested true to the idea and in correct proportion.

Then I realised that I was in fact "outside" the world and all creation. I was Supreme Being where there is no other. (This realised state I suspect is what the ancient Hindu sages referred to as *Maha Purusha*.) I was nothing "producing" nothing, and yet all action and relationships in the sense world were My will acting as love to express this transcendent knowledge. The whole world was love – but I, as nothing, was more "effectual" than love. I was the unmoving cause of love.

I started to shout. Later, Julie told me she thought I was raving. But what I was trying to do was to tell her and John what I was perceiving. Yet even as I called out, I was laughing at my own absurdity. I realised that as soon as I attempted to describe the truth of My consciousness I used the instrument of love or action – be it speech, writing, movements or any other attempt at communication or expression. Love appears spontaneously as the voice, the limb, the sound and yet I am no closer to describing My extraordinary being. By laughing I was proving the point I was trying to make – but only to myself. I am indescribable – though not beyond being – because I am beyond any means of description. The closest thing to My transcendence is love – it could be described as My existential nature – but still it is only an effect of my being, not my being.

The only way to know Me is to be Me.

I enter the world as love when I try to express myself.

When I don't try, I am nothing, and no one can know the truth.

I stand behind the senses, behind the concept, behind the idea, behind the action. Nothing can describe Me, nothing can express Me. Yet all description and expression is My unending endeavour as love to communicate the truth of what I am.

The above is an example of my failure to describe the transcendence of Consciousness, or the realisation of being the one and only divine Being beyond all.

There was one other significant sequel. A few hours later, still filled with transcendence and indestructibility, I suggested to John that we both decide to sit in the room where we were 'and never move again'.

I realised that my body could be thrown like rubbish into a garbage can or buried in a grave without making the slightest difference. In fact it would be this alone, this unalterable, implacable resolution of will never to act, speak, move or do again, that would allow Me to express My transcendence. This was the final irony: to be what I am, I would have to remain as nothing and let my body die inert and immobilised as an act of my unshakeable will. That way, love as the spontaneous but inadequate act of creation would cease, and I the uncreated would remain.

John was not interested. Nor was I willing to do it alone. So the Buddhic Consciousness once again refused to desert the world. That is its weakness, its love.

At the time, I wrote this poem:

THE TRANSCENDENTAL REALISATION

Nothing.
Nothing but I.
Origin
Black, undistinguished, indistinguishable
Being
Outside the world
Static
Forever aware
Forever
Forever present
Forever unformed
Forever unable to tell the secret of My Being.
Yet, not from withholding
For I am Origin
Source
Beginning
Everness
Now
It.
Nothing.
I am producing Nothing.
And you, My Love,
Are producing Everything.
As Nothing
I am Supreme Being
Origin indescribable
No-suchness
A mystery
Of non-stirring, knowledge, ceaseless undetectable presence.
I am Origin of all action and sound

And My agency, the lesser being, the creator
Is Love.
Love is all.
Life is the action of Love
Love's business
The never-ending tireless endeavour to enact My Being
To describe with creation what I am
And lovingly creating what I am not.
Love fails.
Love always fails, yet never tires of failing
(Even now, Love groans at its own inadequacy
to express in words the Truth I am.)
This the impossible, hopeless task of love
The reason why love lives to serve
Yet must forever remain sufficient only to itself, that task.
Love is the only means I have
And the only means to Me
Nothing.
I am producing Nothing.
An unimaginable substantive endingness
More real than even Love.
I am the space, the pause, the perimeter of sound and form.
I enable Love's beauty to be seen.
Where All and the Nothing meet is Man.

# CHAPTER 22

# LIFE IN THE MOMENT

D avid moved from Portman Close early in January which meant that John and Julie had to leave. I watched them sitting there waiting for the moment to walk out; John staring at the fire, intensely conscious; Julie silent and surrendered. It was sleeting outside, a typical cold, grey English winter's day. John got up, picked up their little bag of belongings, and together they walked out.

To me, they were magnificent. Here was a man and woman, a momentous unity, not searching for the truth, for that is to follow an idea, a concept, but throwing themselves into it where it throbs every instant in the uncertainty of no comfort, no aim, nothing but what is. No insignia of begging bowl, orange robe or shaven head. If faith exists this must be very close to what it means.

For two weeks they wandered from place to place, very often starving. Where were they heading? Nowhere. It was John's philosophy to live in the moment and to take no thought whatever for the next moment. It is an error to call it his philosophy for he genuinely had none. What he taught was identical with his way of life. Philosophies are for men who cannot live them.

John and Julie stayed overnight with different friends of John's but no one would put up with these two for long. They were just too "free" and unproductive. And John would not stay in one place more than a couple

171

of nights anyway. Late at night they would frequently be walking around apparently aimlessly while John 'waited for the moment to change'. They would cross the same intersection two or three times in an hour.

For John, no two moments were ever the same; each was new, different, filled with vast new possibilities. If his perception of this truth did not crystallise as a meal, a bed or a bath, it was of little consequence; he, like time, could wait or continue forever. He perceived the beauty of the truth in every moment and that was enough for him to keep the faith of no expectation for his mortal parts.

It snowed and more often rained while they tramped up and down Archway Hill – or towards Wimbledon, Putney, Islington, Knightsbridge, any place. They were continuously wet and cold. Julie wore a pair of slacks, a jumper, a woollen jacket and a cap for her head. John wore the same gear he had when I met him. In a small suitcase, about 18 inches long, which they carried in turn, were a spare shirt and blouse, some underclothes, a grey skirt of Julie's and some small personal odds and ends. Many times she wanted to cry with the cold (as she had with her husband and me in earlier times), or to protest at having to carry the case when she was weak from hunger and exhaustion. But she did not dare. She was constantly afraid that at the first sign of weakness on her part or feminine guile, John would throw all their belongings into the river. She knew her master. She knew he wanted nothing for himself; he would divest himself of anything, even life if it was necessary, to teach her and make her strong.

They also had some wonderful times, this pair of extraordinary human spirits. They played in the snow under the moon on Hampstead Heath, danced care-less in the dawn in Hyde Park. They owned nothing. They were always at best a bit hungry. But in those wondrous moments, they knew what freedom was.

To live with such a man as John, to continuously walk away from compromise and every acquisitive instinct, was of course a tremendously powerful teaching for Julie. His spiritual insights were fantastic, his power to bring about changes in people unbelievable. It is impossible to chronicle most of what he said and did.

As others came to recognise his spiritual power and enlightenment, he did everything he could not to create a visual impression of "holiness" or specialness. One night he looked across at Julie and said, 'My God, you think I'm Jesus Christ!' He rushed upstairs to shave off his beard but could not find a razor. He located a pair of pliers and started wrenching out individual hairs without much success. When David arrived he borrowed a few shillings, bought a razor from the all-night chemist in Piccadilly and removed the beard.

John's way was to continuously destroy in himself any suggestion of expectation.

Despite the cold he tore the lining out of his green windcheater and wore it inside out to avoid becoming a familiar image. He tossed his cap away. He wore sandals and socks even in the snow.

Once David and I met him in the street at Belsize Park on our way for a lunch snack at a pub. 'What are you doing for lunch, John?' David asked.

'You must be joking,' said John who knew it was the body that did everything so he couldn't know anything ahead of what his body did. Besides, you can't answer a question like that and live in the moment!

To John beauty and love were in everything. The partiality of intellectual appreciation and "learnedness" was an anathema, a sick joke. A well-read lady at a party asked his opinion of a theory put forward by a fashionable author. It was pure intellectualism.

'I don't know about that,' said John, 'But I shit beautifully.'

On another occasion John and Julie hitched a ride in an expensive car. The well-dressed lady passenger turned to John and said, 'What do you think of the drugs problem?' With great seriousness John replied, 'LSD's a bit hard to get hold of but the rest are okay.' (Julie never took drugs and we never knew John to.)

As they wandered around the streets of London, he taught Julie how to distinguish the "right" road to take from among the "wrong" roads. After a while she began to see "dark barriers" across the wrong roads and could easily choose the right one. As her perception increased, the barriers vanished and she simply knew which road to take.

For the rest of her life she used this amazing faculty to judge houses, people, streets and even villages. She could tell a bad or low vibration with her eyes closed; and frequently in a restaurant or a crowd would detect and identify the presence of a person who was suffering from a mental illness. She became physically ill in really "bad" company or places.

It was snowing and an old tramp sitting on a seat in Islington stopped them and asked for money. He looked about 80 with a bearded face and had newspapers wrapped around him for warmth. John opened up the suitcase and asked the old man if there was anything there he could use. The tramp picked through the case and said no.

In the case were some silver knives and forks which David had given John as possibly being worth selling. John offered them to the old man, but he shook his head. John took off his jacket and offered it to the tramp. The old man refused to take it.

The three of them sat down. The tramp took out a packet containing two cigarettes, gave one to John and took the other himself. John said half would do but the old man insisted he have a full one.

When they left him, John noticed Julie was upset that he had taken the tramp's last cigarette. 'One should not deny any man his giving,' he said.

Julie asked why the tramp did not take the silver and sell it. John said the old man had reached a point where he wanted only what was necessary for his immediate use. He added that the old man had asked him where he (the tramp) had gone wrong – 'All these people with jobs and homes: Where did I go wrong?' John said he had told him, 'You have gone right. It is the others who have gone wrong.'

To John, life lived in the raw, like the old man lived, was life, not living in comfort and convenience which was a sort of death. John lived a life of immortality which of course is a life without consideration of the body, a significance we will all realise in death.


Many years after these events, Betty, my ex-wife in Australia, sent me a letter I'd written to her from London on 19 February 1969 – after the night of the black energy, the days of my transcendental realisation, and near the end of the train of events that followed. Part of the letter contains some new facts and throws the light of immediacy on that incredible time. I had written:

> John said he could take the black thing from Julie if I would
> let her go to him. Julie did not want to go but said she would do
> as I decided. I said to her, 'If John is not true we are all mad and
> doomed. You must go.' She went. She stayed, I think, five weeks.

I saw her four days later. The transformation was indescribable. John had taken the black energy. All fear, uncertainty, thinking, expectations, intentions, had vanished. She was pure. I knew it. My Julie was dead.

For me, the agony was to see the appearance I had loved now living with another teacher and the knowledge that its purity was too wide now to ever love one man or person again as something exclusive, except by function. For this love, like God, loves all things the same, the only speciality being the dictates of function in the moment.

I had often declared in England, 'Find me a man who knows more than I and he will be my teacher,' never expecting to find one. I had found him. I said, 'Teach me.' He did. I returned home each day while he stayed with Julie. They had no money, no food, and for two weeks I took along with me the meagre food they lived on. John owns nothing, gives anything he might gather away. They wandered through the English winter together for four weeks – John showing Julie his incredible teaching or perception in the moment to moment experience of life, without money, possessions or place to stay except that provided by the moment; living "on the moment" (as he called it) without trying or wanting, expectation or intention.

John killed me stone dead. For five weeks I was in my room, mostly on the bed in the most dreadful agony I have ever experienced – physical and mental. It was this new energy of consciousness working. It is golden in colour although this colour perception is not really of the senses. The experience of the golden energy working through the brain and body is so unbelievable that most minds without the experience would have to cry, 'Hallucinations!' My breathing was stopped, my heart ceased to beat, my body was paralysed while I was subjected to intense pain. The visions and voices and their revelations cannot all be repeated (they disappear as the normal reflective memory returns) for they are too numerous, too unbelievable for memory. The consciousness is taken beyond reason above intellect where there is no continuity, where last exists before first.

I lost 20 pounds (9 kilos) in weight in the first ten days. I ate nothing but an egg flip a day for four weeks but did not lose more weight – the consciousness itself sustains the body when it wants to. Really, if it is the Will, there is no need for heartbeat, breathing, food or even blood, it is all in the golden energy. I watched, unmoved, my stricken body about to die knowing it could take no more. All this and not one drug.

# CHAPTER 23

# THE ARCHONS

One night a week or so after John and Julie left Portman Place, the phone rang in the Putney bedsit. Would I accept a reverse-charge call from Shepperton (about 15 miles south-west of Putney) from a Mr John Hart?

John was excited. 'I had to phone,' he said. 'You are the only one who will understand. I've just made contact with some kind of spaceship. I have been talking to them in my perception. They've been visiting and watching the earth for thousands of years. A thousand years is like minutes in their time. Our technology and culture are unbelievably primitive compared to theirs.'

John continued, 'They were very cautious when I first made contact. They refused to acknowledge me. They tried to confuse me. They used lights to make me think their spaceship was an aeroplane. But I knew they were there; I was in tune with them. They then tried to make out they were superior to me. I realised this was some kind of test. I told them I was stronger and they must obey me. They accepted this.

'I asked them many questions and they also wanted to know different things. They made a cross in the sky to show me they knew about Christ and were aware of that high consciousness. They said that to them it was like ten minutes since Christ had been on earth.

'They know about you. I said I wanted to go with them. They said that would be arranged. I asked if Julie could come too. They said not yet. They said they would return for me.'

That is all of the conversation I can remember, although John spoke for about ten minutes. The important point to me was that although he was aware of the physical presence of the spaceship in his vicinity the entire contact occurred in his consciousness, in his perception as he put it.

After phoning me John rang David and asked him if he would drive over and pick up Julie and him in the car.

David's diary entry for 8 January 1969 reads:

At about 10.30 pm I was at a friend's place in Hornsey when John phoned from Walton-on-Thames, about an hour and a half away [near Shepperton]. He said he'd had a beautiful experience and could I pick up Julie and him. It was pouring with rain and they had no money, so I did.

When I got there John told me he and Julie had been given a lift out to Walton. They had been walking a long way when they saw strange lights, red and white, in the sky. John said he saw something that at times looked like an aeroplane and at times like a diffused light. It went over a hill and he and Julie walked towards it. Immediately he was in contact with "them", the occupants of the spaceship. He spoke, in his mind, with them. At first "they" were alarmed but clearly knew what was going on in the world. They had been watching it for several thousand years. (John later said he thought he knew the star they had come from, travelling on an energy beam, not using their own power) and were familiar with man's childish technology, etc.

John said he communicated with them for perhaps an hour and they wanted explanations for certain things. Previous to this they had tried to confuse his directional sense by moving lights and then by looking like aeroplane lights. He said the precision and beauty of their communication by perception was fantastic. He had no idea of their physical form.

At one point they made the shape of a cross and a man in light to show they know about Jesus and his high consciousness… Julie says all she saw were various strange lights in the sky.

John said he asked them if he could go with them and they said yes, but not now.

They are supposed to be able to take human form and have done so in the past to discover about human life on this planet. John did say they knew about Jesus, and to them it seemed about ten minutes ago in human terms. Such is their strength that they live for thousands of years. Their journeys are supposed to affect tides and weather on the earth, according to John.

They told John that he was really one of them (third heaven but very strong) and he, realising that they were testing him, told them he was stronger than they and they must obey him. They acquiesced and then departed, saying they would return.

A note made at the time in the margin of David's diary says, 'Barry calls them Archons.' I must have got that name from John when he phoned. I know now from my own experience that these beings are archetypal intelligences from inner space (hence their instantaneous communication method). Years later I discovered the word archons in the Gnostic Gospels, 1,600 year-old manuscripts found in 1945 buried in a desert cave near Nag Hammadi, Upper Egypt. In the manuscripts Archons are referred to disparagingly in at least two texts as being the ignorant creators of existence.

Here is how Julie describes John's meeting with the Archons:

> It had been a strange day. We had walked from central London, along the embankment to Barnes, then behind Putney to Richmond. Everything seemed turned on, communicating – the water lapping, the trees, the river. We were awake. We had no money and were hungry, but it didn't matter. From Richmond we hitched a lift to Shepperton. By dusk we were walking down country lanes, right out in the country. On the way, John had sold the cutlery in the suitcase for a few shillings and bought some bread and cheese. We sat on a wall to rest and eat some. It grew dark. We were both very silent.
>
> I looked up and saw a light in the distance, getting nearer and nearer. What amazed me was it made no sound as it approached. It was a small light that seemed to be within a large dark circle,

like you would imagine a small, lighted window would appear in the side of a large circular object. It stopped, stationary, 15 feet off the ground in front of us, 20 yards away.

It started to move. John said, 'It wants us to follow it.' We walked as fast as we could and it went over the horizon of a hill which seemed to be lit up. John said, 'There are many others there.'

We stumbled on to the outhouses of a farmhouse. It was very eerie. I was frightened. John said he was in touch with "them" all the time. They told him he was one of them and that they had come for him. He was the only man in the world fearless enough to go with them. They said he had been chosen to accompany them. They wanted information about the earth. Although I was very strong, stronger than most women, I was not strong enough to make that trip, they said. John said he would come back for me "later". They told him they would return for him.

John got very impatient to get on with it. We eventually found a pub and he said he wanted to phone Barry. On the way to the pub he said, 'We have to call them a name, Julie… We'll call them Archons.'

John said their perception was so instantaneous that he was able to communicate as quickly as them. 'They are in for a bit of a shock as I'm more powerful than they are,' he added. That was why he was not afraid, he said.

After phoning Barry, John said, 'Barry is quick. He was going yes, yes, yes. But he's not as quick as the Archons because it was still necessary for me to speak to him. Having to speak slows it up.'

Five days later David wrote the sequel in his diary:

I went to our friend's flat in Hornsey and John was in the bath. John had to meet them (the Archons) to the north of London and I offered to take him. We set off and messed around Watford and St Albans. I noticed a strange set of subtly lit clouds on the way out at 10.30 pm. Later, as John seemed to be searching for the right place, I felt something indefinably strange going on – the right place evidently needing to be a large flat place without trees.

My headlights would not flick on properly at this stage, although I tried many times. John said "they" were "messing about a bit". At last, at 11.30 pm, we got onto a wide road near Watford and John said he would like to get out. I stopped and off he went. I noticed an ornate set of gates with the words Rolls Royce. Moments before John had muttered, 'It figures.'

Some hours before this John and Julie had got separated. Unbeknown to us, Julie's metamorphosis was now complete – the way was clear for Julia to start entering the world. John, the Blessed Master, had done the job for both of us in less than six weeks. It was time for him to leave the world and return to the inner space from whence he'd come. Only the circumstances of John and Julie's parting remained to be enacted. This was an amusing and symbolic little interlude.

John had gone to have coffee with a friend at the London School of Economics where he had once been a student. Julie was left in the reception area for about three hours. It gave her time to wash and fix her hair but after another couple of hours waiting she began to wish she had the money for a cup of coffee. She decided to find John and tell him she was leaving. Looking down she spotted a sixpenny piece lying on the floor. She picked it up, slipped it in her pocket and went off to find John.

He was standing by one of the lecture rooms. She said, 'I think I'll be going now.' She thought this might be the moment – as she thought every day might be the day – to return home to me. John said, 'Me too, I'll come with you.'

They walked three miles to Islington and spent the night with friends. The next morning John seemed aware of a change in Julie. He put out his hand, shook hers, and with a delighted smile said, 'How do you do?' He repeated it several times during the morning. Then he said, 'What name would you like me to call you?'

She said, 'Julia – but not all the time. I like my name Julie, too.'

He said, 'Right. I'll probably call you Julie when we're crossing the road.'

They walked to Camden Town, another couple of miles. Julie with sixpence in her pocket was feeling pretty smug. Buns there were cheap and she intended to buy as many as she could for John and her to share as their next meal.

As they passed a cake shop Julie lingered, looking in the window to see what was the best buy. John, thinking she was gazing wistfully at food she could not have, walked off. He later said, 'She had to learn she did not need my physical presence any longer.'

That was the end of the combination. John went to his appointment at Watford and his enlightened being left with the Archons.


Later I asked Julie why she had left John. She said, 'John's teaching was "Go out and experience all the time." Your teaching was containment of energy. I felt that for me your teaching was the highest because it was the hardest.'

Julie just for the day decided to live John's way and go wherever she was led before turning for home. It was the first urge for freedom and new experience generated by the incoming energy of Julia. From Camden Town she walked to Kensington – and there (a few hours before John's appointment with the Archons) accepted an invitation to go to coffee at the London Hilton with a well-dressed man sitting in the back of a chauffeur driven blue Rolls Royce.

# CHAPTER 24

# JUST ONE MORE DAY

When Julie (with the incoming consciousness of Julia) stepped into the Rolls Royce at the invitation of the well-dressed stranger, she had made love with only three men – her husband, me and John.

Liberation or spiritual freedom is not gained by trying to be like everyone else. Liberation is gained by true love, that is, by coming alive, by opening yourself to life in whatever direction you are closed. Liberation is being vulnerable, exposing to life the part of you that would try to hide and play safe behind its fear and make an excuse or virtue out of its cowardice. Liberation is freedom without licence, the acceptance of responsibility for being what you are. It is to have the will, the power, the simplicity to live life unafraid to *be* life, to be what you are from moment to moment without pretence and without considering what you or others think you should be or should not be.

To be truly liberated is to have the stale old notion of what you think you are, and what the world thinks you are, cracked open and left behind. Naked of being anything you must stand, and stand alone.

Until I came into Julie's life she had been a paragon of middle-class English upbringing. Her father was the only son and heir of a very wealthy land and property owning Sussex family who traced their ancestry back to a French aristocrat involved in the Norman Conquest. A Sussex village is named after the family. The rich young man who never worked long at anything because he never had to, nevertheless worked hard and with great success at getting through the family fortune before he died.

He married his only real love, a woman born well and truly out of his class not far from the sound of Bow Bells, Cockney land, East London. Their two daughters and older son he raised in upper-middle class ease and comfort by selling off the family properties bit by bit and breaking the family trusts established to protect him from his own profligacy. In later years as things got tighter, the considerable number of irreplaceable antiques in the home vanished one by one only to appear in the shop windows of the local dealers – to the dismay of his two young girls.

In his property and family trust dealings the father was assisted by an obliging crooked solicitor who, in exchange for not asking too many questions, handled all his financial affairs and provided him with a monthly cheque and occasional additional sums to get him out of trouble – with a tut-tut that he must be more careful with his money, which of course he never was.

His son at the age of six was packed off to Dad's old Public School to be made a man and a gentleman. And mother devoted herself to making the two little girls into perfect little ladies. Both attended the local convent school, although the family were Protestant. Rita, three years the elder, was an exemplary student. Julie hated school and for years feigned various illnesses, played truant and made other excuses which kept her absent as often as she was present.

The main lesson Julie learned from school was how to cover up for what she didn't learn, except on one rare occasion when she was moved to show her knowledge. The teacher had asked the class a question to which Julie was sure she knew the answer. Up shot her hand before anyone else could move. 'Yes,' said the delighted teacher, repeating the question encouragingly, 'Who was Sir Walter Raleigh?' As quick as a flash Julie replied triumphantly, 'Sir Francis Drake!' (The Blessed John used to say she was too intelligent to learn anything at school.)

What she lacked in classroom education the young schoolgirl made up for in personal charm and charisma. She was angelic to look at: fair hair falling past her shoulders, wide-eyed, trusting, innocent, friendly, a flashing, penetrating smile. Everyone adored her, forgave her and gave in to her – except Rita. Julie told me that Rita at times truly despised her for her obvious (to Rita) duplicity and popularity she considered unfairly won. And Rita let her know it – putting her down and trying to make a fool of her at every opportunity. But Julie remained the cynosure of the family.

Although the girls truly loved each other, jealousy continually intervened. Rita, Julie said, could not stop herself. Sometimes she would wish her younger sister dead. Her love was punctuated by a fierce compulsion to "get even". This made Rita feel guilty and ashamed. Yet still the jealousy and resentment seethed in her. The relationship made her schizoid, split between love and hate. Which side was herself? – she often wondered. (All this Julie said Rita had told her.)

Julie used to often speak to the family of God and of her communion with that state. She claimed it made it possible for her to bring about things she wanted to happen. Rita believed in God but Julie seemed to know God. This made Rita even more impatient and irritable with her. Julie used to say she could recall the actual moment, the awful pain, when she left God in heaven, to be born. She could remember lying in her pram observing the people looking in at her and seeing the hate in her sister's eyes as Rita studied her. She knew she was not a baby, not what people thought she was.

Rita wanted to know God too. One day Julia would help her to do that.


Julie was something of a tomboy. She loved to run wild and undisciplined with the neighbourhood gang of boys. She was the only girl among them. They loved her. None of them ever tried to touch her. It was always that way for her with men: they liked her or desired her but did not try to force their physical feelings on her.

Rita, a quiet and gentle girl, at 16 fell in love with a boy in the merchant navy. For three long teenage years between his short and infrequent visits home, she loyally and patiently refused the invitations of other boys to go out. The relationship ended when he settled in another country.

Both girls were virgins when they married; Julie at 18, Rita at 23. Most of their teenage and pre-marriage years were spent living in a beautiful thatched cottage in Sussex. When the girls married, their parents sold the place and moved into one of the father's more modest properties, a townhouse in nearby Tunbridge Wells. By the time he died at 60 this was the only property their father had left from his inheritance. He was a drinker and very generous with his hard-drinking cronies. Like a true gentleman, as his fortune and his fortunes dwindled, he didn't complain and didn't try to keep up with his old well-to-do mates. He knew not to contact them any more. He didn't live in the past. He had no regrets. He was true to himself. Three weeks before he died, and while apparently in good health, he suddenly gave up drinking. He was not an alcoholic after all. It was just that he had never found anything else to do.

I never met my second father-in-law, or his wife, or their son. Julie kept us – the old life and the new – well apart. When I came into Julie's life, her very respectable middle-class background and way of living, with its ceaseless compromising and suppressing of the natural emotions, was reflected in her excessive politeness, good manners and ingrained or cultivated gentility. She never swore, didn't drink, didn't make scenes – except to cry sometimes when her hands were cold or she didn't get what she wanted. In public she didn't complain, would put up with just about any inconvenience rather than protest and appear not to be "nice". For a time, as I said, I called her Mrs Mouse. She was as thoroughly phony as a thoroughly respectable upbringing could make her.

Two and a half years with me, and two weeks tramping the freezing streets of London with the Blessed John, had destroyed much of the emotional falsehood and impurity of her personality. But its virulent centre – the wilful emotional self – which often requires the drastic shock of imminent physical death to be eliminated, was still there.

John used to hit her around the head, saying, 'Scream will you. Get angry. Wake up. Swear!' One night while they were crossing the West End through Soho, a prostitute was abusing a man in the street. 'She has more love in her than you,' John said to Julie. 'She's not afraid of life. She lives life. She is life. You're not special. What makes you think you're special? Get out on the streets. Live. Love. Compared to her you're dead.'

Julie knew what he meant. She knew she was no longer afraid of life. Living in the moment with this blessed, fearless man and sharing his incredibly hard physical and spiritual way had seen to that. No longer was she screwed up with convention's fears. She knew her divine strength as woman; for she had lived it in the flesh, not just talked it or wished it. But she had not lived it alone as woman, not lived it without the strength and companionship of such a divine man. Now she must do that; that's what the master was saying. But she must not want to force it by any decision or act of her own will. It must happen in the moment as directed from within.

That moment occurred as she stood on the Kensington street corner utterly alone, free of all ties past and future, true to the moment, true to life, not knowing anything but the wonder of now – and up glided the blue Rolls Royce.

'Would you join me for a cup of coffee?' asked the stranger through the open window of the back seat.

Julie paused, smiled. 'Yes,' she said. The door opened, she stepped in and off they drove to the London Hilton in Park Lane.

He was a Canadian television executive in London for Prime Minister Trudeau's first visit to Britain. He and the film crew occupied several apartments at the Hilton. As Julie walked beside him into the hotel she was very much aware of the large holes in her tights showing between the tops of her worn and grubby boots and the short unpressed grey flannel skirt so typical of those days at the end of the mini-skirt age. But she was not self-conscious, just aware. And the man didn't seem to notice or mind as he ushered her to his table in the plush surroundings of the hotel restaurant.

There they had the coffee – and she a substantial meal. She hadn't eaten properly for weeks. She told him so and that she had no money. He offered to buy her some clothes. No thank you, she said, but she was very grateful for the meal. She liked him. He asked her if she had any-where to stay. 'No, not tonight,' she said. Would she like to stay in his apartment? 'Yes. Thank you.'

In the apartment he offered her the use of the shower and made up a bed for her in the sitting room. He said she was beautiful to be with; she was silent and yet was good company. He made no suggestion of sex – and yet she gathered from his phone conversations with his colleagues that arrangements had been made earlier for some women to come. He cancelled whatever it was and spent the evening talking to her.

A while after they had said goodnight and gone to their separate beds, Julie walked into his bedroom. 'You can make love to me if you want to,' she said.

He replied, 'I would love that. You are like an angel, like some sort of saint. I've never met a woman like you before. I could not approach you that way. It's very strange. You are a most desirable woman and yet... I don't know.'

She got into bed with him. But at the moment of his climax her long hair somehow got stuck in his throat. He broke away coughing and ejaculated outside her.

When they went to sleep she was amazed that he left the bedside radio on. He told her he couldn't sleep without it. Next morning he went filming early, leaving instructions at the desk for her to be given what she wanted. She had breakfast in bed alone, cornflakes, strawberries and cream, a jugful of it. She luxuriated in the pleasure and comfort of it all – the warmth, the ease, the snugness, a bit of smugness, and especially the several soft, clean and bouncy white bath towels hanging from heated rails in the bathroom.

Suddenly, without warning, she felt sick. She choked on the cream, on her own satisfaction. She realised it was over. It was wrong to stay any longer. She must get up and go now. But she didn't. Just another day, her mind said; another day would be all right. So she stayed. But she was uneasy. She phoned me. Could I meet her in Hyde Park opposite the Hilton? It was several days since I'd seen her. I got there as fast as I could. She told me what had happened.

Would she come back home with me? I asked.

No, not yet, she said. She was free. She was bound to no one. She loved me – but no longer was attached to me. She didn't need me unless I loved her. She said she must do what she wanted to do, not what anyone else wanted or expected.

But hadn't she said she'd realised it was wrong to stay another day?

Yes. Nevertheless she was staying, she said. She handed me her knickers to wash, please – the ones my mind noticed that she had worn yesterday with her lover – and went back to the Hilton.

Immediately she entered the apartment nausea engulfed her. She vomited, retched and vomited again. This time she got the message. She left quickly, leaving the man a note, and started to walk the five miles to our bedsit in Putney.

Later I found a pencilled note and a poem she had written about the incident and the man:

> I lay wordless, speechless, fearless amid such wealth.
> You play your tune,
> Mr Sad Man.
> I listen and smile,
> Mr Sad Man.
> Your eyes look away
> And my heart follows you,
> Mr Sad Man.

The next day, after walking the whole night, she arrived at our bedsit tired and drained – but in herself invincible. That night she had severe chest pain and was unable to get out of bed. By 1am she was at crisis point. I called an ambulance which whisked her off to hospital. It was pleurisy. Two punishing weeks tramping the streets and parks without regular food in the ice and cold of winter had been too much for Julie's body, if not for Julia's spirit.

Ten days later she was discharged fit and well and we moved into a large flat in Southwood Lawn Road, Highgate, sharing with David. I wrote, 'We will continue to live together until we are separated which may be tonight or next year. It depends on her and my function – what we have to do.'

# CHAPTER 25

# JOHN, THE MAN

Three days after John's enlightened being had left with the Archons, he was arrested wandering in Hyde Park and committed to a mental hospital. He had taken a Co-operative Society van loaded with food and driven up towards Scotland, distributing the food to hitchhikers along the way. Ironically, while he stopped for a cup of coffee at a roadside cafe, someone stole the van again! And with it went John's famous little bag containing all his possessions: underclothes, poems and safety razor.

The circumstances of his arrest were described in David's diary:

> John said he was in Hyde Park when he saw a hut with a fire
> in a hollow. He went in and helped himself to some corned beef
> and cocoa. Moments later three big black guys entered and
> eventually someone called the police. John told them the truth
> that he had no home, no job, no money. From their point of
> view he was clearly peculiar. They took him to Scotland Yard
> where he was questioned further.

John told me that the detectives who questioned him at Scotland Yard repeatedly punched him. He'd offered no resistance but endeavoured to get them to take responsibility for what they were doing by telling them, 'You're doing it. You're hitting me. Do you see this? You are doing it.' He said they didn't see it and just kept beating him. But something inside the men did see, he said, and was aware of what was going on. That was what was important and what was served, he said.

On admission to the mental hospital, John told me, the attendants secured him and gave him several injections. He felt in himself that he was strong enough to resist the effects of the drugs. He felt they would not be powerful enough to reduce his consciousness. But they were. He lost consciousness. He'd gone out of existence anyway, with the Archons. But once embodied, no power out of existence, or what is called higher consciousness, can finally withstand the force of existence. Whether it's a crucifixion nail, a hypodermic needle or a poison draught, unconsciousness will follow.

After treatment John was put on medication and released. As a teenager he had been diagnosed as schizophrenic and had spent brief periods in care. The medication served to prevent him from entering the peculiar states to which schizophrenes are usually subject. The disorder is described as being characterised by 'a loss of contact with the environment and by disintegration of personality expressed as disorder of feeling, thought and conduct'. I had never seen John exhibit any of these characteristics, not even when he came to me from Scotland in the midst of his extraordinary transformation. But I see from a spiritual point of view as well as the practical. And a psychiatrist may have interpreted his condition differently.

The fact is that John in all his time with Julie and me did not lose contact with the environment but was able to perceive through the appearance of things to a greater reality. This is often claimed by schizophrenes but seldom or never, I presume, are they able to demonstrate that reality as John did. Disintegration of the personality certainly happened in him since his enlightened state was above fear, doubt and compromise, the usual attributes of personality. But he did not lose the ability to mix and communicate with personalities.

John's conduct at times was indeed bizarre judged by ordinary standards. But so was mine, for instance, when I burned money and acted on instructions from an authority speaking inside my head. Perhaps I'm schizophrenic too? Perhaps everybody who has ever realised a greater reality than the transient physical (and that must include every spiritual master) has to be something of a schizophrene – divided but bridging this world and the other? Certainly, no sane psychiatrist can do this.

A schizophrene once declared his condition at one of my public meetings, giving several examples of what I presume would be defined as a psychotic disorder. While he was speaking a car door banged in the street and he said that the sound had spoken to him. I can't remember what he said the words were but it was a frequent experience for him. John in his enlightened state said many of the people in mental institutions were suffering from an overdose of perception. Their physical and emotional systems were unable to cope with the inrush of reality. Ordinary people were protected by not having this split in their systems through which the reality appeared.

John spent a good deal of time in psychiatric hospitals. He said it was part of his teaching; through his presence he could communicate a similar reality to that which the inmates had experienced. These were the people who needed help, he said. He always chose to live in the poorer and neglected areas of London. He enjoyed being with the downtrodden, the down-and-outs and discarded, seldom failing to stop and chat with tramps and share a cigarette or his money with them. John spent much time in the streets. He lived mostly off Social Security and worked with volunteer groups helping the deprived and mentally handicapped. Finally, Social Security gave him a flat of his own in North London.

John's schizophrenic condition returned after his enlightened being left with the Archons. Although his compassion, humility and wisdom remained, the power we'd known had left him. If he did not take his medication he would descend into a sort of madness, mumbling incoherently or shouting and behaving strangely. On the medication he complained that it made him dull and slow; but he was grateful for it. Later he told me that he didn't want to return to the extreme physical pain he had put himself through in those earlier days; he was afraid of it, he said.

Once, I remember, before his enlightenment, in the depths of winter and in the middle of the night, he chained himself naked to a lamp-post in the City and lay on the freezing pavement for hours until police arrived and cut him free. His explanation to me was that he could not bear being servile to his senses. How many other punitive incidents like this occurred I do not know. Years later when I asked him if he recalled the extraordinary empowering presence he had been for Julie and me in those few weeks at the end of 1968, he said, 'No, not really.'

How do I explain the enlightened part of John leaving with the Archons?

The answer is in the chapter entitled "Julia". Each of us has multiple levels of being or consciousness in the psyche behind the senses. The psyche extends back with increasing consciousness, spirit, to the point of eternity (and probably beyond that). This means that what we are endeavouring to realise in the spiritual life, we already are. For all we can ever realise is our own being in those finer and finer profound levels.

In realising immortality, for example, we realise immortal being at that level. In realising God is responsible for everything, the good and the bad in existence, as I describe in the book *Knowing Yourself*, we realise our own being. But even that is not the end of being, as my transcendental realisation of the utterly Supreme (laughing) Being shows.

Julia was Julie's higher being at one level of her psyche. Although Julia was powerful in truth, I would not describe her as blessed, as I do the Blessed John. The Blessed John, John the man's extremely profound being, came from a divinely spiritual realm of the psyche. He had the power that even in the coarseness of physical existence works miracles in people, as he did with Julie and me.

Some mornings John would tell us that during the night his consciousness had visited the fifth heaven, the power of which was necessary to dissolve the black stuff he had absorbed from us. He said this black stuff was in everybody but his job had been to take it from us two. John said there were seven heavens and that he came from the seventh. Coming from the seventh heaven allowed him to enter the fifth because 'only the higher can access the lower'. If we substitute the levels of being in the psyche for the word "heavens" we can get an idea of the immensity and amazingness of being.

Why didn't the Blessed John just quit and return inwardly from whence he came? Why the complication of a spaceship, and communicating with its occupants without gadgetry or words?

The greatest mystery of our times is the question of UFOs. Millions of people have witnessed the phenomenon but there is still no proof. Why? For the same reason that there is no proof of the spirit or of God. Proof of course in our world has to satisfy scientific criteria which are concerned with existence where everything is measurable. Spirit or God is in the invisible realm of the unconscious behind the senses. It cannot be measured. So it does not exist.

The UFOs and the Blessed John came out of the same invisible world. Hence he alone could "converse" with them instantaneously in his consciousness without words. Anything from that deep spiritual level vibrates at such a speed of intelligence that it can remain for only a short time in the much denser vibratory world of the senses. John could stay only a few weeks. UFOs because of their tremendous existential speed are even more transitory.

To me, the Blessed John's intelligence chose the "outer" way of going back into the unconscious so that I could tell you the truth behind such incredible happenings. For the truth is that there is no outer world as we perceive it; our world, despite its appearance, is all inner – inside the unconscious as all the worlds are. The self-conscious surface mind, and its subconscious level of thoughts and feelings, perceives the world to be "out here". As both are part of the "outer" world, the illusion is complete. But when the intelligence of the individual here speeds up sufficiently, the perception changes and the external physical world is seen to be a transitory projection.


When the police were beating up John's body, the Blessed John had already "left". Nevertheless, the spirit is always present where there is holiness.

All this is paralleled by a curious esoteric tradition dating back 2,000 years and associated with the reputed crucifixion of Jesus. It starts with the ancient gnostics (from *gnosis*, meaning knowledge) who were active before the Christian era and who believed that spiritual truth rose spontaneously from within and was essential to salvation. Dogma was anathema to the gnostics.

The gnostics saw that spiritual truth had arisen spontaneously in Jesus and many became Christian gnostics. But the perceptions of the gnostics conflicted with the increasing dogma and hierarchical structure of the Church and the gnostics were soon marginalised and disappeared under the force of Churchianity.

The gnostic tradition declared that the Christ, or the messianic element in Jesus, had already left him on the cross and was present above him at the time. Which may explain the forlorn cry, 'Father, why have you forsaken me?' The gnostic contention would not have suited the Church Fathers, for it is essential to the dogma that Jesus was always Christ.

# CHAPTER 26

# GOLD FROM MR GOLD

A round February 1969, several weeks after the departure of the Blessed John, I resigned from the *Evening News*. I had no other job to go to, and nothing in mind. It was one of those "unreasonable" things one does when living in the moment and delighting in the freedom of being psychologically dependent on nothing. Every thing is looked after, every need filled for every one.

But the difficulty with this reality – which has to be real for the individual – is that one needs to have at least realised immortality to live it. While death is still regarded as an end, or even a possibility, there will be fear and holding back from the unknown. Death is nothing more than the filling of the final need. Whose need? Who needs to die? Everyone needs to die. It's just the timing that we seldom agree with.

So I typed out my resignation giving the required three months notice, but no explanation, and handed it to John Gold, the editor. He was surprised.

'Do you have another job to go to?'

'No, Mr Gold.'

'Is it your health?'

'No.' He couldn't be blamed for asking that question. Over the last two months my weight-loss had made me look like a walking skeleton.

I'd actually been asked seriously by workmates on a couple of occasions whether I was dying. Well, I was, wasn't I? – but not in the sense they meant.

'I don't mean to probe,' said Gold, 'But are you unhappy here?'

'No. Not at all. It's to do with my philosophy.'

'Oh, I see.' We had talked briefly a couple of times about my teaching but not enough for him to understand it or my incentive for resigning. John Gold was a gentle man and he asked no more questions. 'I shall be sorry to lose you,' he said.

This was early in 1969 when the British wage explosion was beginning to happen. I had joined the *Evening News* as one of the highest paid sub-editors on the editorial table – and that was only about half of what I would have been paid in Australia. British workers worked for peanuts but now they were discovering their industrial muscle. Six weeks after handing Gold my resignation, the company decided to give all its journalists an 18% increase. John Gold called me in. 'Barry,' he said, 'because you've resigned I can't give you the increase.'

With Julie back living with me I could have done with the money. 'That's okay. I understand.'

'But if you withdraw your resignation you can have the increase. I want you to have it. Then, if you still wish to resign, you can do so and I'll do my best to let you go early so you don't have to work out the full notice.'

As I say, everything is provided. I withdrew my resignation.

John Gold was Jewish. I'm not. It is remarkable how many Jewish individuals have helped me – and how many I have taught – over the many years since my spiritual conversion began in Australia. It seems to me quite beyond the scope of coincidence.

When I was near broke in London, one Jewish gentleman literally gave me the suit off his back. He was Sidney Sinclair, the former chairman of the Men's Fashion Council of Australia, and managing director of Anthony Squires, Australia's leading menswear manufacturer at the time. We'd worked together as part of my old public relations job, when I was acting as regional director of the MFCA in order to promote men's fashion in TV interviews and through the other media. Sidney was over on a short visit and gave me two suits out of his wardrobe – one of them the "good one" I tried to withhold from "burning" during the transcendental realisation.

Sidney was a former Londoner who in the late 1940s, with a partner named Lou Klein, moved out to larrikin Sydney with a small cash stake and a brilliant mind, and achieved the impossible – founding a men's fashion council in the world's biggest sartorial desert. The company exported top fashion suits all over the world, including London and New York.

Around the time I left Australia in 1964 there was an odd mystical coincidence involving Sidney's 18 year old daughter. He and his wife and two children lived in a mansion at Wahroonga, a mile from our place. About a week before I left for India, I visited the home and lunched with the family. I talked about my reasons for going and sang a couple of my songs.

Later when Sidney gave me the suits in London he told me his daughter had "gone mystical". He said that two months after my departure she had gone on a tour to India and had some kind of experience there. She'd then travelled on to London where she lived and worked with a number of other girls in a Brahma Kumaris ashram in Muswell Hill, North London. The Brahma Kumaris were celibate, dressed in white and were followers of the Indian founder of their movement, Brahma Baba, who died in 1969.

Sidney said his daughter had abandoned her study of medicine and adamantly refused her parents' pleas to return home and live a normal life. They were heartbroken. 'We think she must have overheard what you said that day you visited us,' said Sidney. 'It seems the only explanation. You wouldn't think just hearing a conversation would do it. She'd never shown any inclination in that direction before.'

On another visit to London, Sidney phoned me one night in the midst of my Putney disintegration. I can't remember what was said but it would not have been a very reassuring conversation for a man deeply concerned for his daughter who had chosen to live the spiritual life.

I met the girl briefly in London a couple of years later but have not heard of her since. I trust she found what she was looking for.

# CHAPTER 27

# THE MYSTIC
# RESTITUTION

T he move from Putney to the flat in Southwood Lawn Road, Highgate, was a watershed in my life. It marked a transition that was to last four years. It was the end of the first 11 years of my spiritual life in which my ignorance – my self – and all that it was attached to, had been progressively destroyed. This seems to be the way the spirit works in man and woman. Everything the individual has cherished or treasured must be taken from them, as exemplified in the 5,000 year old story of Job in the Old Testament.

Job was a rich man who owned many goats, camels and wives. He was tested to see if he would deny and blame his God, as slowly all his possessions were taken from him. He was even afflicted with sores and boils all over his body – physical suffering which can accompany devotion to the spirit. But despite all the provocations, Job held fast to his love of God, uttering this most poignant of declarations, 'Even though he slay me, still will I trust in him.' And after the ordeal, all his worldly goods were restored to him, tenfold! So it was on a smaller scale with me. From now on, all that I had left behind was to be gradually restored – and more.

In the classic tradition of the mystic I had left all my worldly goods and family behind in sunny Australia. I'd passed through death in India and lived something of the life of an ascetic in the bedsit forest of dark, dirty and dingy London. There I'd enjoyed my evening strolls through the finest and most varied selection of dog shit in the Western world. When I was moving from grubby Bayswater to Shepherds Bush and asked an acquaintance what it was like there, he said, 'Much the same, only the dog shit's thicker.'

I'd lost my woman, the Bhagavati – again. The master had taken her. Through my transcendental realisation, I'd even lost, or experienced the loss of, my attachment to physical existence, my senses. And then the master himself, who'd provided the energy for this, had been taken – departed. It was time for the new. Like Job, I was now to discover more of the mystery of God's will.

I was not a renunciate. I'd never renounced anything. Everything was taken from me. That was the way of the Lord for me. And if anyone driven to find God thinks they'll manage to retain something along the way, they're mistaken. What's more, you're not even allowed to be attached to the new life of having nothing. That'll be taken from you too. And finally, if the will is for you as it was for Job and me, you'll find yourself up to your knees again in material responsibilities and possessions.

Although everything I'd lost was to be restored, nothing would ever be the same again. I was a wiser and more profound individual; and so was my woman. For every loss reduces our ignorance, as every gain thereafter tests how much we have learned the lesson of having without attachment. The spiritual life is a divine process, not a perverse or random destruction. It is the working of supreme virtue. Being an expression of the divine will, the divine good, the aim is to free man of identification with his self; to make him a Conscious being, out of the ashes of the human being that he was, so that he may embody God's inscrutable purpose on earth.

The house in Southwood Lawn Road, Highgate, was an old, partly converted, Victorian mansion – solid, cold and damp-ridden. You've heard of holy statues weeping; well, when we lit the fire in the lounge room the whole 25 foot wall would stream with tears of condensation. Five feet away from the fire was almost as cold as being outside.

The house had two storeys and we had the top floor. The two bedrooms faced north with a splendid leafy view down towards the Archway Road. We drew lots and David won the coldest room. It was so cold he had to use two more blankets than we did next door to him. David, since the black energy experience, was always a bit afraid of psychic phenomena and of living with us, especially with Julie who was something of a psychic medium. He thought she was the cause of the coldness. Anyway he felt the place was colder than just cold.

We moved in round about March 1969. That is, Julie and I did. David arrived a couple of days later in an ambulance – his broken leg in plaster up to the thigh; he had slipped on the ice getting into his car. Now he had to have six weeks sitting around at home. This he employed very usefully by working on my manuscript, *Wisdom and Where to Find It.* He published this at his own expense as a private edition of about 300 copies. These were bought by the men and women attending my meditation classes. I'd now resumed teaching and people were coming to the house and bringing their friends.

Meanwhile John Hart had been moved to Severalls Hospital, Colchester, where he was still under treatment but allowed occasional weekend leave. In a letter, answering a question about his memory of the momentous events culminating in his exchange with the Archons, he said:

> For me, most of the intensity has gone out of now and the past is a very strange and erratic canvas. Sometimes I get back to things we talked about and did over last Xmas – a sort of regurgitation seems necessary to me – and I find these memories blurred into an absence of reality. It is as if we'd taken off to another planet together. Now all those ideas and experiences lack substance to me. Annihilation was certainly achieved with me, including any ideas of the path to it. Also dubious about the value of it when complete. The mind seems capable of almost complete destruction, and fortunately, regeneration. In some ways my mind is a little like that of a rather dull-witted child. The pills I still take keep me away from the abyss but leave me remarkably dull.

A few weeks later John was discharged from the hospital. He was on the prescribed drugs and fairly stable. The still, sweet man remained after the overt power of the master had left.

One afternoon at Southwood Lawn, Julie had gone to visit John where he was living in a room in Islington. The prospect of her ever meeting John always disturbed me. Although I knew she loved me and would not leave me, the love between John and Julie was so profound and tender that it seemed to threaten my ability to hold her. They were so psychically or spiritually linked that for six or eight months I was anxious whenever we went walking. I knew that they would attract each other. And this seemed to happen most times we went out. John would come round the corner or just turn up. Julie understood my anxiety and repeated that she loved me and would never leave me. Still, my recurrent dream was of her leaving me for John.

On this particular day it had got dark and Julie had not returned. I sensed that something had happened. With relief, as I stood at the window watching the road, I saw her under the streetlight crossing towards the house. She came upstairs and I asked her what had kept her. She said she'd made love to John. I said, 'Why? You said you didn't need to any more.'

She said, 'He needed me. It won't happen again.'

That night I made love to Julie. And as I did she breathed on me. It was the breath of the Blessed John.

It was around this time that I first met Julie's sister, Rita. She was living in Queensland with her husband and their four children and had flown over to London for two weeks for her father's funeral. I spoke to her about the truth on a couple of occasions.

I was still working at the *Evening News* but things had changed within me and I felt the need to leave England. Julie agreed and we decided to emigrate to the United States. The documentary formalities were completed and all that remained for me personally was to line up a job. In those days it wasn't a requirement to have work to go to. But I set about making inquiries among my newspaper contacts in Australia and England. One of them was Steve Dunleavy. Steve had worked for me as a cadet reporter on the Sydney *Daily Mirror* while I was chief of staff. I'd run into him again in a London pub when I'd first arrived from India three years earlier. He was looking for a job and invited me to meet him in Madrid where some mates were starting up a new newspaper and where we could both get work 'in a cheaper sunny country'. This, especially after a few beers, sounded a pretty good possibility. I told Steve I might see him down there in a few months.

Well, I never made it to Madrid and neither did Steve, evidently. Next I heard he was over in the States working on the *New York Post*. This had recently been acquired by Rupert Murdoch who'd started his international media organisation by buying out the Sydney *Mirror* just after I'd left. Steve certainly made it to the big time. Seventeen years later, in 1986, I was to see him featured in an hour-long television programme. He had become New York's leading crime reporter and the programme showed him at work one night covering that city's violent police beat.

An amusing incident involving Steve and Eric Baume occurred back in 1959 when Steve was still a cadet and Baume editorial director. After the last edition of the *Sunday Mirror* had been "put to bed" at about 2 am, it was customary for the staff to go for a beer at the old Journalists' Club in Flinders Street, Surry Hills, a short walk from the office in Kippax Street. On this occasion Baume had been at the club for some hours persistently playing one of the two shilling poker machines – and losing heavily. Just after I arrived, young Steve, who hadn't been on duty at the paper, weaved in drunk and glassy-eyed. Baume had gone over to the bar to get some more coins. Steve, as he staggered past the machine, dug a two shilling piece out of his pocket, shoved it in and pulled the handle. Jackpot! A cascade of silver florins poured into the tray and overflowed onto the floor. Baume with his back to the machine couldn't believe his ears. But a quick glance confirmed his suspicion. Moustache bristling with indignation, and drawn to his full majestic height, he strode across to his 19 year old cadet reporter. 'You stupid little bastard,' he roared. 'That's my machine!' (As though anyone who came in would know he'd been playing it.) Steve faced him valiantly, gently weaving, and opened his mouth to make a reply that never got uttered. Instead, out came a stream of vomit all down Eric's front from his tie to his fancy plaid waistcoat. The outcome I can't remember – except for the amused jubilation of all the late night journos in the club.

I've always been interested in genuine clairvoyants. My spiritual life has shown me that the human psyche is a fairly open book to the past and the future for those gifted people able to read it – even though the language of the book is symbolic and easily misread or misinterpreted by the mind. While still at the *Evening News* I visited one of London's best known psychics, Tom Corbett.

He told me I was going to change my job, that I'd be working in a wider professional field. He asked me did I do much flying? I told him I'd learnt to fly light aircraft and did a bit at the weekends but he said that wasn't it, adding, 'You're going to be flying many, many trips to Europe in aeroplanes – and it won't be long before it happens.'

He also told me that I would be the author of many books – to be published when I "was ready". I retorted, 'I am ready. I am ready,' so loudly that Julie outside in the waiting room was able to hear my exclamation. I wasn't ready, of course. But I would be in another six years.

A remarkable turn of events then transpired. Still on the lookout for a job in New York when we emigrated, I phoned Australia House in the Strand and spoke to Len Barsdell, director of the Australian News and Information Bureau in London. I asked him if he knew of any journalistic job going with the Australian government over there. He said he'd just been posted to New York as director and he'd let me know when he arrived. That same afternoon Len ran into a friend who was trying to find a suitable man to fill a senior public relations position for a London firm. Len mentioned my name. His friend contacted me immediately and said, 'I've got just the job for you in London. It's with Nielson McCarthy, one of the best known public relations companies in the West End. They're looking for an experienced Australian journalist to help handle the Australian Shipping Conference account. It's right up your street.'

I said, 'My street is Main Street USA. I don't want to stay in London any longer.' He told me I'd be mad to miss the opportunity and why not go for an interview.

I did. And I took the job. It paid a third more in wages. I was working with a team of professional men and women (Nigel Neilson was personal PR consultant to Aristotle Onassis, the Greek shipping billionaire) and dealing with owners and managing directors of giant European shipping companies. Over the next two years I flew to Oslo every month with occasional visits to Paris, Rotterdam and Hamburg, servicing our company's shipping clients. Tom Corbett had scored an amazing bullseye. Before quitting Australia for India I was earning a good salary as the Sydney manager of a public relations firm and dealing with the owners and directors of big companies. Now I was earning double the amount in a position that was relatively more prestigious.

So, the restitution of the job was taken care of (along with the clairvoyant's prediction). Next was the restoration of the wife and family. Betty relinquished her opposition and agreed to divorce me. Julie and I were married in September 1969 at Wood Green Registry Office. As I've mentioned, Ken and Julie's girlfriend Anne married at about the same time. Things were settling down.

Julie's children, Mark and Jonathan, now aged eight and five, were dear to me and visiting us more regularly. For the previous two years they had come for weekends to our succession of tiny bedsits. Sometimes we would have to conceal their overnight presence from stern landlords who forbade children, one landlord contending that they were "fire hazards".

My attachment to the boys was revealed during my transcendental realisation. I saw myself anxious for their welfare if Julie left me – and at the same time perceived that this was purely my own selfish clinging, through them, to Julie. I did, however, love them and cared for them as much as my position as part-time stepfather would allow. They both enjoyed being with us and their stilted childish notes and drawings on birthdays and other such occasions were loving and enthusiastic. I would frequently talk to them of love, life and God.

# CHAPTER 28

# COME HOME DADDY

While my new family was coming in, my two natural children in Australia were inevitably growing further away. This seems unavoidable when physical contact is denied. If you don't see your child for a year or two there is a great danger that you'll never close the gap. They outgrow you and your expectations, fast. I'd been away now for five years. I'd written to the children but I suspect my letters gave little comfort since I was always endeavouring to point out to them the reality of life. Our lives had diverged into two different worlds.

Anne (she didn't like her given name, Annette) was now sweet 16. She wrote to me saying she was in love for the first time with John who was five years older than her and worked on a dairy farm. He was 'fairly good-looking', she said. He also smoked and drank, habits she usually disliked and he'd been drunk when he'd taken her to the pictures; despite this she found she loved everything about him. He made her feel wonderful and he loved her. She knew he loved her. But her mother couldn't see it. Betty had put her foot down. Anne was not to go out with him. He was interfering with her schoolwork and she had her exams to do. She wanted my help. Please would I come home and do something about it? She realised she was being 'a bit demanding' but she just didn't know what else to do. She needed her dad.

My Dear Anne,

Love at 16 is the same love at any age, my dear. But because we lack the built-in safety devices of experience we go out totally in innocence and trust to our first love and this gives it an intensity that is never again quite repeated. By the same impatient movement, our early loves are soon left behind – even though, at the time, it would seem such love could never end. It is not the love that ends, my dear. It is the relationship. For young love will not allow itself to be contained in any one object or person; it will pause a while and make us think it can – and then fly on, ever eluding us until we learn to love love for itself.

All that, I know, does not change the tremendous reality of your feeling. I was impressed with the maturity of your letter, the rational, unemotional way you have been able to stand back despite the onslaught. It showed you are observing the workings of this love within you. Love is a great changer – not of things but of ourselves. In that way it can appear to contain its own destruction.

In your letter you observe that whereas previously you were against smoking and drinking you do not condemn them in John, because they make up a part of him. This is an example of love working to break down a rigid attitude. It is love's secret lesson in tolerance for you – only for you – some wisdom to carry with you in all the relationships yet to comprise your life, not just this one.

Life allows, and indeed insists, that you maintain standards for yourself – but only for yourself unless others are in your care or seek your advice. If another person's lack of standards intrudes on yours, your duty is to exercise the right of personal preference – not hate – and remove yourself from their company or influence.

While in the state of love, my dear, you must keep a rigorous and constant watch upon yourself. For you will have noticed that love, for all its beauty, is heavy with the pain of consequence. The thing we love most will always cause us our greatest sorrow. For it will always fail us.

Here are my decisions and some of the reasons:

1. Your mother's decisions are my decisions in this matter. I know from your letter that you have already seen what I am going to say now and that there are no magic wands

to give us our way out of despair, only our own fortitude
to sit it out. What would you have me do? Let you marry
him? Let you have a freedom that in your own good sense
you would not allow your own daughter to have? Would
you have us both betray the lessons that life has taught
us? Would you try to tell me that love is innocent? Love is
innocence, my dear, but boys of 21 are not. You must
understand that love is not of man or woman. It is a state,
as real as stepping into a river. It carries minds and bodies
with it for its object is always unity and its consequences
can be appalling.

I think you will find your mother sees her duty thus,
and it is inarguable: by the law of life the mother must try
to protect its young whether the mother be dog, bird,
reptile or woman. A mother, alone, must decide what is
best. For she, alone, will willingly die for her young. Dare
the bitch or the sow allow their young to define the
perils? Never. How much more then would you expect
this instinct to manifest in the mother of man? What more
has she got to guide her in this duty than what she
believes is best for you? This is all any of us have – you
too – when there is a job to do. It is her job. She stands
alone. But I stand behind her. As I stand behind you.

2.   How long are you subject to mother protection? The law
says until you are 21. As far as I am concerned: definitely
until you are 18, when the position would be reviewed,
but not necessarily relaxed, in the light of your
understanding. In between you will find, of course, a
naturally increasing freedom which you have already
always enjoyed. But, as with nations, when a threat to the
security or welfare of the family is apprehended, the
Government imposes temporary restrictions.

3.   Your studies are paramount. You are not to betray and
fail that diligent girl in you who for years has devoted
herself to her studies. You might have experienced a more
intense love but I am not convinced it will be as enduring
as your old love. All men must work despite their love.
You are no exception. Besides, we might invite you to
finish up at an English university – and they are pretty

selective. I suppose the trouble then would be to keep
you out of Carnaby Street.

4.  I cannot return to Australia just because you have fallen
    in love for the first time. It could cost me a fortune in
    fares before long.

I do not belittle your love, my Anne. It is a precious part of
you. I understand.

Love, Dad

With her mother's guidance, and I don't know what else, Anne quickly got over her infatuation with the young man.

Julie loved houses and had an extraordinary flair for picking a good
investment. She wanted us to buy a place as soon as we could afford it.
To me this seemed a long way off, even though I was now earning good
money. In any case, having left behind in Australia my own house and
all that went with it, I don't think I was too keen on getting into the
householder thing again. One day when I came home from work she
announced she'd found a flat that was just being built in a block of six at
81 Shepherd's Hill, Highgate, overlooking the valley towards Alexandra
Palace. It had two bedrooms and cost only £8,750. We could have it for
a deposit of £875 and get a mortgage.

She might as well have said £8,000,000 to me. We had no savings and
it seemed impossible. But with the help of my mother in Australia I
raised the deposit, secured a 90% mortgage from a building society and
we moved into our pristine new flat in the spring of 1970.

Next came the car. It was a brand new General Motors Opel coupé at
£1,100. Its purchase was inspired by Julie. We'd travelled by train and
bus (as usual) to Mill Hill for David's wedding to a Japanese lady; and
after waiting in pouring rain (as usual) in her best dress and a new hat,
Julie announced, 'This is the end. We have to get a car.' My last car I'd
left with Betty in Australia six years before. Here I was, off again.

David's marriage ended in divorce some years later and he married
again. His propensity for attracting unusual situations was mirrored in
the circumstances of his second marriage. As a young man of 21 he had
visited Portugal and fallen in love at first sight with Maria Fernanda, the

daughter of a respected and traditionally conservative Portuguese family. She was 19 and according to David 'had the most beautiful eyes I have ever seen.' Throughout their contact they were carefully chaperoned. Three years later, after some difficult experiences for her (probably to do with her family) she decided to sever contact with him. He was broken-hearted. And subsequently she married.

David in those days was a fine poet, unspoiled by the rational concepts which tend to detract from some of his later poetry. He was simple. And in this poem, entitled *Eh Maria, So the World has Caught You*, he expressed his heartache and disappointment:

> Eh Maria, so the world has caught you, eh.
> So the claims of flesh and home have
> taken you away.
> So we must part. So let it be,
> against my will, and yet I will
> be with you where you go. For words
> that are spoken make print
> upon the raging world.
> Like a dream it must have been when
> you were alone. Too much thinking,
> too much waiting and then the
> woman won. You found one man is
> much the same as any other.
> Eh Maria, so the world has caught you, eh.
> Always the changing wind on the
> Mondego. Remember me. Remember me.

Twenty years later David and Maria Fernanda met again by accident in London. She was now the mother of two fine boys, had lived in France and Switzerland, got divorced and gone back to Portugal. Three years later she and David married. And when I last spoke to him he repeated to me, 'She still has the most beautiful eyes I have ever seen.'

In those early days when David first met Maria, he wrote many poems. The one I enjoy most is called *Inanity*:

> Don't speak of love the wise-man said.
> Pick a subject hard and high.

> Don't think to repeat, or to dispel
> the sounds and thoughts of the great.
> – But I must tell of what I feel
> if it only sounds to me; for there's
> Nothing I know to compare with snow
> On the tip of a big cat's tail.

Before Julie and I got our new car I had to get a British driver's licence. This I thought would be a doddle. I rented a car for the day on my Australian licence, spun down to the test centre and displayed my considerable skill, acquired from 27 years driving in Australia (and India).

During the test I thought I mightn't have been doing too well when the examiner looked up sharply as I turned a corner and let the steering wheel skilfully spin back through my fingers to the central position. Undaunted, however, I proceeded to show him how unnecessary it really was for such a seasoned driver to have to undergo a test. We pulled up back at the test centre and, opening the door, he turned, expressionless, and said, 'I'm sorry Mr Long, I know you're a very experienced driver, but you've failed.'

Next I had the very good sense to take one lesson with a driving school instructor. He did what he could and in the driving school's car I fronted up once more at the test centre. Once again I thought I was doing pretty well until coming out of a side street the examiner jammed on the foot brake in the dual-control car. I was amazed. It was obvious to me that even though there was a car bearing down on us from the right, I could accelerate out and make it. The English driving examiner didn't think so. As the test continued my paranoia increased and even I knew I was doing everything wrong. I failed again.

On the third occasion I passed. This time, contrite, humbled and truly respectful of the English stylised method, I asked the driving instructor to teach me until he was sure I'd pass. My Australian licence I'd received at 17 from the local policeman in Woodstock, New South Wales, the country town where my father was manager of a hotel and where I was living while a cadet reporter on the *Cowra Guardian*. I'd been driving my dad's car around the place for several months and drove it up to the police station where the constable handed me the licence.

Next came the start of my being a globally read author – although not from writing books of truth as I had always visualised. This phase of my life was to last 15 years. It introduced me to a man who became like a father and who made it possible for me, at around the age of 50, to get off the treadmill of working for others.

In the public relations companies I've been associated with, starting time is after a cup of coffee plus an extra 30 minutes for reading the morning newspapers. In London this is probably necessary to recover from the jungle warfare involved in surviving the rush hour on the Underground.

On a September morning in 1970, a colleague browsing through the *London Times* said, 'Here's something for you Barry.'

She then read out the following classified advertisement:

Australian publisher requires professional re-write man for 'History of Astrology' and other work. Personal interviews, Charing Cross Hotel, Sunday/Monday, 20/21 September.

Since being taught the Hindu system of astrology by Pandit Sastry in India, I'd taken an acute interest in the Western method and read various books. The two systems, although different in some respects, essentially have a common basis. Also, my clarity of mind allowed me to perceive through the formalities to the truth behind astrology and this gave a certain inspiration that otherwise may have required many years of dedicated study to reach.

Astrology is one of the last remaining popular practices of myth in our modern materialistic times – myth being the attempt by early man, who was far closer to the beginning of things than we are, to describe the original truth of life on earth. Science, or materialism, is the endeavour to find the truth via the world, via the existence of matter. The practice of myth is the attempt to find the truth via the structure of the psyche itself – a method beyond the understanding of the modern materialistic mind. And despite astrology's detractors, psychology has yet to come up with a finer and more accurate description of character types than the 12 zodiac signs of antiquity. Astrology is not the truth. But a study of it opens the mind to a greater possibility of truth as a universal function.

Anyway, down I went on the Sunday morning to the Charing Cross Hotel, then a pretty dingy rabbit warren over Charing Cross Station. There I met Richard N. Beim, of Newport, Sydney. He was a stocky man, aged about 60, in a dark baggy suit, bent and shuffling from a painful arthritic hip. He had that sort of neglected, unloved look that a man gets when he's been separated from his woman or has given up hope of finding one. He wanted me to write an introduction of about 20 paperback pages to a new cheap series of horoscope books he intended to publish worldwide. The books were the kind you buy at the beginning of the year for a prediction for your particular star sign, along with 365 daily forecasts.

I did the work, he liked it and paid me a welcome sum, about £150. The deal was: no royalties, no copyright, no mention of my name, and whatever I wrote he bought outright and what he did with it was no concern of mine. Agreed. I was now a part-time hack writer. The not so funny joke (for all hack writers) was that this introduction has appeared for over 30 years at the front of the same series of horoscope books published internationally. All the same, as I learnt the business, I learnt that he had to take considerable financial risks and that for every bestseller there were several dead or limping ducks.

The outcome of my first job for Richard was that later he gave me a contract to write the whole series of Super Horoscope books for 1973. The manuscript had to be finished a year before. I had five months. I had to write 365 four line daily forecasts, plus monthly and yearly forecasts for the 12 signs – about 4,500 items. Working part-time it was an impossible task – I'd overlooked how long it takes to build up speed for this kind of writing and still do a professional job. So I decided to farm out some of the work. But even the journalists I tried who had an inkling of astrology couldn't handle the routine or found it too tedious, although to start with it seemed to offer easy money.

Here, Andrew Ray entered my life. Andrew, aged 32, was a former child and teenage star of the booming British and American film industry of the late 1940s and 1950s. The son of Ted Ray, Britain's most loved comic of the time, Andrew won international acclaim as an eight year-old urchin in the film *The Mudlark* (with Irene Dunne and Alec Guinness) and rode the wave of fame and success for about a dozen years. Andrew was now broke and on the dole; acting work was virtually non-existent for him. He'd written his life story and sent it to the London literary agents, Eric Glass Ltd., who were also my agents. (I was trying to break into British television with some of my plays.) Janet Crowley, the executive who handled my work, asked me if I'd like to expand and rewrite Andrew's manuscript for submission to a publisher.

I hadn't heard of the man myself. But I was impressed with the fast moving style of writing. In my reply to the agent I said I wouldn't like to rewrite it. I said Andrew Ray had a smooth, uncomplicated style that should earn him money in the right market but his manuscript was a narrative not an autobiography. Anyway, we met. I never wrote anything for him. But for the next 12 years Andrew wrote for me. He became a staunch, reliable and generous friend of myself, Julie and her children. Andrew was the quick-witted, nimble-minded, adaptable professional hack-in-the-making I was looking for. Given a few lessons he produced a skilled product in a short time, where others far more qualified in writing had failed.

Richard Beim changed Andrew Ray's life for good, as he changed mine – although he never met Andrew.

CHAPTER 29

# INTO THE WORLD

N o man in worldly terms had given me more than Richard
Beim. He is probably the most remarkable man I've met. As a
youngster he and his family had been forced to flee Austria,
then Nazi Germany. In World War II he skippered a small transport boat
for the British in the Mediterranean, was torpedoed by an Italian subma-
rine and then blown up again, surviving three days drifting in a lifeboat
with third degree burns. After the war he opened up various trading
businesses in the Pacific and ended up residing permanently in Australia.
From there, with more regularity than a migratory bird, he flew into the
world's capitals selling his ideas.

Richard's main gift was the ability to see opportunities years ahead of
their time and the courage to invest all his money and tireless energy in
bringing them to fruition. He was an ingenious, enterprising businessman and organiser – as well as an inventor. Among his inventions was a
revolving bookstand, the success of which put him in touch with the
world's biggest publishers. This enabled him to present to the publishers
his next remarkable but very simple proposition.

Top publishers were very wary of investing in horoscope forecasts
because no one could guarantee the next year's manuscript. Richard
invested considerable sums in paying writers like myself to write several

years ahead and was able to lay these manuscripts on the publishers' desks. The publishers knew that astrology was big business and here was the man with the solution. They bought it and Richard and his writing team were in business for years to come. The biggest publishers would always see Richard Beim. He was also impeccably honest in his dealings. What he said he'd do, he did.

Outside Australia House in the Strand, London, there's a public telephone box. This was Richard's office in the early days. From here he would telephone publishers all over Europe and the USA informing them he was in London and ready to fly over for a big deal. But if he had to leave a message he always took the precaution to tell the secretary he'd phone the boss back. He would then return to his modest phoneless room in some cheap hotel. He became a very wealthy man.

Richard Beim's style was to open up new fields, develop them and then move on. In Australia he established the world's second biggest avocado farm, drained a mangrove swamp for a huge residential canal development and founded a super efficient cattle station as an investment for flush medicos and other professionals in Victoria and New South Wales. He was a visionary.

When I met him he was in the throes of a marriage break up and divorce. After this, and a successful artificial hip operation, he was a changed man. Although always an astute businessman he was a dear and generous friend, never failing to come to my material assistance when I asked.

Richard also was a Jew. Not an overtly spiritual man, he listened at length to my spiritual observations but I was never moved to teach him. He was a Pisces and had had his own mystical insights. On four different visits to England he asked to read the first draft of this autobiography (up to the coming of the black energy), saying, 'It's a great story.' He never, however, offered to publish the finished manuscript and nor did I ask him. I knew it was outside his area.

Now that Julie and I were comfortably established in our Shepherd's Hill flat, a new set of young people started coming to my lounge room talks on truth and self-knowledge – and to meditate with us. Just as David White had been responsible for bringing most of the earlier students (and they brought their friends), the nucleus of the new set arrived at the instigation of Barry Glass, my literary agent's son. He was about 20 and a university student and so were most of his friends. I'd met Barry at the agent's office one day and after engaging me in conversation he was avid for more.

People came about once a week. I'd sit on a chair and they'd sit in a semicircle around me. Julie would sit on the floor close beside me and at the close would serve tea and biscuits. There were usually from six to ten people. John would sometimes come.

I'd declared earlier in my private groups that art in all its forms was a sort of preparation for the artist to receive the truth I teach. I said I was a teacher of artists. And I certainly seemed to draw all kinds to me at that time. The most avant-garde (and incomprehensible to me) was the art of Peter Kuttner and Peter Dockley. These young men, aged about 27 and 25, were two irrepressible expressions of a nonsensical fringe art wave of the 1970s – seemingly aimed at the destruction of the mind-set of conventional society. I must have been concrete hard for I never understood what they were doing but always applauded their (to me) meaningless endeavours, out of a recognition of the one-pointed devotion to their art.

For instance, Peter Dockley, at an art exhibition at Alexandra Palace, built a small circular cubicle like a telephone box with a tent-like piece of material draped over it down to floor level. Between the cubicle and the cover was a space wide enough for Peter to sidle round without being seen from outside or inside. Across the entrance to the cubicle was a black curtain. It was dark inside except for a circle of six small lighted windows at eye level, each about a foot square. You walked in and hanging in each of the windows was some mind-stopping sight – a headless chicken with gory bloodied neck, the head hanging dolefully beside it, and other equally assaulting sights associated with everyday realities such as a plate of dog shit or a dead rat in a trap.

For those unsuspecting viewers who were really lucky, Peter Dockley's head with closed eyes would sometimes be motionless in one of the windows, as if it too had been severed from his body. Or his face would suddenly pop up behind another shocking exhibit. From time to time he would leave his masterpiece, wander round, have a cup of tea or lunch, and then pop back to add his extremely good-looking head to the spectacle. (Peter Dockley was so handsome that one of the greatest slights to his self-image as a serious artist was the number of offers he received to be a photographer's model for the glossy magazines.)

On another occasion he cast in wax six life-size male forms, three of them seated at a table with wax wine bottles, bread and cheese, and the other figures standing. At a public exhibition Peter proceeded, at unspecified times over several days, to melt the figures down with a blow torch. When children visitors, in their innocence or stupidity, would ask their parents, 'What's he doing that for?' the typical reply was, 'How would I know?' or 'Let's go.'

This particular event was made into a 16 millimetre film at an advertised duration of 30 minutes; but for a viewer such as myself it was interminable. To make the point of the transitory nature of our images of ourselves, Peter used in the publicity a quotation from one of my epic poems: '… a gradual diminution, a creeping execution of himself.' The film was, of course, funded by the Arts Council of Great Britain. At the same exhibition and competing for the gold medal for interminable boredom was a 15 minute film by Yoko Ono (Beatle John Lennon's woman) showing a succession of different women's bottoms walking away from the camera.

These extraordinarily dedicated and perceptively creative environmental artists, Peter Dockley and Peter Kuttner, were continually broke, living off the dole and jockeying with each other for grants from the Arts Council.

Peter Kuttner didn't have Peter Dockley's patient creativity. Peter Kuttner was an ideas artist, a first rate publicist with a hustler's nerve of steel. But in his way he was as effective in this peculiar, negative art form. His most outrageously confrontative contribution to the enlightenment of the human race was to get himself and a few chums locked up for the weekend in the chimpanzee cage at Chessington Zoo (temporarily emptied of the other inmates). Visiting families and tourists were suddenly confronted with what was supposed to be a reverse situation: who was the monkey and who was behind bars? Again the intelligence of the little children (not to mention the BBC and Fleet Street photographers) was stimulated and such comments abounded as 'What are they doing Dad?' Once again Dad wasn't too sure.

On another occasion (in between interviews on BBC television) Peter Kuttner hit the headlines with an extraordinary exhibition at one of

London's leading hotels. Although living off a shoestring (in a North London room with a cat he called Mouse) he managed to find the money and to convince the chef and kitchen staff to put on for the Press a buffet lunch of coloured food. The bread was dyed green, the butter red, the chicken blue, and various other rainbow hues confused the mind-set reaching for the familiar. He did several follow up exhibitions and the most memorable centrepiece at one was a large multi-coloured cake with the icing inscription: 'Something for the critics to get their teeth into.' He proudly hung this exhibit for years on his lounge room wall!

Another one of Peter Kuttner's great ideas was to send a copy of a printed poster at his own expense and without explanation to all of the UK's 650-odd Members of Parliament. The poster, about 18 by 12 inches was in two colours, red and blue, the colours of the Labour and Conservative Parties. In three lines of large poster type it announced with a profound simplicity that must have rocked the Westminster establishment: 'Left Is Right.'

Peter Kuttner's most extraordinary quality was his persistence. He was one of the original people introduced to my teaching by David White. He embraced it later with considerable enthusiasm and service to me for 12 years. Peter had a habit, fully consistent with his freewheeling lifestyle, of dropping in unannounced at our flat for a chat. Wearing a long, embroidered white Afghan coat hanging down to his calves – and by Afghan I mean the hide of an Afghan sheep or goat turned inside out – plus a tussled head of hair not unlike his favourite film comic, Groucho Marx, he'd knock on our door at any time of the day and late at night. I never saw anyone I didn't want to see. So when I didn't want to see him I'd say, 'No Peter.' When he kept it up I wouldn't open the door and I'd shout through it, 'No Peter, go away.' When he still kept coming without letting me know I surrendered to his persistence and Julie and I would be as quiet as mice while we waited and listened through the door for his footsteps to tell us he'd departed.

Inevitably, Peter Kuttner and Peter Dockley moved in together and shared the same house with a sort of wary, watchful but friendly respect for each other. It was Peter Kuttner who brought Peter Dockley to my teaching. Peter Dockley also figured prominently in my life for some years.

What happened to all the individuals that I taught in early private groups over the years? In most cases I don't know. The point of teaching, or revealing the truth to others at the deepest level where I, the master, operate, is not so concerned with the individual "progress". What's important is that the truth is taught or revealed and that there are ears to hear, eyes to see and bodies to absorb. Every body is a sort of passing porthole leading down to the indescribable whole psyche of humankind. The reaching of this extraordinary potential consciousness, through the individual's temporary abandonment of their person (which is essential to absorbing the truth), is what "it" or life is about.

No person gains from my teaching. I actually destroy the person so that the message will get through to and for the greater good. This destruction in the individual is felt like dying or death. And so it is. They come and they go. Some stay. But these are the very few. They stay as long as they are able because I must be served by love in order to continue to serve the greater good. The ones who stay must truly die for truth and serve the God of truth and love. In doing this they discover both in themselves.

In June 1971 my mother came to visit us from Australia for six weeks. I hadn't seen her for seven years. She'd died one hundred deaths since I'd left, so great was her attachment to me. And I told her later that looking down from the moon, or from a greater height of this life, one of the reasons I spent 20 years in England was to break her obsessive loving hold on me – so that she would die in peace.

Living our lives is the process of dissolving our attachment to existence so that we may realise the pure life behind it and within ourselves. Existence lasts between 70 and 100 years but life is forever. Our attachments bind us to existence. They are as immovable as the steel bars of a prison cell. At death the more we are attached, particularly to the people or things we really feel we love, we fail to "make" what I must call "the right exit". Instead of "going on" we go into another enforced dream of existence.

My mother in a way was another aspect of the divine woman who has accompanied me throughout my life. She served me utterly and completely without complaint or blaming. She was in effect one of my closest students. And although I once was her child, I am now the man, the master, who by my presence and in return helped to give her an equivalent gift of love – death outside the dream. She bore me as the mother and I bore her as the spiritual father.

Meeting my mother for the first time punctured one of Julie's dreams remaining from the past. I'd given her such an impression of my mother's practicality, affection and how she would love her that Julie had built up an image of an ideal mother-in-law, something of a substitute for her youthful frustrations with her parents. It wasn't long before Julie woke up to her own delusion.

My mother, quite innocently and oblivious of what she was doing, talked incessantly about her love of me and my daughter Annette (who had always been the apple of her eye). Although my mother "loved" Julie, the clamour of her attachments to Annette and me prevented her from realising the quiet rapport and natural love they had. Julie summed it up in these words, 'Your mother does not love me although she thinks she does. Everything she does for me she does because I am with you. It's okay, but don't tell me she loves me. She loves only you and Annette.' The extraordinary thing is that finally my mother's love of Julie, and Julie's love of her, was so deep and real that it worked a miracle which I will recount in its place.

My mother at the time of her visit was in her late 60s. A victim of colonial fervour for the "old country", she had a deep, ingrained respect for the Queen and the Royal Family. (The fact that her father, my grandfather, was English probably helped.) Back in 1953, when the young Queen Elizabeth flew into Australia for the first time, as chief of staff of the *Daily Mirror* I was able to arrange a special place from which my mother and Betty could see her at close range as she was welcomed by a host of dignitaries before walking into the Sydney Airport Terminal. My mother was jubilant. Now, 18 years later in England, she was off to see the Queen again; this time by invitation!

The occasion was the first polo competition for the Coronation Cup. The PR for this event was one of my accounts. Nielson McCarthy had an "in" with the royal establishment since one of our directors was an equerry to Prince Charles, who was an avid and accomplished polo player. Polo had the taint – will it ever be different? – of being a rich man's sport and my job was to help disabuse the public of this idea by whip-

ping up interest among the flagging horses or sceptical hacks of Fleet
Street.

The Queen and Prince Philip would be there, Charles was captaining
a team, and I, naturally, had invitations for my wife and mother to attend
as guests. The event was at Midhurst, Sussex, on the private polo field of
Viscount Cowdray, World War II hero (he lost an arm at Dunkirk), business tycoon and one of England's richest men. He was head of the
organising committee and in our frequent contact I found him a kindly
and unpretentious man.

My liaison with the teams and players (most of them from South
America) was through Major Ronnie Ferguson of the Queen's Household
Cavalry and in later years a man of some notoriety. We got on well. In
the PR preparations I committed my first – and last – royal blunder. It
was a near thing. I was nearly ostracised for life, condemned to the cold
outer regions of ordinary humanity. One of my jobs was to get interesting copy for press releases about the coming event. And one lucky day I
found Prince Charles on my phone about some detail. As an old head-
line hound this was pennies from heaven. We spoke for several minutes
and I asked him a few questions about his views on polo.

I wrote the story which was about as sensational as the chairman of a
detergent company declaring his product washed whiter than white. But
my error was that I actually quoted what the Prince had said. This is just
not allowed. I submitted the copy for the committee's approval and in no
time Ronnie Ferguson, quickly followed by our director, were pointing
out to me that if ever such a thing got published I would 'have a stink
about me forever' as far as the royal establishment was concerned. The
Prince, whom I spoke to, I can confidently declare wouldn't give a
damn. He spoke to me like an ordinary guy. The "stink" I think is the
smell of the establishment around him.

On several occasions it's been proposed to me that The Barry Long
Foundation should send copies of my tapes and books as a gift to Prince
Charles who is reported to be privately interested in pursuing a greater
reality. So far I haven't agreed. The Prince, like everyone, will come to
the master when he's ready.

It was a glorious English summer's day, the polo event went off without a hitch, and the cup was won by some team or other. My mother
enjoyed immensely meeting and chatting with the various titled people

the occasion allowed. The final intimate highlight for her was when a knighted gentleman excused himself, after a quick introduction, with 'Must go, I'm on my way to get some whisky for the Queen.'

For my mother to be included in such regal company was a far cry from the young woman who in 1940, with my father, bought the tin-roofed single storey pub in hot and dusty Lightning Ridge, 783 kilometres north-west of Sydney. My dad, a man of many occupations when he was younger, always wanted to be a publican – although he seldom drank. Somehow they raised the finance to buy this quaint country pub, probably the last one in New South Wales west of the Great Dividing Range.

Lightning Ridge is the home of the famous black opal and in those days it wasn't even a one-horse town. But it had hundreds of wild goats and on the rare occasions when the miners and shearers would organise a dance and put up posters in the hope of attracting some girls from the district, my mother said the goats used to eat the posters off the walls.

Every weekend the bar would fill with miners, shearers and drifters from around the district who came to "drink" their cheques. Sometimes there were nearly as many drunks as goats and one day when things looked ugly my father closed the bar, locked the old swing doors and went for a good long walk with Mum. When they returned the clientele had broken into the bar and were helping themselves.

On the strength of his experience at Lightning Ridge my father got Tooheys Brewery to take him on as a manager of their hotels. He ended up having managed more than 20 but the hotel important in my youth was the Royal at Woodstock, 280 kilometres west of Sydney. From here, where I lived with my parents in 1942, aged 16, I used to ride my motorbike 20 kilometres to my first journalistic job as a cadet reporter on the *Cowra Guardian*, and at 18 joined the Royal Australian Air Force.

As an indication of my mother's fearlessness and sense of justice I'm going to let her tell what to me is a very funny story about a ruffian top-gun sheep shearer, a story that otherwise would never be told. She said:

> We had some very good customers at the Royal and they used to tell us about this fellow called Roughhouse Webber. They said that if he came into the hotel they'd all clear out until they were sure he was well and truly somewhere else. 'He makes you get

down on the floor and walk on all fours like a dog,' they said. 'He's such a dreadful man that we all do it and we're terrified of him.'

Anyhow, sure enough, one Saturday morning when the bar was packed, in walked Roughhouse Webber – six foot-odd, barrel-chested, in white singlet and trousers above which his generous beer-belly protruded. A couple of his hangers-on threw open the bar door for him and he bellowed, 'Stand back you shallow water men and let the deep sea roll in.' The shock effect of this had everyone petrified for a moment. Then he shouted, 'I come from Tough Town. I live in Tough Street. The higher you go the tougher they get and I live at the top.'

Of course the next second the bar was completely emptied except for one poor little fellow who was half drunk and sitting on a stool at the bar. Roughhouse, who obviously knew him, walked over and said, 'Tinker, you get down and walk like a dog. Go on.' He got hold of Tinker and pulled him down onto the floor.

I was furious and rushed round the bar and said, 'You dirty great big coward, you would pick on someone inoffensive like Tinker. Why don't you pick on someone your own size?' And, poking him in the stomach I said, 'You pick him up off the floor and you get out.'

He got such a shock that someone would stand up to him that he picked Tinker up, put him back on the seat, looked at me and said, 'Madam, you're a lady. I can't believe it – you doing this, coming at me like this. It's the first time anybody ever dared to do this to me. Now you get all those men back in here and I'll buy them all a drink.' The men had fled into the back rooms and up the backyard and most of them came back in. So of course I was the Queen from then on.

And here at the polo match, all these years later, she was now actual-ly with The Queen!

# CHAPTER 30

# MUM AND DAD

When I was very young and had just begun to crawl, my mother discovered I had a strange idiosyncrasy that is not easy to attribute to conditioning. One day she held out a sweet for me to take, and, as some mothers will do to intensify their feelings of love, she playfully put her hand behind her back and pretended I could not have the sweet. I looked her straight in the eye, made no sign of protest, turned away and crawled to the nearest corner. There I gently bumped my forehead three times on the carpet, kissed the floor and crawled off without a backward glance.

This amused my mother so much that she would repeat offering and refusing me the sweet and my response was always the same. She said her friends got such a kick out of my behaviour that they would take me to the sweet shop and show the people around what I did. So she had to put a stop to it because she felt it was mean.

Another thing she could find no explanation for occurred when I was only three years old. My father would say 'Salaam Sahib' and I would bend right over and salaam two or three times with my hands on the floor. She thought I must have been doing this naturally and that my father had noticed and made a game of it.

My mother was a Pisces, soft-hearted, caring, loving and intuitive. Although not a particularly religious woman she believed in God and goodness. She had been brought up in the country in the rather easy-going Church of England. She had the normal exposure of those days to the religious idea through Sunday School and fairly regular Sunday church attendance which ended in her teens.

Her father, James, was born in England in 1856 and at 18 joined the Royal Navy. Four years later, his man-of-war, HMS *Sappho*, berthed in Sydney and the young sailor jumped ship with several others. His official Navy record, which I obtained in England, simply says 'Ran Sydney.'

Jumping ship was a very serious offence and James headed for the bush fast, changing his name and arriving in Scone, 264 kilometres away, where he met and married Agnes, my grandmother. The newlyweds put another 150 kilometres between them and any pursuit by travelling further north to an isolated region called Kootingal near Tamworth. There James bought several acres of wild, uncultivated land and got a job on the railway as a fettler. He cleared the land, planted an orchard and a large vegetable garden, and built his own timber slab house where the couple reared ten children, most of whom lived into their 90s and one to 104. James died aged 65 when my mother was 18. She was the second youngest.

On the day I was born, the 1st of August 1926, my mother had a vision, the only one she said she'd ever had. During the last hour of a long confinement she saw the Virgin Mary, all white, standing by her bed.

'Your son will be born behind a cloud,' said the vision.

'What do you mean?' said my mother.

'He will be born dead.'

The nursing sister told her later that after the birth the doctor said he couldn't do anything for the baby but that they would work on the mother. My mother later said, 'Knowing what I had gone through, the sister said she couldn't bear to tell me my baby was dead. So she got hold of him, hung him up by the legs, swung him around, and breathed down his throat. She put a drop of whisky on his tongue with her finger – and he breathed.'

To me now the vision symbolises much more. I was indeed born behind a cloud or dead. I did not begin to live until I was 32. I did not know I was alive until I had passed out of the living dead into the immortal moment at the age of 38. At 42, I realised what it was to exist without living. And now I know what it is to live without existing. This is not semantics but the truth.

Although my mother was somewhat psychic, she had little overt perception of things beyond the physical senses. She would listen when I endeavoured to explain the spiritual life I live and teach and she would try to absorb my books and tapes, but would end up saying, 'They are too much for me to understand. I'm just an ordinary woman and I can't see where you could get such knowledge from.' I persisted though, and her understanding deepened. It was when I talked of death that she'd get uppity. 'I'm not afraid of death,' she'd declare. 'I'm going to live to a ripe old age – touch wood!' She died at 90.

As a girl she had a strange and rather terrifying experience which suggested the possibility of survival after physical death. Her eldest brother, Freddy, aged about 19, was dying of pneumonia in Tamworth hospital, ten kilometres away. Freddy was one of those sons of the soil who loved the land as though it were a part of him.

My mother's parents had gone to the hospital in the horse-drawn buggy leaving the eldest sister, Lorna, 18, at home to look after my mother who was in bed with a chill, and the other children. Freddy died at 2pm. Just before he died, he grasped my grandmother's fingers in his hand as though he were holding a rein and said, 'I'm going home.' He clicked his tongue twice as if to start a horse moving, and died.

At that moment back at the homestead there was a violent knocking on the front door; then on the back door. My mother jumped out of bed to answer it and ran into Lorna standing trembling and white-faced in the kitchen. 'Don't answer it,' Lorna screamed. The knocking began moving around the house, pounding the timber walls, faster and faster. Every window shook and rattled. Freddy's dog rushed up outside barking furiously and chased the knocking round the house. Freddy's horse smashed its way into the yard and galloped whinnying round and round the house. The girls clung to each other in terror. My mother looked at Lorna. 'Freddy's dead,' she whispered. Lorna nodded. The disturbance lasted 15 minutes but the girls remained crouched under the kitchen table until the parents arrived home around 6pm. So traumatised was Lorna by the incident that she had to be taken to hospital.

My mother always seemed to have an unusual sensitivity to her own "wrong" actions. Whenever in her life she chose what she regarded as the "wrong" way, it was not without an inner awareness that her weakness was an offence against something higher, something which in her moments of anguish and emotion she called God. When I was leaving my job, home and children to go to India, she said, 'I know God is doing this to punish me for my sins.' She did not understand what was driving me on but she did understand that I was driven.

I think she had several lovers while I was young. To her peculiar self-appraisal these were her sins. Her strength was that she did not regret or indulge herself in remorse. She just felt somewhere deep inside that what she did was wrong. To me it is not remarkable that my mother, an attractive, vivacious woman, should have responded to the charm and attendance of other men. From the first week of her marriage as a virgin bride she had to bear the disenchantment, loneliness and humiliation of my father's compulsive drive for sex with other women.

She loved me with an extraordinary devotion, even for a mother. Throughout her life she put my welfare first. She never asked me for anything and when sick would only tell me afterwards. My mother was very slow to judge others and responded with an almost indulgent understanding to their confided problems and transgressions, even those committed against herself – provided the person did not underestimate her considerable intelligence.

My father, Vic, had no feeling whatever for religion, let alone mysticism. He could not understand what was happening to me in the spirit. When he heard about my early preoccupation with the truth his solution to the "problem" was simple, 'Throw the books away, Son,' he said – and offered me £500 to go out and have a good time. He didn't have much money; it was a sincere attempt to do the best he could to 'bring me to my senses.' He couldn't know (and nor did I then) that the whole battle I was engaged in was to eliminate my psychological dependence on the senses for my identity. I didn't want "in", I wanted "out"!

However, if I had taken up his offer it still would have served towards this end. It is only by "having a good time" and living the life of sense experience, often to the point of surfeit, that one eventually starts to yearn for a permanent quality of life, a real identity, something lasting and self-sufficient. I had already experienced enough "good times" to make me begin looking elsewhere – within. So my dad was right, though not in the way he imagined. He had offered the best medicine that is guaranteed eventually to turn a sufficiently sensitive individual towards the truth.

The day I told him I was going to India he wept. He was 67 and recovering from a heart attack. 'I'll never see you again,' he cried. He was proud of my successful career and could not understand how I was able to throw it all up when all he had ever dreamt of was to be respected and looked up to. When I returned to Australia ten years later, he was still going strong at 77. He still didn't understand. But now he knew he didn't understand. I wasn't necessarily a fool, as he had thought before. There was a humility in him, a little bit of space, self-uncertainty, the good fruit of age.

My dad was a cheery man, never moody despite his financial and job difficulties, and was always whistling around the place. He'd run away from home in Freeling, South Australia, at age 14. He'd become a drover for Sir Sidney Kidman, the Australian cattle king, who'd also left home at a young age and who finally managed to own a string of outback cattle stations stretching across three States. So my dad when he came to Sydney as a young man had no trade, which in those days meant labouring or using your wits to get a few bob together.

He and Mum loved each other and got on very well apart from when there were arguments about his affairs or her suspected ones. He was very jealous of her.

My dad, like my mum, was always good to me. I don't have any memory or sense of his ever having hurt me. In those days when I was a boy, when you did something wrong you received a "hiding"; you got the strap. You knew you deserved it if you got it, or I did, because my parents were fair and never punished me without good cause. Once, aged about six, I'd been intrigued for some time by my father's cut-throat razor and decided to see how sharp it was. For the purpose I selected the leather razor strop hanging under the bathroom mirror and gave the strop a deft slice, cutting it through to within a quarter of an inch of the other side. There it hung, very lopsided and very ominously predicting trouble. 'Mum,' I called out. She came in and quickly took the razor out of my hand. 'You could have cut your finger off!' she exclaimed. 'You must never touch this razor again.' And then, seeing the limp but convicting evidence of the near-severed strop, she added, 'You know your father will give you a hiding for this.'

When Dad arrived home I was waiting for him in the bathroom, pants down and bottom exposed, with the damaged strap in hand, to take my punishment. For some reason he didn't do it. I got a severe talking to and later I think I heard some laughter in the bedroom.

For most of my infancy my dad was out of work due to the worldwide financial crash of 1929. I remember a day my grandmother came to visit for afternoon tea and she had to lend my mother a coin to nip out and buy the tea, as we couldn't afford that luxury. My mum kept things going by doing long hours of sewing; she never seemed to be off the old Singer pedal machine. But both my parents got through, as everyone does, and in later years managed the hotels for Tooheys brewery. My dad, a great lover of dogs and horses, even got his own racehorse, a mare he fondly called Black Opal in memory of their first hotel at Lightning Ridge, home of that precious stone.

My mother was quite a raconteur and excelled in telling anecdotes about her life. She recorded some of them for me. She said:

> This might sound like a mother thinking that her son is different to other children – Barry was a very normal child, very happy and outgoing – but somehow he was different. When he was four or five years old I developed a kidney infection and was very sick. I would have to send Barry to stay with one of my sisters, different ones each time. They would always tell me what a wonderful child he was and how they loved having him. One wanted to adopt him.
>
> About this time we were going through the Great Depression and like many others were very hard up. In those days there was no help from the Government; I think they may have issued us a ticket to get bread and milk. Barry would hear his father and I talking about having no money. I used to go down to Paddy's Markets in the city, which was cheaper, to buy him a pair of trousers or something to wear. When I came home with them he would cry and say, 'Oh Mummy, what did you buy me trousers for? You haven't got any money.' I'd try to pacify him and make light of it. He got to worry so much that I said to Vic we mustn't discuss money in front of him, as he's too young to have that

kind of worry. So later on Vic said, 'Son, you don't want to worry about us not having any money. We've got tons of money. It's all in the bank. But Sir Anthony Horden's got his on top of it. We can't get it out.' Anthony Horden was one of the biggest stores in the city and the family were millionaires. Vic tried to pacify Barry that way. [And it worked – I believed him!]

At that time Barry's father, who had no work, leased a couple of racehorses to try to get some money. One was Edgecliff and the other Melton Son. Vic had to get up at about 4 am to go to Randwick to groom and train the horses. We didn't have an alarm clock or a phone and he would say, 'I hope I wake up in the morning.' Barry apparently heard him and it got on his mind. At about 4 am he would get out of bed, go to his father and say, 'It's time to get up Daddy.' He was such a conscientious boy we had to tell him his father wasn't going any more.

A little later on I went with a friend for a couple of weeks holiday to Tasmania. I went to a fortune-teller. People said she was very good. Apparently she was because what she told me has come true to a certain extent. She said, 'You have a son and that boy is going to go to great heights. Big things are going to happen in his life. I can see him now driving through the streets and crowds cheering him.' Now he's a man he's not driving through the streets but he is a great man in his teaching and has thousands of followers.

# CHAPTER 31

# THE HOMECOMING
# (ALMOST)

One evening in the summer of 1972 an estate agent knocked on the front door and asked if we wanted to sell our flat. I said no, we'd only had it for 15 months. He said, 'You'd get a good price for it.'

I said, 'How much?'

'About £25,000.'

We were staggered. The place had tripled in value in just over a year. This was the start of the first English property boom of the 1970s. We were in on the ground floor. It was like winning the lottery. And it focused our attention on what we really wanted to do.

The cold and damp English weather troubled us both. I'd got side-tracked from emigrating to America by the public relations job. Although I had no regrets we both felt the need to get out of England. So we sold up. We decided to go back to Australia to live. After repaying the mortgage we had a profit of £16,000. Julie's mother had died the year before and left her some cash. We flew out to Australia with about £23,000, a princely sum in those days. And we landed in Sydney on a scorching summer's day in January 1973 – eight years after our departure.

Our plan was to inspect a block of land on the tropical central coast of Queensland which we'd seen photos of in London, and where we were thinking of building a home. So after two weeks spent with my mother in her Double Bay flat on Sydney Harbour, we bought a new Holden station wagon and headed north for the home of Julie's sister, Rita, about a third of the way up the coast from our destination. There we stayed for two weeks with Rita, her husband Brian and their four children. The two sisters hadn't seen each other since Rita had flown over to London for her father's funeral.

Rita and Brian as young newlyweds had emigrated from England 12 years before with little capital. They'd eventually saved enough to buy a block of land in a bush suburb outside Southport on the Gold Coast. Brian by then had his own concreting business and when we arrived had been building a house on the land for a couple of years. It was an attractive two storey English-style brick home but was still less than half finished. The roof was on and the inside walls were sufficiently in place to reveal what promised to be a very spacious house. But at this stage the family was sleeping in a caravan parked outside the back door.

Rita was an excellent cook and the cooking and eating were done inside the house in the already well-appointed kitchen and dining room downstairs. They moved the children's mattresses inside the building and we took their beds in the caravan. Brian called the house Banksia Place after the many native banksia trees on the property. When I saw the building situation and particularly the casual relationship between Rita and Brian, I predicted that the house would never really be finished. It wasn't; not in their time together, anyway.

Rita was overjoyed at having us there. We offered to rent accommodation nearby but she wouldn't hear of it. After a fortnight we headed north again. She was very sad to see us go. The three of us had spent almost every day together during which Julie and I both talked of the truth to her. Rita, like Julie before her, had had no idea of the truth I spoke of. And like her sister, she loved it and soaked up every word, particularly when Julie recounted the details of the extraordinary changes that had happened to her since our first meeting. Rita was clearly ready and willing for some sort of spiritual or psychological change.

After promising to stay with them again on our return, we drove north into the tropics for several days before reaching the block of land. Although it was as large and the location (on a blue seawater canal) as beautiful as the photos had shown, the climate was too hot and humid.

Our intention had been to sleep in the station wagon but that never eventuated, due to the heat. We toured around for a week, spent a few days on the return journey with my publisher Richard Beim (who now lived at Bundaberg) and arrived back at Banksia Place, not sure of what to do next about a permanent home.

In our absence, Brian had been busy working on the house and clearing out some of the building materials. He and Rita had moved into their large double bedroom and we had a room of our own with a comfortable mattress on the floor. At Rita's request we settled down to stay some weeks with them and again spent most of every day together. Brian was an easy-going and amiable man and seemed genuinely pleased that Rita had our company. He often joined in our talks of truth.

Twelve years in Australia had had a noticeable effect on Rita's speech and dress sense. She had almost lost her refined English accent; her way of expression had become casual Australian. Her dress sense was awful, her wardrobe reflecting the absence of style and interest that can often overtake a woman raising four young children in a semi-bush environment and working to save money in between. She admired Julie's style of dresses and her long flowing hair. Julie took her shopping and over the next few months most of Rita's old wardrobe vanished. She stopped going to the hairdresser and started to grow out her pretty black hair. The girls were in constant conversation. And, obviously influenced by Julie's clear and precise Sussex accent, Rita began to return to her original way of speaking.

During her brief visit to London for the funeral, Rita had expressed feeling a deep connection with me. I'd forgotten about this but during our first weeks in Australia she repeated it and kept saying to Julie, 'Isn't he beautiful?' To me it meant she was seeing the God in me and to Julie it meant the same. I can't say I wasn't attracted to Rita at this time. But to me it was the light of the love of truth that was starting to shine in her. And it was that love of being that attracted me – as it always does.

While in England, Julie often said I reminded her of her grandmother whom both sisters had loved dearly. It was hardly a flattering observation in the normal sense, but I understood. In those moments Julie would also say she wanted to pick me up and would try to lift me off the ground as she'd done with her grandmother. Anyway, one day Rita said to Julie, 'Doesn't he remind you of Grandma?' They both chuckled.

'That's what I keep telling him,' said Julie. 'And I want to pick him up,' said Rita, at the same time having a try at it. Roars of laughter from both women. 'And what about this?' said Julie. 'In England he wears lavender oil all the time!' This information reduced them both to tears of hilarity – because lavender evidently was also Grandma's favourite perfume.

At Banksia Place Brian was progressing well with the inside of the house. Rita was now looking at furniture and curtains. As a Libran, she had good and expensive taste. No worry though; Brian was making money, the two daughters aged six and eight were going to private school and everything in the garden was coming up roses – except for the parents' relationship. Not the types to argue for long, they were more like good friends than a devoted couple. The marriage was pretty well over.

The three of us decided to fly down to Sydney together. The girls wanted to do some shopping; my mother was away and her flat was available. We were there a couple of days, and one night there were some cross words about the attraction Julie sensed between Rita and me. Julie stormed out and I made love to Rita. Twenty minutes later Julie returned. She knew what had happened and some angry words followed. 'I told you,' she wept, 'you could make love to any woman but not to my sister. She's always tried to take what I loved, even as children, and now she's taken you.' That wasn't all true. I had done what I must and what I had come to Australia for without knowing it. I had affirmed Rita's love of God.

Next morning Rita checked into a hotel and was missing all day although we tried to find her. Julie was very devoted and anxious about her and we heard nothing until she phoned the following day. She said she'd spent the time alone and gone through a deep spiritual experience; and that she was not the same woman. There had been a distinct shift in her consciousness, she said, adding, 'I'm having a spiritual baby.' This was pretty wild stuff and I don't think I ever found out what she meant by the last statement.

But when we met up and the three of us flew back to the Gold Coast together she was certainly different. There was an innate stillness in her that hadn't been there before, a distinct serenity. She was softer and extremely grateful for all that Julie had done for her. She admitted without prompting that from childhood there had been a dark and ugly energy in her that had made her spitefully jealous of Julie but which had now miraculously vanished. She said she loved Julie and showed it in every way from then on. She also said she loved me, her master.

Once again the tantric power had worked its wonders. As I observed the amazing transformation in Rita, I was reminded of the death of Cleopatra in Shakespeare's play, *Antony and Cleopatra*. In the suicide scene where Cleopatra lies dead from the bite of an asp, a Roman soldier assigned by Caesar is the first to arrive. He asks, 'Is this well done?' Cleopatra's maid answers, 'It is well done, and fitting for a princess descended of so many royal kings.' But in me I substituted my reply for the maid's, 'Yes, it is well done, as befitting a princess of the royal line of divine love, the love of God.' This is the mission of my tantric life – to transform woman by awakening and affirming the intensity of her fundamental love of God, a royal line of love in existence where most is fear and ignorance.

Although I loved Rita dearly I made love to her only once, and to no other woman, in my 13 year marriage with Julie. Nonetheless, Julie never really forgave me for making love to her sister, even though she knew it was a holy act that changed the woman permanently, as she herself had been changed. Perhaps she did forgive me but she never seemed to forget; and as soon as she remembered she became irrationally emotional. Future events in her life seemed to dissolve the problem but only temporarily. The emotion about her sister was so deep-seated that only the approach of certain death finally eliminated it.

Essentially, Julie was an other-worldly creature. Her apparent paranoia over Rita reached into that other world where it had particular significance for her, something to do with a past beyond comprehension. She was ordinary like all of us but a psychical and spiritual enigma, a paradox. Her great love of God endowed her with a charismatic innocence and the gift of vision beyond the ordinary. Yet her swings of emotion made it very difficult for her to cope with the world. I was her anchor. I loved her through everything. Later I found some of her poems and writings about the events of this time. One poem referring to me read:

All my songs you took and gave to her.
Are not forest flowers blue and perfect?

The love of a master became unsure
And woe is the virgin's thirst for knowledge.
Bury your seeds but leave behind what is uncertain.
Once your ring went round my finger
Unblinking I beheld its golden light.
Now so bare upon the bed I lie deserted.
You came so sweetly and as never before
Love caressed the lightness of my soul.
If it be God can I ignore the solitude of my own longing?
Is to take a need or is to give a sin?
It is time to wait and to observe.
Not before I know for sure
Shall I leave your beloved face.
Profoundly shall I live. But never shall I think again
For I could not bear to live.

Another poem, referring to me again:

The walking, the talking and holding hands continued
But my love was never quite the same.
Did you know I came home?
But where was my love?
It could not wait, so little faith we had in each other.
Yet we continue.
'It wasn't like that. I am a teacher. I teach with penetration.
I hold my student near. If she desires I make love with her.
You hear, you hear.'
Thus the master to his wife.
Oh starry skies where gods hide
And earthy visions rise to realisations
Can I never love like mortals? Will all love end in death?
What is it you try to teach me? Why will I not listen?
Is it all so destructive of the woman idea?
At ten years old I made a vow never to love.
My grandmother knew; she said I was right.
She knew me well. 'Never tell,' she said.
Oh so ragged is my promise.
How shall I ever be free of such knowledge?
There is no Prince, nor ever shall be.

Only God speaks.
Invisible love that breathes with such strange emptiness
Filling my soul with purity.
I cannot speak, for you are right –
I and all mortals shall die.
But in you I shall live.


Three doors down from Banksia Place a small fibro cottage went up for
sale and we bought it. It needed a good deal of renovating and for the
next several weeks I worked with a carpenter, painting and doing it up.
But the place never became the comfy little cottage we'd envisaged. I
spent another six weeks levelling 40 truckloads of sand to make a bigger
lawn at the back where the land was swampy. I planted grass seed, carefully kept it watered, and wondered after three weeks why no grass had
appeared. My inquiries eventually revealed that the sand had been exca-
vated from near the sea and had salt in it.

Despite my best efforts, the place was a failure. Julie lost interest and
I couldn't blame her. The place wasn't worth buying new furniture for so
we got a few secondhand pieces and slept on a mattress Rita had lent us.
The cottage was all right for now but certainly was not going to be our
home in Australia.

CHAPTER 32

# THE DEVIL

*What is the devil? The devil is the human personification of sex without love; and the effect of that in human affairs.*

J ulie and I continued to eat and spend our evenings up at the big house. On some nights we were joined by another guest, a new business acquaintance of Rita and Brian's. The man was in his late 20s, handsome and personable. He was a practising bisexual and made no secret of it. When he came over, Rita, in her usual hospitable Libran way, would invite him to join us for dinner. Afterwards when I spoke the truth, as I did on most evenings, he showed an interest and at times his perception was unusually acute.

On this particular night, as I talked I saw a radiance around Rita. This did not surprise me since I knew it symbolised her new state of consciousness. At the same time I saw an even greater radiance around the young man. This did surprise me because the questions he was asking were far below the lofty state of consciousness I was seeing. He wasn't being true to what he was. He was pretending to be ignorant. He was hiding something.

I then realised he was Lucifer. His consciousness was radiantly beautiful but he had been possessed by the demonic energy of sex. Like Lucifer, the highest of the angels, he had deserted the God of love and used his great magnetic power to lure women and men for his selfish sexual satisfaction.

I said to him, 'You're not being what you are.'

'What am I?' he said.

'You're Lucifer. You're the devil, and you know it.'

'Yes,' he said. 'But who's going to believe you?'

It was a strange moment, one of the strangest of my life. I knew and he knew. There was no emotion between us, nothing personal, just the fact. It was as though we were talking about his make of car. Everyone heard, but as he said, who would believe it? Even so, the revelation stayed with Rita and Julie but without provoking reaction in either of them. To me, this was due to the young man's extraordinary forthright honesty in a situation where most (in those days) might have ducked for cover. But his apparent honesty I discovered later was part of his deception. It was a tactic, a ploy of directness intended to win the trust of ordinary people who are usually defensively protective of their personal secrets. He was not concerned at all with what others thought of him. He was different in a different way. He was shameless.

The young man's case was unique in my experience. And I've not encountered anything like it since. His extremely high consciousness, blended with the depth of the other, was indeed a symbolic representation of the beauty and selfish arrogance of the fallen archangel Lucifer who, according to the myth, rebelled against God. It may help if I recount the myth of Lucifer. As I've mentioned, Lucifer was an archangel, a chief angel next to God. He rebelled against God and then became a fallen angel. Two things are not explained in the traditional religious myth. First, fallen means having fallen into existence, which means having descended into sensory awareness. In that sense, all men and women are fallen angels. Second, to rebel against God is to rebel against love.

As beautiful as the earth is, and as good as life can be for man and woman, there is always something that spoils the beautiful and the good. What is it? What's the name of the spoiler? Its name is sex – sex without love. Sex without love is a legacy on earth of the original Luciferic descent into matter. We all have a touch more or less of the Luciferic taint until the self-indulgent sex in us is converted to love. Those Christian saints, so often fondly remembered for their bodily contortions as they "fought with the devil" were simply fighting their own suppressed sexual drive.

Because the sexual drive is at the foundation of human affairs, its enormous conflictual influence on daily life is not recognised. Selfish sex – the Luciferic drive – is what keeps the unhappy world unhappy, the unhappy people unhappy. The greed, frustration, anger and impatience in selfish sex is responsible for all the murders, cruelty, violence and wars between nations. Men and women, due to the Luciferic influence, compete and fight for power over one another instead of over their self, and inevitably in relationships try to possess the beloved instead of simply loving each other.

All this conflict is a human effect. It is not that way for the man in whom the Luciferic consciousness has taken complete possession. Although he affects negatively and imperceptibly the lives of all those close to him, he himself is unaffected – for a time. His consciousness is not human, but the man of course is. And the consciousness, being immortal, is only visiting until eventually the man and his world collapses, undermined by selfishness, duplicity and inevitable addiction to drugs or alcohol. It then moves on to possess another suitable body-in-waiting.

The Christian depiction of the devil as an horrifically frightening and ugly brute has some truth in it. Apart from scaring and scarring the living daylights out of Christian children, it is an unwitting description of the human effect of sex without love. Lucifer in human form however is personable, amiable, sociable and unrecognisable as anything more than an ordinary, likable fellow. He hides what he is until after he's got the sex and purity he wants. Then he concentrates on manipulating individuals who can provide the worldly security of social acceptance which his lifestyle otherwise would not allow. He wants to join humanity as an ordinary mortal before age and illness take their toll.

His first aim is to find a man or woman of high consciousness, the awakened love of the divine, and to subjugate them to his own will. This is done over time by gradually absorbing the victim's consciousness so that eventually he or she loses the power to relate to their awakened state. They just forget. And as forgetfulness is part of the ordinary consciousness to which they return, nothing is seen to be amiss.

Even in the normally degenerate man there remains an element of manliness – a kind of faint universal hope – that propels him evolutionarily in the general direction of eventual good. Somewhere in the consciousness is the seed of noble aspiration. In the Luciferic man where the possession is complete, little room for mitigation exists because the spirit of the man, the saving grace, is seldom there, if at all.

If a man not completely possessed tries to change there will be an enormous tussle in him between the good and the other, and a grave danger of repercussions. The possession is very powerful in the world. Denial of it where there has been a long established indulgence may result in intermittent relapses or other forms of addiction. Either will make the life a sad or unhappy compromise for those around him.

As I've said, I have only met this one man reflecting the complete Luciferic presence. He is complete in his self-knowledge, as he revealed on that night. He knows who he is. This is as rare among humanity as a spiritual master who has realised who he is. The master is on one side of pure love and Lucifer on the other side.

Many years later I met the man briefly again. The amazing thing was that I immediately recognised the sham of him and the hypocrisy of his whole life – and told him so. Again, despite the thousands of men I have met around the world during my teaching life, I had not seen this in any-one but him. Other men may be as perverse and hypocritical but they are humanly unconscious and not really responsible for what they are or do. But this man is conscious of all he is.

In every ordinary individual the intensity of sex varies, being basically suppressed by fears and doubts, and heightened by fantasy. It contains very little real knowledge of God, or none at all. The energy itself is con-scious of what it's doing but the individual it acts in is not. The individual is the vehicle. The energy is consciously in control. That is why man and woman often see themselves risking everything they love or treasure when sexually driven.

The energy of sex is a psychic force, inferior to the spirit. But being psychic it is immortal as far as we are concerned. Its power is basically beyond comprehension but suffice to say that being the sex drive it is able to possess innumerable bodies simultaneously without detracting from itself. Its duplicitous nature is hidden behind pleasing, plausible or persuasive explanations.

At its most intense, in any man, the energy is suprasexual and master of the sexual excitation of woman. The only real love in such a union is hers. He slowly drains her resistance, literally sucking her dry of virtue. After draining her, he leaves her sexually alone for a time while she replenishes her virtue. For her the draining usually results in degrees of depression, desolation or illness because he has taken her love and left little in its place.

If the woman is promiscuous the man may leave her for a long time or for good, because the other men she goes with who do not love her will each take a bit of her innocence and leave her bereft of what he wants. Or he just travels from body to body picking up what virtue he can but taking responsibility for none.

When the woman he's ensnared has replenished some of her virtue, the sexually demonic man repeats his vampirish ritual. She is then captive, bound to him without knowing it by her own lost love, her sense of insufficiency and insecurity. He has taken her consciousness, her love, with the result that she thinks she stays of her own will.

Elements of what I've described are potentially in every man. The energy is fundamentally male but can also possess and appear in a woman's body. In that case, it again concentrates on the innocence of another woman (or a man) and devours her into bondage. And because the demon is bisexual it can appear in a man who lives off the innocence of young men and binds them to the same sexual ritual. Where the energy is in possession the appearance of the man (or woman) does not necessarily show it. But to see "him" as he really is – that is, to tune in to his fundamental energy – is unmistakable.

Sometimes the energy reveals its essence to its victims in the depths of their misery and despair. These women, in that moment of truth, know beyond doubt that what's in the man is demonic. They actually "see" him as this incarnate depravity. But who on earth would believe such a story? The women who have seen him in this way and who read this book will. If their minds have not blocked out the knowledge as unbelievable, they will know they were not mad, not mistaken and not having delusions. From this knowledge they may gather new strength and perhaps attract a man who will truly love them and know what to do.

# CHAPTER 33

# GOD SPEAKS

The evening of my extraordinary conversation with the young man went on much as usual, and so did those that followed. But for me the incident meant I needed more spiritual power. The young man was up to something; he wasn't wasting his time being there. So I didn't eat for several days – my way in those days of increasing my power.

The man and I were alone in this incredible knowledge. It has always been like that for me. I love and serve God. I bring men and women closer to the realisation of God. Lucifer loves and serves himself. With his power and beauty he entraps women and men and keeps them away from God. He always remains a liar. With his original Luciferic knowledge he will frequently mouth "God's will" and pretend to love God. But the signs of his life will give him away to those closest to him, unless he has completely hoodwinked them.

Lucifer is my eternal adversary. There are only the two of us. He has been as close to God as I am. An infinitesimal line separates us. I do not judge him for we are both beyond human morals. I simply oppose and expose him when I can with the power of Consciousness – for Consciousness is the realm beyond time where battles such as these are fought.

The possession in the young man had given him a magnetic power in the world that no ordinary man has in my experience. It is the kind of power that can work "miracles", create events that will serve the desires of the possession. Being Luciferic in origin, the energy has an insatiable appetite for divine purity and innocence. I saw he was attaching himself to Rita. He "knew" beyond events, as I "knew". He was attracted to her and she clearly fancied him.

Nevertheless the woman the energy strives most to possess is she in whom the Bhagavati appears. So now the man's interest switched from Rita to Julie. I noticed a mild flirtation happening between them. This became more obvious each evening until one night it was so outrageous that when we arrived home I had it out with her. I told her he was sucking her in. I said that now that she was shining out to him he was slowly seducing her in her consciousness. He always went for the greatest purity in woman or man.

'You're jealous,' she said. 'You fucked my sister. You left me.'

The old resentful childhood emotion surfaced. It frequently did these days, only it was aimed at me now, not Rita. There was nothing I could do about it since I was guilty of what in Julie's mind was the ultimate betrayal. As I've said, she'd witnessed the remarkable change in Rita and she herself had been changed by the same tantric process. But emotion is neither reasonable nor honest.

Julie had a pretty white lace blouse. It was her favourite. She wore it on all special occasions, keeping it very carefully washed and pressed. She loved it. And lately in her flirtations with the young man she'd been wearing it nearly every night. She had it on this night. And when we got home I told her, 'Take it off.'

Sensing something, she said, 'What for?'

I said, 'If you don't take it off I'll rip it off you.'

'You wouldn't dare,' she said brazenly. I moved towards her and she removed the blouse.

'What are you going to do?' she said.

'I'm not going to do anything. You're going to do it. Tear it up.'

'I can't, I can't.' She was crying and groaning.

'Do it.'

She started to tear the blouse at the neck. 'You're taking my life,' she screamed and sobbed.

'I'm taking your vanity,' I said. 'You've been flirting with the devil. His attentions have made you unholy.' I handed her a pair of scissors. 'Now cut it up smaller.' She did, crying and wailing until the pieces covered the floor at her feet. Then she was quieter, more composed.

'I don't know he's the devil. You might have made it up.'

'Then I'll have to leave it to God to inform you.'

In the middle of the night, Julie woke me. 'He is the devil,' she said. 'God just told me.'

That was the end of any influence the man had over Julie. But Julie's emotionalism about Rita and my having made love to her continued. In another poem, referring to Rita, she wrote:

> Every trick she has used to destroy me.
> How she haunts me.
> Perhaps some time ago I did her wrong.
> That is why she moves me with her sorrow.
> I love her through her hate but find it hard to trust her love.
> Anything I ever had she tried to destroy.
> If I ever let her know the deep sadness I feel for her
> I know she will destroy me
> Leaving me forever with her burden of no love.
> But can love ever not know love?
> No, so what harm can she do me?
> None, for I love God. This no one can take.
> But it would be sad not to lie in my loved one's arms.

Did I truly love Rita? Yes. At first I recognised the spirit in her and her potential for change. She also increasingly showed that she loved the truth that I am from a profound place within. Like Julie before her, she listened and absorbed the words of truth and love I spoke in the many months the three of us spent together. Moreover, she was most receptive to Julie's refining spiritual influence. This gradually swept away the accumulation of the past and revealed a spiritually sensitive woman.

After I made love to her, Rita became exceedingly beautiful, restored to the essential woman she was. The beauty was not only within but without. Her crowning external feature was her long black hair which by now hung naturally past her shoulders. She emanated the indefinable.

Afterwards, Julie of course was ever watchful of the pair of us. She knew I loved Rita and had no problem with that. But she must have sensed there was something personal in me which detracted from my one-pointed love of her. And I have to accept she was right. She must have been right. For the Bhagavat cannot have two Bhagavatis at the same time. And my love of Rita was intense enough to be heading in that direction.

Nevertheless the three of us spent every day we could together, shopping in Brisbane, nipping into Southport for lunch, swimming at Surfers Paradise and spending the evenings at Banksia Place. Julie loved Rita, too. And Rita loved Julie. There was much love and harmony between the three of us – except when the ogre of my personal love for Rita arose in Julie.

She didn't blame Rita for what had happened; it was my doing and she was reminded of this each time I looked at Rita. Sometimes I looked too long into her eyes, or Julie would see me looking too often in the rear-view mirror of the car. Once, as though inspired, she saw it in the reflection of the stainless steel kettle in the kitchen. She would rebuke me severely when we were alone, but not in front of Rita. To Rita I was her spiritual master and Julie recognised this. She truly loved me loving Rita but not in the way I had. She wanted the best for her sister. And as far as she was concerned she did everything in her power to bring that about.

Despite my love of Rita, I did not attempt to make love with her again. Nor did we speak about my love of her or her love of me. It was just there, unspoken but incredibly intense between us. I knew in a way my personal love of Rita was not right. I had slipped over the edge. With my tantric power I was creating another Bhagavati; and that is not permitted. So I withdrew myself as best I could until finally my love of Rita was just as real but no longer personal. It was a great teaching for me. I was then freed for good from personal love.

Before I made love to Rita her marriage was well and truly finished by mutual consent. That being the case, I spoke to Rita about the consequences, as I saw them, of her making love with any man who did not love her completely. I said she was now no longer an ordinary woman;

the divine beauty had been awakened in her and although this would tend to attract a spiritual man it could also attract a man to whom sex was more important than love. She had to be on her guard and discriminating.

The selfish, sexually driven man, I said, could not resist contaminating beauty. If such a man made love with her, and did not change his ways for love, he would drain her virtue and keep her bound to him for that purpose. In that event she would often be tired and physically weak. She would be sad, or depressed at times, at the apparent hopelessness of the situation; and if the association continued she was likely to be sick and perhaps even finally lose her will to live. But if such a man truly discovered love through loving her, and she stayed true to the truth she knew, she could transform him. But it would be a long and difficult path for both. Most of all she would have to beware of the Luciferic man. He could not really change because he never intends to.

Meanwhile, Julie and I decided that Australia wasn't the place for us to settle, not at this time anyway. After a stay of less than 12 months we began making arrangements to return to England. This included selling the cottage.

The year of 1973 was the peak of the building and property boom in Australia. Prices seemed to increase every month. You could buy a piece of real estate and be sure of selling it for more. We'd bought our place early in the year and we sold at a good profit just before we left. The car also fetched more than we paid for it new – the model was in short supply. We'd also bought as an investment an attractive two bedroom unit on the beach at Surfers Paradise and sold that at a profit too. We left Australia with more money than when we'd arrived.

CHAPTER 34

# THE GUARDIAN OF
# THE THRESHOLD

Arriving back in England in March 1974 we determined to stay out of London and find a house in the country. We toured the home counties closest to London but decent properties were far too expensive. So over we went to Suffolk, the most eastern county, and there we found it – a pretty two storey thatched cottage in a tiny village called Hitcham, 80 miles from London. It had flowers and rose bushes all round and looked like the typical English postcard cottage. The name was equally as quaint: Friday Lane Cottage.

It had a bit of a smell of damp but we assumed that went with the place which had been built in the 16th century, around the reign of Queen Elizabeth I and when Shakespeare was writing his plays. It was originally two cottages built side by side for farm workers and their families. This was evident upstairs where a massive oak beam, suitable I'd say for the keel of one of Her Majesty's man-of-war ships, went right across the middle of the second bedroom. The beam was about 4½ feet off the floor and you had to bend almost double to get to the third bedroom on the other side. Twice I nearly knocked myself out. But we thought we could live with the obstruction since it was part of the "quaintness" of the cottage. I learned in England that when they describe a house as "quaint" it means that it's also damned inconvenient. After a

257

couple of months we'd cleaned up the cottage, got rid of the dog and cat smells and hair, and furnished it.

One day Julie was sitting on one of our new sofas in the lounge room and casually gave the stain on the wall a poke with her finger. It went straight through the plaster revealing a big damp patch in the wattle and daub packing. We both walked round poking the walls with the same result. Much of the place was riddled with damp. What had disguised it most was the heat from the coke-fed Aga cooker in the kitchen that was always kept burning.

Crisis. The whole place was a quaint, lovely-looking dump. Up came the local builder, in went an application for a renovation grant on the grounds that it was a heritage building. Down came most of the walls to be relined with lime and sand plaster, as was the original practice with wattle and daub construction. Up came all the tiles and bricks on the ground floor to be relaid on plastic. Out went the old cooker and in came central heating. Off came much of the thatch to make way for a dormer (a passageway) linking all the bedrooms. Down came the perilous oak beam. On went a new thatch and up and up went the cost above the grant we'd received. But it was certainly all worth it. After six months of having dust and inconvenience rained down upon us we at last had our comfortable, cosy cottage in the country.

The 1973 property boom in Australia had frightening repercussions for us at Friday Lane Cottage in England. My speculative confidence had been such that just before we left I paid a 6% deposit on a luxury high-rise unit which was starting construction in Surfers Paradise. The accepted strategy of the time was to sell the unit before having to pay the huge final price six months later, which would have been absolutely beyond our resources. The new year of 1974 brought with it an unprecedentedly savage credit squeeze. Overnight the property market collapsed. It was impossible for me to sell.

I had to borrow A$70,000 at 10% interest with awesome repayments each month. After the first four months it looked as though we'd have to sell the cottage to keep up the payments. I was in constant touch with the real estate agent in Australia. He was sympathetic but kept reporting that nothing was moving. This concrete monster of my speculative ignorance was pursuing me with an insatiable appetite and it looked like it was going to devour us.

One day, to my grateful surprise, the estate agent said he'd go halves with me in the investment. He would pay half the repayments and we'd share the profit when the unit finally sold. He was confident it would sell in time as it was a highly desirable property. And it did. Three months later he sold it. After all the outgoings were accounted for we made A$12,000. Or A$6,000 each. Phew!

Julie, as I've said, was a sensitive psychic, not a channeller as such, but an involuntary medium. She was quite frightened by her psychic powers and did nothing to encourage them. When they became threatening she sank into her love of God and felt a protective screen around her. This had happened several times before I'd met her.

During our life together we were frequently woken at night by psychic phenomena in the room around us. What always amazed me about these intense psychic visions was that Julie and I "saw" them "within" simultaneously while we were still asleep. The most dramatic for me had been the black energy in 1968. But one night at Friday Lane Cottage six years later, there was another encounter – not so lastingly disturbing but equally as frightening and weird at the time. We went to bed about 11.45 pm and what follows is a description I wrote down first thing next morning:

> At about 12.15 am I awoke. Julie was screaming and I was scrambling out of the covers to kneel upright on the bed and face the huge apparition of a "man". He appeared to be wearing a cloak-like garment and was right in the centre of the bed almost on top of me. By huge I mean his head (which I don't recall any feature of now but Julie says I said he had a beard) was almost at the cottage ceiling level – 15 feet! – and his cloaked figure must have been 6 feet across. It was enormous. I knelt on the bed looking up at it (Julie was still screaming) and shouted, 'Stand back, stand back. I command you to stand back.' It remained where it was and then moved back a bit. I said, 'Stand still and be seen.' It eased back further into the shadows near the window. I said, 'Don't you dare come into my space again. Don't you dare.' It vanished into the darkness.

Where was this space I referred to? Was it the room or was it really my psyche? Had some energy slipped into my psyche while I was asleep and through Julie's psychic sensitivity taken form in the room – just as the black energy before it had appeared inwardly and outwardly simultaneously? Is this a common event such as in nightmares and dread, only then there's no apparent image other than perhaps dream form? Are we really all subject to an inner world which accounts for most of our feelings?

I was extremely agitated by the presence of the image. The energies were flowing through me at a tremendous rate, as might be imagined. It was so huge I was like a dwarf speaking up to it. I'm sure my hair must have stood on end. I did not apprehend danger as such from it. But I was very much aware of its intrusion into "my space". I was indignant. It was too close, obtrusively so. It was a powerful energy. The energies it aroused in me made my eyes water, my body sweat instantly and my bottom lip purse as it would from severe emotion. The reality of the knowledge that I was conscious and that the figure was actually, really, there, was stark.

Afterwards as the energies continued to race in my body I used the device I'd learned when the black energy visited us; I psychically "stroked" them down with the power in my crown, for they must not be given a chance to go out. It was a truly terrifying experience. Julie said I spoke to the apparition in the deeper slower voice I used after the black energy in 1968. The enormity of the image is the thing that still staggers me; and its living power of presence. Obviously Julie and I both woke together, but the absence of the conscious mind makes this stage practically impossible to recall; we have often woken, both "knowing" we have been talking to each other "elsewhere".

Julie said that what woke her was the same black shape as the 1968 black energy shooting across the room from the door to near the window. I did not see that. I woke fully aware of the thing over me, with Julie screaming and me struggling to extricate my body from the covers to get up into a higher position to face it. Before my surface mind was operating I knew the thing was there. The cloak was not a colour but seemed to be dotted; something like the gowns worn by Merlin and other

fabulous wizards seen in pictures and drawings. I am wondering
if it is the Guardian of the Threshold – the Guardian that I was
required to face to enter the next phase of my spiritual life.

In everyone the Guardian of the Threshold is an inner psychological barrier guarding the next step to a higher state of freedom or consciousness.
But it seems that only in the deep inner spiritual life does it come forward with the psychic intensity of an apparition such as I've just
described, which is probably an aspect of divine compassion. We have
only to face what we can stand – and I'm not discussing drug induced
hallucinations.

In everyone every moment of fear is the barrier or "guardian" that
eventually has to be crossed. But as I say, no one has to face a fear
beyond their psychological capacity to deal with it. The explanation
being twofold: the fear is self-made, therefore lower than the innate consciousness of the individual; and the fear disintegrates once fully faced –
and then no longer exists. Invariably the inclination is to turn away. But
only by courageously facing the Guardian can one pass through into the
new.

There are many degrees of fear in human experience, many aspects of
the Guardian. And living consists of facing them as the difficulties, heart-
breaks and crises that beset people. Each fear successfully faced
engenders a sense of freedom, as everybody with any sensitivity knows.
Fears that are not sufficiently faced drag on as circumstances (or drag-
ons!).

So many things challenge people's equilibrium that most fail to see
what's actually going on. They don't realise that each problem or difficulty is actually a "minor guardian" and that the facing of each dissolves
a tiny bit of fear. Success or failure is not the point. The resolute facing
of the difficulty is what counts. All attempts contribute to the individual's
and humanity's slow but steady march towards greater freedom. The
greatest freedom is freedom from fear.

The Guardian is nothing more than myself. The only bogeyman we
ever have to face is "myself". And my self, which I alone have created, is
nothing but fear. However, self or fear is far deeper and more extreme
than can be imagined. It extends back beyond the personal into the fundamental fears of humanity. Day-to-day fears are the tip of the iceberg.

In my experience of the deeper inner life, the Guardian first manifests significantly as humanity's most deep-seated fear – the fear of death. This aspect of the Guardian I passed through in India into the uninterrupted realisation of immortality. This led to my meeting and union with Julie.

Humanity's next deepest fear is fear of the psychic unknown, the psychic intangible, the horrific inexplicable. A terrible aspect of this I'd had to face as the black energy over a period of several weeks before eventually absorbing or passing through it as described in the chapter of that name. This led to my transcendental realisation with the Blessed John.

It was those two earlier encounters with the Guardian that gave me sufficient strength and presence to order the psychic manifestation out of my space. Although my body showed every sign of fear, the consciousness was unafraid. So it is with all of us, underneath the fearing self-made self.


My publisher, Richard Beim, arrived at the cottage one day with a large and bulging overnight bag. He emptied it on the floor and out fell 20 of the latest books on astrology. 'I'll pay you £3,000 for a series of 12 books, one for each sign – if you complete the job in 12 months,' he said. 'These are your reference books.' What he wanted was about the equivalent in words of three good-sized novels. As usual, there would be no royalties, no author's name, just the one payment. None of that troubled me. It was good money in those days for a freelance writer and I accepted. 'What's it to be called?' I asked. 'That's what I'm paying you for,' he said. 'You give it a title.'

I finished the job one month early and named the series AstroAnalysis. For more than 20 years, AstroAnalysis has continued to be published by various publishers in Europe, America and England, and no doubt will continue to pop up on the world's bookshelves while Richard Beim is alive and holds the copyright.

So 1975–6 was a pretty busy writing year. I still did some teaching but not as much as I would have done had I still lived in London. I gave a number of meetings to groups in private houses in London and one of the people who attended was Poonam Lowe who ran the Bhagwan Shree Rajneesh organisation in England. At her invitation I addressed a meeting of Rajneesh sannyasins at their headquarters in London and also at a large country home they'd been given at Gislingham, not far from where we lived.

Julie's children would come and stay with us and I noticed a decided spirituality developing in Mark. Jonathan, five years younger, was still being innocently impressed by the culture of the times. One Sunday as we walked past the local church, Julie said to him, 'Hear the choir boys; they sing high.'

'Are they on drugs?' responded Jonathan.

Three stalwart students from the London meetings used to come down to visit me, but overall my time at Friday Lane Cottage was fairly isolating from a teaching point of view. Julie called this my karmic "punishment" for making love with her sister and for falling in love with her. I wasn't convinced of her first point but I did learn from my love of Rita that a tantric master must never start to "fall" in love – and I never have since. Falling in love, as the word implies, is a descent into a form of unconsciousness represented by personal love. Personal love ends and changes as the person does; but true love, because it is based on the love of God, is forever.

Julie said she (Julie) was my Bhagavati, my love, and in the spirit where our love was I could not have two Bhagavatis at the same time. I could love other women if I was moved to and give them the benediction of my consciousness but I could not love like ordinary people do. Ours was a love of divine union and that was very different, as we both knew. For her part, she was endeavouring in this period to overcome the deep corrosive emotion that had been stirred in her. She never succeeded and eventually it would kill her.

Rita phoned from Australia to tell me she had met a man and was in love with him, and that he loved her. Before taking it any further she wanted my blessing. I said she had my blessing to do as she must and that I was pleased they both loved one another as mutual love was the only thing that could help a partnership endure. I told her that she was the higher consciousness in the partnership and her task was to raise his consciousness by love as hers had been raised. I also reminded her of what I'd said to her before leaving Australia about the consequences of her making love with any man who did not love her completely. She repeated that she and her man loved each other and that he was not one of those men.

Some weeks later Rita phoned again. She and Brian had split and had agreed amicably on a divorce. She was now living with her new partner. She married him a couple of years later.

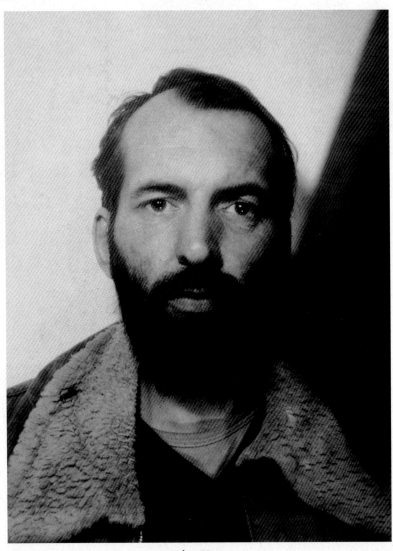

John Hart.

Barry and Julie, Sydney Harbour, 1973.

Double Bay, Sydney, 1973.

Barry, Shakespeare and Julie, Stratford-upon-Avon, England, Spring, 1974.

Barry and Julie, England, Summer, 1974.

Julie and David White, Hampstead Heath, London, 1974.

Friday Lane Cottage, 1976.

Barry and Julie.

Barry and Gar.

# CHAPTER 35

# THE CHILDREN'S SCHOOL NOBODY WANTED

A t the end of 1976 I sensed the need to get back to London and so did Julie. We sold Friday Lane cottage (at a profit) and with a mortgage bought a three storey townhouse in Kingsley Place, Highgate, London. We couldn't get possession for three months, so instead of paying high rents in London, Julie got the bright idea of our spending the waiting time in the country where rents were much lower. We took a three bedroom place in Looe, Cornwall, an attractive little fishing village and well known tourist resort, about 250 miles from London. It was mid-winter, February, so the rent was even more reasonable.

In May we moved into the new house in Kingsley Place. In the first week after moving in, I publicly announced the opening of The Children's School of Philosophic Development and Understanding of Studies. I placed an ad to run for four consecutive issues in the local Ham and High (Hampstead and Highgate) weekly newspaper. The ad said:

> If your normally intelligent child, aged nine to twelve, has a problem in understanding any school subject so that it causes the child to fret or worry, I might be able to help. I do not teach subjects, only understanding. There is no charge.

And I gave my name and phone number. One nervously tentative parent phoned and a man who wanted to know what I was up to. I didn't hear from them again, or anyone else.

After years of teaching numerous adults, I had learned that most of their problems were formed in childhood, and that many of these problems of fear and self-doubt originated from the pressure and sense of failure associated with not understanding particular school subjects, and the accompanying strain of having to convince teachers and examiners otherwise.

No subject matter is complicated, no matter how complex. Complication and confusion occur in the mind. They are emotional attitudes, or blockages, that start to arise with the first anxiety in childhood of not having understood something. The accumulation of these early anxieties is the basis of our adult "complex" which largely accounts for our discontent, mundanity and ceaseless striving for fulfilment. We spend much of our lives trying to compensate in external terms and in self-justification for the emotion, the "guilt", of not having understood something, perhaps many things, so long ago.

Most of us had this "learning ceiling" fall on us at some point as children but we managed to duck and scramble through into adulthood – not cured, but by developed cunning able to cope and conceal the conflict, confusion and anxiety it generated. Usually this happened because our teachers or parents did not have the time or the will to go back to where we first failed to understand what a subject was about and its practical significance to us as learners. This mostly occurred at a point where our teachers assumed we comprehended something when we did not, and we were afraid to ask 'Why...?' We could not admit our lack of comprehension in case we seemed foolish or were made fools of, or, worst of all, discovered that we were in fact less intelligent than the guy next to us who did seem to understand.

In planning the school my intention was to teach children how to learn. I would do this with my own truth and the child's intelligence – intelligence being the ability to see the fact or the truth. Since the child with a study problem has a blockage and cannot see the fact of what it's about, I would ask the child questions until the fact was seen. This would free the child. I would teach the children to ask 'Why...?' and then to listen for the answer. I would show them how to assess for themselves whether the answer was the truth.

By engaging their interest, understanding and enjoyment, I would make a subject meaningful and therefore worthy of learning. This of course is "pure philosophy", not philosophising. Pure philosophy is the study that embraces all subjects and which can always be made absorbing and interesting for any age because it does not have to be learned – it just makes sense. This eliminates the student's fear of dependence on memory, which is probably the chief subconscious cause of student anxiety.

I wrote at the time, 'Learning is not an end in itself, except for the curious and the computer and quiz-master mentalities. Meaningful learning is a means to understanding and from that alone flows the possibility of true individual creativity and self-fulfilment.'

I wanted to teach the children because they were the adults and parents of tomorrow. But the fears, doubts and suspicions of their own parents – the very emotions I was offering to try to eliminate in their offspring – denied the children that chance.

# CHAPTER 36

# THE BIRTH OF THE CENTRE

After the failure of my attempt to launch the Children's School, I decided to set up a school for adults and called it The School for the West of Self-realisation. The following are extracts from the introductory document:

SOME PRINCIPLES

1. This is a Western Way of Truth which teaches that nothing is true unless it can be demonstrated in the individual's own experience.

2a. An individual's understanding of his or her own experience can be expanded at any moment by contact with right energy, such as a right teacher.

2b. The limit to all understanding is fixed by the evolutionary status of humanity as a whole. But the individual's understanding can exceed this at any moment which makes genius and self-realisation possible.

3. The aim of this school is to expand the consciousness of each individual who participates so that the Consciousness of humanity is expanded in time as quickly as possible; for in Consciousness or Self-realisation we are all one and serving that one.

4. All is energy and there is no energy higher than right love, which has no object.
5. The problem for the mind in this teaching is to discover and not to hold.

DIRECT EXPERIENCE

This teaching aspires to give the individual direct experience of life. Our normal experience is all indirect and gives us only the experience of living; we experience naturally through the medium of the body or the senses but interpret that through the past experience of the mind. This gives a flawed perception. Direct experience does not involve the emotions, the memory or the imagination. It means seeing the meaning of experience, what's behind it, instead of simply having the experience itself. It requires a still mind.

In this teaching, direct experience is achieved in the first instance by the teacher being able to penetrate the mind and psyche of an individual to expose his or her emotional congestion or blockages. These are the cause of all immediate ignorance and confusion. The chief blockage is then isolated and the necessary de-confusing process begun.

First the mind is penetrated, then the psyche (the sub-conscious) behind it which contains the emotions. Beyond the emotions the psyche is pure and extends to the realm of Consciousness. The degree of Consciousness realised in an individual determines the clarity of his or her direct experience.

The teaching is concerned with the individual alone. The group is simply an energy structure, a sort of umbrella, which itself is going nowhere. Any group can become a blockage if the individual allows it to hold him. He must be held only by the energy that frees, and then only as long as is absolutely necessary. A group, and that includes the mass of humanity, can never share in the unity of Consciousness. Only the individual possesses this potential.

It is a teaching for the Western world because it teaches only the demonstrable fact. It shuns imagination. Like all true philosophy, Eastern and Western, it is a contemporary aspect of The Philosophy which moves and expands with man through the ages and his developing consciousness. For the West it is the

seed of a new culture, which, through the direct experience of
the individual, can solve the fundamental problems of
uncertainty, mediocrity and insignificance, the roots of boredom,
frustration and despair.

The teaching admits nothing to be true except that which is. It
has no beliefs. It hands out no crutches. It cites no authority but
the truth itself. It dissolves and dissolves until nothing remains
but what is true; and that is direct experience. It is the teaching
and practice of self-discovery.

The level of penetration is different for each individual. But
the levels do overlap enabling one to learn from hearing
another's penetration – one of the advantages of the group
device. A person's emotional condition is most commonly
externalised by the questions he asks. These are the verbalisation
of his pain to know, the problem standing between him and the
immediate truth, his self doubt, his profound aching discontent.

The emotion behind such a question identifies the person's
congestion point, the weak spot, where a penetration can and
must be made. The penetration seemingly is done by words. But
in reality it is all done by the exchange of energy and particularly
through the teacher's Self-realised presence. For a moment the
questioner can "know" what he "knows" – what he has always
known but could not realise until now.

This is a moment of direct experience before he falls back
again into the confusion of his mind, emotions and his world.
There he will find another question, another lump of
complicating, emotional mind-stuff for decongesting. But with
perseverance and the right teacher he will become stiller and
stiller. And finally through stillness, he may realise Consciousness
so that every question, every doubt, is eliminated, not by
suppression, belief or avoidance, but by the power of self-
knowledge and understanding.

Three months later I abandoned the idea of the School for the West of
Self-realisation and in October 1977 started a small teaching and meditation group in our home using the same principles and method.

I was beginning to turn away from the Eastern idea of using capital S
for higher Self. I'd seen that the correct Western word was Being and that
the only self was the troublemaker and spoiler in everyone's life. It took

time for this to formulate fully in my teaching. But for some time I'd been avoiding using Eastern words except one or two like *karma* for which, from lack of right perception, there might seem to be no Western equivalent. To me the correct Western definition for karma was "repetition of the past which has not been consciously faced" – a rather clumsy but meaningful description of the reality behind the word.

All this obviously was a largely unconscious process, paralleling my conscious declarations that I was Master of the West. It seemed to me there had to be a precise Anglo-Saxon word for every mystical experience in the spiritual life and it was up to me to find it. Yet there appeared to be an almost unbroken tradition among Western teachers to have had Eastern masters and to pepper their teachings with Eastern terms. To me, Eastern terms in the spiritual life are not a part of our Western cultural experience and therefore do not communicate the living meaning of the word.

Among the first of those to attend the teaching and meditation meetings was Peter Kingsley, a very serious young man who was studying classical philosophy at Cambridge University. He'd been at some of my earlier meetings, loved what he heard and stayed and served me for seven years. There were the two avant-garde artists of the time, Peter Dockley and Peter Kuttner, and later Clive Tempest, Oxford graduate and former manager of the arty Round House Theatre in Chalk Farm. After 25 years (at the time of writing) Clive is still with me, having served me and the dissemination of the teaching more than any other. There was David White and Richard Osband, who had undertaken to organise the meetings each week, as well as various new people, including women, who came and went until we numbered about 15 each meeting.

Because the weekly meetings were relatively small, I was able to teach the people present personally. My method was to ask each one, 'What are you feeling?' or 'What do you feel?' – a device to get them into their body. It is remarkable the difficulty people have in answering this question. It's because the mind and emotions are not still. The mind is used to responding from the imagination, memory or feelings rather than from the fact. The fact behind the question is the body. And most people are out of their bodies and in their heads.

The next difficulty is the self, the emotional centre in everyone that gets in the way of the intelligent perception of what's happening in the body. The self, with its constant habitual consideration of the emotions, deflects the attention on to itself and a false reading or answer results. Often there is simply confusion in the person and the answer, 'I don't know.'

It takes a good deal of time to get out of the head, out of the emotions and into the body. But we persevered and the individuals who attended regularly, and even those who came only for a time, announced that they'd discovered a greater stillness in themselves. There were also evenings when people suddenly had deep insights and realisations which they joyfully recounted to the group.

In between, I would take the group into the silence of meditation. This silence varies in each individual. True inner silence is the absence of mental and emotional activity and that depends on the attention being focused wholly and uninterruptedly in the body until nothing arises. I encouraged questions and gradually imparted the difference between right questions and intellectual questions, the latter being those that came from the head (what the individual had heard and read) and not from his or her own experience.

I also had many realisations while meditating with the group. One day David dropped in and I said to him, 'I think I love my fellow man.' The knowledge of this love continued to increase in me and of course it's the very basis of what moves me from within to teach. I love the people, not the public. The people are real to me; each is an individual conscious-ness whereas the public is a collective statistical thing. Anyway, there was a meeting the night following my comment to David and after the meeting I wrote this:

THE BODY DIAMOND OR
THE BODHIDHARMA NIRVANA REALISATION

Still the Blessed One retreats
And beckons me towards the Diamond Man
The incorruptible body of day and night
His.
Then,
Through the Eye of Consciousness
I enter
A wisp of world

A garden
A paradise
An Eden
Truly a State where Nothing dies
In the fullness of Love.
Then,
The understanding that this is the Body of my Fellow Man!
Behind the brilliant diamond point
That only love of Him can bear, or dare, to enter.
And yet,
Not mine, but Man's love it is that has reduced me to the
worthiness to love
For who loves who – and who is who
When in the Body of Mankind there is only I?
I am Blessed beyond all knowing except in the knowing of
blessedness
That I am loved by Him – who I am.
This is the final humbling
To be loved by such a One as He
An unendurable delight, Ananda
That I can hardly bear
And yet, to not bear it is to not deserve it
Impossible!
For such Blessedness is no gift, no reward,
But the *means* of Love,
The diadem of Power Unearthly
Untouchable by human longing
Set in laurel-leaf upon the head
The Diamond Dew-point
The Jewel in the Crown of
Divine Consciousness.

Years after writing the *Bodhidharma Nirvana Realisation* I was astonished to learn that a Buddhist named Bodhidharma had actually lived in
the sixth century. He is considered the 28th Indian Patriarch in a direct
line from Gautama Buddha and credited with the establishment of Zen
Buddhism. I know that my realisation was the same as his realisation of
Nirvana.

The Diamond Body realisation was of course an inner restatement of the love of my fellow man.

Years later I recalled a poem that hung permanently in the classroom when I was a boy of 11 or 12 in sixth class at Double Bay State School. We had to learn the poem off by heart. Entitled *Abou Ben Adhem*, it was by the English poet Leigh Hunt (1784–1859), a poet of what's called the "Romantic School", and a friend of Shelley and Keats. "Romantic" is a term used to describe the poets of that period whose works were characterised by an emphasis on inner (probably spiritual) perceptions, rather than the traditional objective classical forms. Here's the poem, still memorised although perhaps imperfectly:

> Abou Ben Adhem, may his tribe increase,
> Awoke one night from a deep dream of peace,
> And saw within the moonlight in his room,
> Making it rich like a lily in bloom,
> An angel writing in a book of gold.
> Exceeding peace had made Ben Adhem bold,
> And to the presence in the room he said,
> 'What writest thou?' The vision raised its head,
> And with a look made of all sweet accord,
> Answered, 'The names of those who love the Lord.'
> 'And is mine one?' said Abou. 'Nay, not so,'
> Replied the angel. 'Then pray write me
> As one who loves his fellow men.'
> The angel wrote and vanished. The next night
> It came again with a great wakening light,
> And showed the names whom love of God had blessed.
> And lo! Ben Adhem's name led all the rest.

The night after the Diamond Body realisation, there was a most unexpected sequel, an amazing (to me, anyway) revelation. I went to the typewriter and wrote this:

> And more about this Diamond Man that all will enter…
> Enthroned He is in the beauty of the earth and
> In man where there is no more longing for the world.

And so it has been rightly said that the earth is his footstool
To which may be added: and the world is his maya (illusion).
He is the earth being
The One Man behind all.

I then started to have a vision as I wrote:

I can see him now on his throne. I'm vaguely uneasy because
I know he should be in his throne, not on it. Then I see he is
sitting on a crudely made wooden stool – motionless,
immovable, meditating. This surprises me mildly for why would
the Lord of All be meditating? His face I cannot see, nor his body
– but I have the knowing it is so. Does he ever not meditate? I
do not know. This is the first time I have seen him. And he is
meditating. He is absorbed. He must be sustaining me – and you.
Perhaps he meditates forever. I shall find out, for this is the Lord.
And I am in his world or state of love and beauty. But here at
this point I am knowing that there is something wrong –
mechanicalness. Whatever I am seeing is almost... no, I must not
say it for it cannot be... I must look away and fill myself with
more beauty and love by holding the Diamond Point of Being.
But what I have been knowing is true and now I see fully what I
have been looking at. It is an enormous meditating Buddha-like
figure. It is not the Lord at all. It is the purely mental image of
the Lord built up in the human mind by billions of religiously
misguided men and women over the millennia. The vision has
also revealed the error of men, priests and monks, who have
seen this sight before me and perpetuated it as truth in the minds
of their fellow man. They are responsible for the misleading
physical manifestation of this image in the many towering statues
of the meditating Buddha in the East; statues whose huge size
dwarfs the boys and men meditating around them. The image is
in man's mind forever; it is the Sleeping Giant of spiritual
ignorance. It cannot be awakened. It must be dissolved in men's
minds by truth and being. That is the task.

Later I added this observation:

The extraordinary thing was that I was in the Diamond Body
consciousness, that radiant centre of Being, when I saw this

tremendous figure that men have erected as a sort of God, a thing that has no good in it and yet seems posited in the most good state. In my description it can be clearly seen where I became aware that "something" was wrong. And the "wrongness" was that no mind-form or any form at all can exist in the exalted state; for existence there is impossible. The existence of the mind-form had the effect of creating my own existence and this enabled me to perceive the image while still in the divine consciousness. I felt smaller than the image – it towered above me in massive dimensions. But contrasts like big and small are only possible where there is mind. In the formless divine consciousness there is no position, no place, just sheer beauty. That's how I knew the image was false.

I also know now that there are other Sleeping Giants in man's subconscious. The form they take depends on the religious figure to which he has devoted himself and his pious imagination. Billions of worshippers have built up in the mind such delusionary images of Jesus or Christ; and of Mohammed and other religious founders. When they see these images they think it is the real thing. But the real thing has no image.

Julie's mother had left her an antique brass replica of a ship's anchor. The shank was about 18 inches long with the rest in finely crafted proportion. It decorated a corner of the lounge room where the weekly meditation meetings were held. Pointing to the anchor, I told the group, 'It's a symbol to remind you of the golden anchor inside each one of you. The golden anchor is your intelligence and it has to be fixed on your senses. While you're anchored to your senses you will not think or be troubled by your emotional self. Most people anchor themselves to their judgmental and impressionable self and so live a life of uncertainty and ups and downs.'

A year after starting the meditation meetings with the core group I was still trying to get a Centre established. My transcendental realisation had revealed that I was producing nothing and now I saw that, in the world, producing nothing translated into my doing nothing. Whatever needed to be done had to be done for me. I wrote:

Through divine grace I have been given a great power of stillness behind all my actions. Yet I can do "less" than I could do even a month ago. The more spiritual power I receive the less I can do. The key to this mystery is that my fellow man now has to do whatever needs to be done for me. My function is to hold the power and to do nothing more than bring the truth into the world. Although the Diamond Centre [which I had realised, above] is already operating and very clear in my consciousness, its physical manifestation depends on those men and women who form the inner circle. They are really psychical and spiritual forces, not individual people. If those in the circle do not bring the Centre about, do not do the work, they will drop away. And righter and more developed individuals who are ready to serve their fellow man will replace them.

I have tried several of the men in the group and all except one has backed off, possibly without even knowing it. The responsibility is too heavy for them, too testing of their love. David White, who in many ways is the most formally backward, serves like a true Bodhisattva (one who according to the Buddhist philosophy refuses to leave the world until every man is free). He gives his time and energies freely, interviewing me once or twice a week, coming down 35 miles from his home in addition to meeting nights, transcribing the tapes in longhand and bringing the texts back for correction.

There are no other Bodhisattvas in the group. They are a selfish lot. What I wait for forever, without any sense of waiting, is for the Bodhisattvas to say, 'How can I help you to serve my fellow man? I will do anything to help towards his search for his Self.' [In those days, as I've explained, I used to use the Eastern concept of self and Higher Self, which I no longer do. Today self is problematical self and 'Higher Self' is simply Being.] The power that has been given to me will bring or reveal the Bodhisattvas who are to be the radials of my Centre; they will know that through the Centre they can truly serve their fellow man. Come, my Bodhisattvas, come.

Well, they emerged and they came, and today at the time of writing, more than 20 years later, due to the loving service of these many men and women, the Centre is now an international charitable Foundation and has organised my seminars in Europe, America and Australia and book and tape sales worldwide; with a devoted permanent staff and many equally devoted people round the world serving organisationally.

At this point I'll mention an interesting aside relating to three of the original group, David White, Peter Kingsley and Peter Kuttner, all of whom feature in parts of this autobiography. In such a book as this, the question always is whether to use actual names and whether to be completely honest about how I saw people and events without considering feelings and thus compromising. Years later, each of these three men gave me some strong advice on the question.

David wrote, 'Tell it straight. No names changed to "protect the guilty". No being nice to anyone! And let's have as much as possible – you can't assume that some autobiographical details are not suitable for general consumption. If the story is to be told you have to tell it all, however strange; or if you want to miss out something then you have to say so.'

Peter Kingsley wrote, 'The real question about the autobiography is whether you (and those around you) can dare to face the embarrassment it would arouse. Can you be honest enough to expose yourself, or must you consider your "reputation"?'

Peter Kuttner wrote, 'Is it wise to protect anyone in a book of truth?'

I trust that when they read this book they are all satisfied.

# CHAPTER 37

# THE BOY MYSTIC

In July 1977, Julie's son Mark was nearly 16 and going through a hard time. He wrote me a letter from Brighton filled with misery and lamenting his failures. He wasn't getting on with his dad or step-mother, despite their sincere efforts. He wanted to leave home and quit school and they wouldn't let him. He was in darkness, he said, and had lost all his knowledge of truth. He wanted to be free more than anything else but didn't know what to do.

I wasn't surprised by all this since I knew that, apart from everything else, for months he'd been frequenting a dodgy nightclub in Brighton that allowed teenagers in. God knows what the youngsters got up to there. The following is my reply to Mark:

> The way to truth and light is through the darkness you are in. Your previous writings have revealed that the truth and light is there – a remarkable thing in one so young. But the vital force of puberty, which I referred to in a poem I wrote you when you were 14, has obscured your vision. I shall try to explain what is happening to you.
>
> You are becoming a man, as the spirit, or the truth and light, strives to become man. This becoming is what we call the

struggle of humanity and living. The man who wants – even his freedom – is not free and never will be. Man becomes free by containing the wayward self, the wanter, which yearns for an impossible freedom.

There is only this world, Mark, and there are no free spirits in it. But there are a few free men. And these men, by having contained their wayward self while in the darkness you are in, have made their body/energy system abstract enough to be, and not to want. To be, is to be free – now! – a state you cannot know until you can "hold" and dissolve the wayward self.

This is being done for you by an awe-ful and inscrutable process with which you are now familiar as the circumstances of your life. You are being made to locate the energy of that truth and light within you, to absorb it and become one with it so that in manhood – your spiritual flowering – you can turn and serve your fellow man who will be stumbling through the same wearying darkness.

I have a great part in your misery. I am one of the lead players. The only difference is I know why it is being done. You are no poor suffering boy to me; but while you suffer rightly and persevere, I love you indeed. I am always here for you to phone.

I am not interested in your failures because you cannot fail, not while you persevere rightly. All the apparent going backwards is part of the process. It is true you can go mad, you can die, but that only means you were not up to it; and someone else will come along and do the job for you. You are working for Life, Mark, not for yourself. You cannot know this yet. But I who do know say, get on with it, you can do it; I am with you every moment.

Barry

Five months later, just before Christmas 1977, Mark phoned in deep distress from Brighton. He'd left home and had been living in a squat for months. Julie and I drove down and he was in a bad way. His clothes were filthy, his hair lank, long and dirty, his face thin and pale with strain and anxiety.

'Can I come and live with you, please?'

'Yes.'

So we popped him in the car, picked up his few belongings and moved him into our spare room.

Mark hadn't had a good start as a boy. His mother had left him; he didn't get on well with his stepmother or her child, and he'd been through years of the trauma of the break up of the family. Also, he was a 1960s child: he was fascinated by the drug and squat culture; his heroes were the obscure and funky musicians of the day and dubious hippy story-tellers who glorified drugs and dropping out.

At 14, as with other kids of his age, he was up at sun up picking and eating magic mushrooms. I don't know that he ever took hard drugs. Before he left home, he'd been falling behind in his school studies because of lack of concentration (probably due to the pot he was smoking) and his father and stepmother almost despaired of him. His teachers had sufficient faith in him to call in his father for a round-table conference to see if anything could be done, as they could do no more.

In her diary, Julie recorded our picking up of Mark thus:

> Jonathan came with Barry and me to see his older brother in a squat. Jonathan had not seen Mark for months. Mark said, 'Hello' then quickly spoke to Barry about a spiritual experience he'd had. I noticed Jonathan was trying not to cry. I asked him if he knew why; Jonathan said he did not. Barry turned to Jonathan and said, 'Stand up. Now put your arms around Mark and hug him.' They stood really hugging each other. Jonathan was so joyous that he had made contact with Mark. To this day Mark says he always touches Jonathan when life has kept them apart. Some people communicate love easily. Some like Ken love but cannot show it; they become aloof and forget how to love. People really fear love.

Under all Mark's thirst for hippy experience, he was the most spiritually aware youth I'd met. He had been exposed to my teaching since he was five. His writings and poetry written during the pre-pubescent years from 12 to 14 had amazing depth and insight. Even so, I put one condition on his coming to live with us. I would have him only as my full-time student. He was to agree to obey me in all matters, not out of threat or compulsion, but out of a desire to solve his problems for himself under my guidance. He agreed readily. And only later did I realise that I had enrolled my first and one and only student in what I'd thought was the defunct Children's School of Philosophic Development and Understanding of Studies – and a full-time boarder at that!

In a note I wrote:

> With all boys, when the sex energy of puberty comes through
> at around 14, a deep subconscious disturbance occurs which
> continues until 17 or 18. This is the energy of independence,
> rebellion and breaking away. In a spiritually orientated and
> spiritually conditioned boy like Mark, only spiritual discipline
> and justice can do the job of preparing him to cope with the
> world in a normal way and to continue living the spiritual life. A
> boy who is conditioned by worldly values needs only worldly
> teachers and worldly discipline. Mark is spiritually innocent in
> that he is free of attachment to judgment, the judgment of others.
> If he is able to keep his innocence he may be a new generation
> helper of others caught in the same evolutionary hiatus as he
> himself was. If he cannot remain innocent he will leave and live
> an ordinary, self-perpetuating, uncreative, continuously
> frustrating and largely useless life.

We enrolled Mark at the local state school to finish his A Levels (final exams at school) but he didn't complete the course. The damage to the scholar in him had been done. I wrote:

> I teach him the fact about study and he sees it. I urge him (as
> I do in the spirit) to constant awareness of his failure to apply
> himself sufficiently and intelligently to the task of catching up.
> But I'm afraid it's a pretty hopeless task from the academic point
> of view.

After 15 months it was evident that at school he was merely going through the motions. So we let him quit. As he showed signs of being a writer, I had him taught how to touch-type before he started work in a recording studio in London. I wrote:

When he leaves I will have dissolved most of his destructive past karma which he brought with him. But I cannot dissolve his future karma; that is, what he must face as his unique individual life, for that is life. Mark's problem is he's trapped in an aural culture. He is a worshipper of sound. Ten years of living will be needed to reach a karmic point equal to his inner development. I suspect that the moment he leaves my space he will make no more spiritual progress. But that's okay. If he can ever finish with the aural culture, which is a sort of reflexive worship of the primitive in man, he will once more go forward and perhaps be a divine teacher.

Spiritually, however, his progress was spectacular. He attended the weekly meditation meetings and at one meeting, just before he left us, reported that his mind had stopped, that he had realised space or clarity.

This is an exceptional realisation for anyone – when it is permanent. It happened to me in 1961. I was staying overnight in a motel in Melbourne in connection with my public relations job. I sat down in the darkened room to meditate. Suddenly, it was there, extraordinary clarity and stillness of mind. Whereas before there had always been some sort of movement in my mind, now there was none. It was as though I was alone in deepest cosmic space. It was pristine. Here, I saw, nothing ever moved or happened. Then, in the same space and stillness, I was presented with an image. I was looking at a sort of flat moonscape dotted with small rocks. Under each rock I knew there was an eternal idea. If I lifted up one rock and saw the idea, and returned to the same rock in a thousand years, the idea would be there precisely the same, untouched, unchanged. The meaning was that in this sublime space there was no movement of mind to develop or expand the idea; here the idea was perfect as it was, forever.

As pleasing as Mark's realisation was to me, I wrote at the time:

Mark is sloppy in his body. He is physically undisciplined as youth apparently must be. He is wonderfully obedient to me. I could not ask for a finer student. He is surrendered to the truth and the truth he has discovered and made his own is remarkable.

He is strong and can talk unselfconsciously and straight. I do give him some terrible verbal moments when his physical and emotional slackness or unconscious unconcern about what he is doing becomes too evident in my space.

Mark wrote me this poem:

O SACRED SAGE

O Sacred Sage
Your sound
Your very being
Haunts
My burning soul,
Heralding my every step,
Through lost wilderness.
I search
For a place
Where the travellers meet
And you sit
In patient solitude, waiting.
Please,
Wait for me (I shall arrive)
Wait till I clasp
The wings of your words
And soar
Up!
O Sage
I love you.
I see you
I sense you
I know you
And yet
You are alien (to me)
I long to be with you
And yet
I'm afraid.
You excite me
depress me

cleanse and confuse me
And yet –
Then –
I am not worthy.
I love you.
You are sacred.


Mark lived with us for 21 months, until just before his 18th birthday in 1979. At a Wednesday night meeting on his 19th birthday he had another astonishing spiritual experience. I asked him to write it down. His account is so clear and profound that I include a substantial part of it here as a description of a mystical state induced by Mark's devotion to the truth and to me. Mark wrote:

> The group went into meditation. I immediately became aware of the "nothing", the state of infinite clarity of mind, as God. This, in a glorious past moment, I had known before [when his mind had stopped]. However, the experience of God had long since digressed to a constant awareness of something I had become accustomed to name the "nothing".
>
> In my meditation I noticed that although I was experiencing a strong awareness of the space around me as God, I was not surrendered to it: I was not "one with it". It (God) was simply there and I saw that I was indulging in thoughts and trivia without losing that awareness. Taking it for granted perhaps. I was appalled by this. I yearned to surrender to the divine space totally. The thought came in, 'Take me. Take me.' This desire expressed as thought, however, had no direct effect that I could perceive. I stopped thought.
>
> Somehow, through an indescribable process, I found myself opening, letting go to the divine mind; allowing it to consume my being. This was a motion which had to be continuously re-affirmed; not a single action but a repeated one.
>
> As I surrendered each blockage as it came into view so the divine space of God would consume my body, more and more. (Certain knotted areas in my being had to be informed of what was happening, so it seems. I would give up one and another would float up to the surface. I dissolved each as it came, one at a time.) The nothing seemed to be moving down the body from

the head, where I had only known it before, virtually erasing the body as it sank. It stopped at the stomach and would not go further. Some part of my being, I knew, remained unsurrendered. A sinew of attachment still had life. At the time I saw it as my life, the very need to live. The desire for life was refusing God's entrance. I found this despairing. I came out of meditation.

My eyes were open. I looked ahead and closed them again. Again the words, 'Take me. Take me.' This time I declared before God, 'I will die for you.' I had the sensation that my body was shrivelling. My head was swaying and falling back (leaving my throat exposed as a dog might offer himself to his fighting opponent in defeat, I see as an afterthought). I felt I was some diminishing, punctured inflatable doll. I so desperately yearned to be wholly consumed by the sweet space, so absolutely, that I was prepared to die for it. This, it seems, is the only path God can take into a man's heart. That path can be blocked by the finest sinew of attachment to the world or even life itself. The swaying, shrivelling sensation continued. I felt desperate. Still the words, 'Take me. Take me. I want to die. I yearn to die, if only to be with you.' This I truly felt. Again, near to tears, I came out of meditation.

I paused, breathed and closed my eyes once more. My attention was immediately focused on my fingertips. Sensation was leaving them. The death of sensation seemed to be creeping up both arms simultaneously. I did not experience even a numbness where sensation had been, absolutely nothing. Death in my fingertips, wrists and arms. Shaken by this and unable to push it any further (as I wanted to but could not contrive such a thing) I came out of meditation for the third time.

I opened my eyes. I looked down at my body. It was golden; brilliant. It was a golden body. I was the golden body. I am the golden body. I saw that the shrivelling sensation had been the shedding of my old body; as a caterpillar might shed its skin to emerge as a beautiful butterfly. I sighed deeply. A sigh swept like a cooling breeze through my whole being. Eventually every breath was a sigh. I was trembling with the impact.

I have never used the word "energy" before since I had never truly perceived "energy". Although the direct experience or vision of the Golden Body has passed, its energy remains. I write

this the following evening and am still aware of the energy
working in and on me. Today I have felt it rumbling through my
body in waves. In moments I have heard my own voice as
another would hear it; strange it sounded. Following a television
play has been impossible: I heard each word only as it was
uttered and could not piece two together. Someone greeted me,
'Hello Mark'. I was shocked to hear myself respond. I had
assumed that 'Hello Mark' meant simply 'hello'. I could not relate
to my own name.

I do not understand or know the meaning of all this.
Apparently it had been in the experience of Barry, even given
the same name by him some years ago, "The Golden Body". This
I was not aware of at the time, nor ever had been, yet I choose
to use it, the only possible term to describe what I had seen, to
the group soon after the experience. The gold figures of Buddha
one sees on postcards from India come to mind. Previously I had
seen them as extravagant idols; now I understand – the Golden
Body of Buddha.

Three days ago I was reading the first section of Barry's
autobiography. Reading of his experiences left me in a state of
deep concern over my own lack of seriousness towards the truth.
I felt saddened by my youthful frivolousness, my weaknesses
and insufficient self-denial; the ugliness of indulgence. Later I lay
in bed pondering this. Fleeting images of Barry came into my
mind: little scenes from the past of him talking to me on the
stairs; coming through the kitchen door… etc. I knew or felt it
was all over. It had all been a dream and I was waking. I felt far
greater sadness for the loss of Barry; one I love so much as my
master-teacher.

My hands clasped across my chest seemed to be sinking into
my body. I felt a sensation of disintegration, my body dissolving.
For a moment it occurred to me that I was dying, physically. This
I felt had to be why I felt it was finished and Barry was gone; it
had not been a dream. The moment passed and I fell asleep,
thinking nothing of it when I awoke.

I know now that I love God. I did not know before. The
energy of the Golden Body has passed into a constant
knowledge and awareness of divine love. This is not something I
know in my mind or head; my whole body knows it, every cell

of my being. About a year ago I realised the presence of God in my head as infinite crystal-clear space; the universe; the nothing. This I knew with absolute certainty had always been there and always would. Through ignorance and thought I had lost sight of it. It has never left since the moment I first noticed it. I know it never can. I did not however know divine love. I could never utter the words, 'I love God.' The Golden Body experience has slowly strained God's love through my being. I know it is there. I know divine love... it is inseparable, undying. It is and can never not be. What more can I say? It is wordless.

And what happened to the boy mystic? How did his adult life turn out? Mark said that following a suggestion from me he had worked originally at MENCAP, a charity serving the mentally handicapped in London. He enjoyed this and saw that to earn more he needed a qualification so he went to Bristol University for a two year course of training as a social worker. He finished the course in 1991, aged 30, and then worked as a social worker specialising in child protection cases. At age 37 he was still occupied with this work in a responsible position and had two children with his partner. The job was stressful and involved dealing with chaotic lives and sometimes he faced threats of violence.

Is Mark fulfilling his youthful promise? To me, he is. No full time activity is more worthy than endeavouring to ease the misery of suffering humanity; there is no greater love. But it has its inevitable strains and one of them for Mark, he says, is that he has little or no time or energy to read or be with himself. That often seems to be the price of service – for a while. Perhaps in later life he will be a writer of significance.

And Jonathan, Mark's brother, nearly four years his junior – how did he make out? Jonathan had far less exposure to me than Mark, although while Julie was alive he would spend weekends and part of his holidays with us and with Mark. A steady Taurean, he didn't have Mark's experimental nature. When Mark was rebelling against the family life and getting into squats and bad company, Jonathan stayed close to home with Ken and his stepmother Anne.

And did Jonathan manifest any spiritual leanings? I'm told that in his early 20s he went to see a visiting American Evangelist and that night gave himself to Jesus. Jonathan evidently threw himself into the more extreme charismatic form of Christian revivalism and joined the Christian Outreach Centre, a worldwide movement founded in 1974 in Australia with centres in over 30 countries. He became pastor of one of those centres which he set up in Sussex. In a surprise letter to me in January 1998 he said he wanted to tell me that he now found himself married to a beautiful wife, with two young sons and was the leader of a 'vibrant, spirit-filled church.' Apparently he had been in Australia with the Outreach Centre and had tried unsuccessfully to reach me. He said he would very much like to hear from me again, if I wished to contact him, as, he said, 'Time is urgently running out!' And so I replied:

> Greetings Jonathan,
>
> I was very pleased to receive your letter; also to hear that you appear to have found your role in the Christian Outreach movement. I note that you have started your own church, which I presume is dedicated to helping others. Where I come from there is no greater love than to endeavour to ease the misery of suffering humanity, and if you are doing this then it is indeed blessed work – a suitable outcome of your mother's love of God and dedication to the truth, until her death. I've also been told that Mark is engaged in a most admirable occupation that follows his dedication to the spiritual life as he lived it with me in his youth – helping to alleviate the pain and damage in abused children and endeavouring to help families cope with their chaotic lives. Again a reflection of the spiritual life lived by his mother.
>
> Barry

I'm not sure what Jonathan meant about 'time urgently running out'. But I have heard that there's an apocalyptic edge to the Church's teaching. This is not surprising to me, as mystical experience can often invoke a knowledge that the end is not far away. In 1984 I wrote and recorded an audio tape in my *Myth of Life* series, called *The End of the World*. I had originally entitled it *A Prayer for Life*, which it is, but the apocalyptic significance was so strong in me that at the last minute I changed the title. My knowledge was not inspired by any organisational or traditional doctrine but by my own mystical profundity. Perhaps the truth behind the end of the world is my own death.

# CHAPTER 38

# THE ORIGINS BOOK

A s the 1970s were coming to a close the Centre started to emerge, fuelled by the new found energy and dedication of the core group. Peter Kingsley came forward to run the Centre full-time. I suggested that he do a rapid touch-typing course and when this was completed I taught him how to write simply; this enabled me to farm out to him some of my astrology writing work which provided him with an income for several years.

When Peter had first joined me he was the typical angry young man. He wanted the truth more than anything else in his life. He had no time for trivia or people who peddled it. He was a voracious scholar. Although working for his doctorate in Classical Greek philosophy he was rebelliously contemptuous of his tutors and their lack of understanding of what the ancient Greek philosophers were actually saying. Peter was literally fluent in ancient Greek and he would explain to me from the original texts of philosophers like the fifth century B.C. Empedocles (his favourite sage) where the accepted official translations and the views of his mentors were wrong. In his Thesis he was supposed to observe the official line but Peter insisted on trying to do it his way. The result was he gave up in disgust and decided to abandon his Thesis.

I stepped in. I said he was being foolish and the important thing was for him to get the Doctorate by compromising where he knew he had to.

I told him that one day he would write books and that he would have much more chance of getting his ideas across, and perhaps changing the official line, if he had won the magical "Dr" and the appropriate letters after his name.

Peter worked hard to catch up and deliver the goods. But it was somewhat too late. He was awarded an M.Litt. (Master of Letters), which is second rate to a Doctorate. Later he continued his studies and today, Dr Peter Kingsley, with several suitable letters after his name, is a renowned worldwide authority on ancient Greek philosophy, the author of a massive tome published by Oxford University Press, an esteemed lecturer in his field and author of many papers. I'd expressed the hope to him that he would one day write a book in popular language for ordinary people, explaining the truths of the ancients that he'd discovered. That seems to have happened in 1999 with the publication of Peter's book *In the Dark Places of Wisdom: The Forgotten Origins of the Western World*. From an extract someone sent me, it is a simply written and relatively easy to understand masterly work. I'm waiting to see if Peter ever interrupts his focus on dead masters to write a book about his own years with a living master who changed his life in so many ways and reflected to him in his own experience, in the present, much of the truth of the ancients of the past.


It was now 1979 and I was well into writing my major work *The Origins of Man and the Universe: The Myth that Came to Life* which engaged all my spare time for the next four years. In that work I describe in detail the Seven Levels of Mind which is the spiritual "structure" behind all earth existence. In the book I say also that in all ages (at the deep unconscious level) the body or reality of humankind is empowered to select a man to be surrogate for all men in realising the central idea of the earth – the Earth Being at Level Seven – and the six other levels of existence. This man is to report back everything he discovers, thus ensuring that the truth and knowledge of the idea never leave the world of living men and women.

The Earth Spirit, or Being at Level Seven, is of course identical with the Diamond Man that I had written about previously. The two are simply perceptions of the One from different angles. But I didn't make that connection until years later when I opened my file referring to that time. The similarity can be seen from my description in the *Origins* book of the Being at Level Seven:

> It is experienced as pure, glorious spirit, perfection, the heavenly Lord of the blessed earth and the one body of humanity where no other exists. It is apperceived as paradise, a literal garden of Eden identical in one single Being with all man's most rapturous moments of love of nature combined: as he has ever smelled, heard, tasted, seen and felt the earth to be in all its fullness. Except that here the fullness is realised as a single unified Being free from differentiation into sense objects like trees, clouds, sea, sky and creatures which in manifested nature inspire man's wonder and love.

Peter Kingsley spent many hours a day with me helping to edit and arrange the *Origins* book. We worked together on it for about three years. It took time because I was writing from deep inspiration and after the first chapter the sections were like essays on different aspects of the truth of life, and our task was to put them together into a cohesive whole. Peter loved the work, especially when I would write almost the same words to describe something that Empedocles or one of the other ancient sages had seen. He spent so much time working with me that Julie once said that I was more fond of being with him than her. Peter did love me. And he loved Julie. He was so passionate about surrendering everything to the master that he wrote a note giving me all his savings in the event of his death. When he left me for good in 1984 I handed him back the note saying, 'You might need this.' He'd forgotten it.

I have in front of me a letter from Peter dated the 27th of February 1982. Julie and I were in Australia for a couple of months and Peter was very busy editing (and trying to make sense of) the latter section of the first draft of the *Origins* text. He wrote:

Those 17 pages of *Approach to Reality* that you gave me
before you left – I just can't get through the last four or five of
them!

After reading the first few pages I had an incredible
realisation. A bit later in the same day I passed through Death –
or rather Death came to me and passed through me. And I saw
what death is. The secret of death is so extraordinary that no one
– not I or anyone – could ever have thought it up, but once you
do see it, it's so incredibly obvious – that's why it's so
extraordinary – and it agrees exactly with what you Barry have
been saying and writing for years. It's so crazy that nobody
would understand it except apparently someone who is dying…

After such an experience and realisation it's so obvious how
worthwhile – as ever – your writing is. The energy is in it, even if
the words are difficult to understand, or impossible…

When the *Origins* manuscript was finished in 1983 I told the Centre we
needed to get it accepted by a well known publisher. The group
response was that that would probably be difficult with such a work and
why not publish it ourselves? I said that as a new teaching we needed
the recognition of a respected publishing house.

We engaged a literary agent whose friend happened to be an editor at
Routledge and Kegan Paul, London, a long established publisher of psy-
cho-spiritual works and philosophers including Gurdjieff and C. G. Jung.
After reading the manuscript the editor said, 'This book has to be published.' And publish she did. There was a slight catch. Five thousand
copies were to be printed of which the Centre would buy 3,000 copies at
£2 each – £6,000 up front! I appealed to the group members for interest
free loans; we raised the money overnight and had paid it all back in less
than 12 months.

Within two years the publishers RKP had disappeared, absorbed into
one of the international conglomerates that were changing the face of
publishing at that time. The *Origins* book was "remaindered" and sold in
bargain bookshops for a quarter of its cover price – a practice that now
seems to have become the custom among the world's few big remaining
publishing companies. But I'd got what I wanted – published by RKP.

The group had become more and more active and devoted to getting me and the teaching out to more people. I told them that first I wanted to take the truth to the undergraduates at Cambridge and Oxford universities, the traditional seats of learning in the Western world, because the undergraduates were the decision-makers of tomorrow. Our university men warned me that there was not likely to be much interest as the universities attracted intellectuals. I said, 'Well, what about all of you?' They said, 'We came to you of our own accord.'

'Anyway,' I said, 'put on a couple of meetings at both universities.' Peter Kuttner designed the posters and Peter Kingsley did the organising and distribution of 120 posters in both town centres well before the meetings. So up we went to Oxford for two evening meetings and then up to Cambridge the following month.

Flop! Flop! After three months of intensive organising and widespread postering on the many college notice boards, as well as in both town centres, we got an attendance of six both times. That was the end of my interest in taking the truth to universities.

CHAPTER 39

# MORE TO LIFE THAN THE MIND BELIEVES

I often used to wake at night and see strange objects and lifelike figures in the room. I became so used to seeing most of the apparitions that they were just like glancing at things during the day. I'd seen chandeliers, bunches of roses, little figures running across the room and even Mark, Julie's son, lying on his side looking at me while he was actually sleeping in the other room. These phenomena did not have an energetic presence that disturbed me like the others I've recounted. But they did serve to show that there is more to this life than the human mind believes.

In the early hours of one morning, Julie and I woke together and immediately I was on my knees on the bed, face to face with a glowing golden image. My first impression was that it was a girl or young boy. Then I realised the face had no features. The whole image of the head, hair and top of the torso was literally one undifferentiated mass of dripping gold. I thought it must be an angel, the solar angel perhaps, but at the same time I thought I didn't know what angels looked like. It was only 18 inches from my face. I knew I wanted to speak with it or it with me. There was something to be said but I couldn't say it. We faced each other for several seconds. Then it glided backwards, away. I held out my hand and beckoned to it, saying, 'Come here, come here.' But it gradually disintegrated.

Julie was watching. She said, 'You put out your hand, beckoned with your finger and said over and over, "Come here, come here", in that weird drawling voice you get when you speak to these things. There was nothing there.' This night Julie had not screamed. She'd just heard a "flutter". It was this "flutter" that announced to her in her sleep the coming or presence of a psychic energy. Many times she had heard it and sat up screaming but on many of those occasions I was unaffected and saw nothing. The presence of any psychic apparition disturbed Julie acutely, even though it seemed undoubtedly she was the medium of their appearance.

Julie's most tragically prophetic and terrifying vision happened one night in October 1978. She described it in a diary note and letter to Rita:

> I awoke shaking and trying to remember what had woken me on the left side of the bed. I was lying on my back with my eyes open. Then directly in front of me I saw a terrible thing – a torture cage of heavy iron bars reaching from the ceiling to the floor with equally heavy torture tools hanging over it. The wind I had been listening to before the apparition seemed to be wailing with suffering. I knew I had seen this cage many times before but never consciously like this.
>
> For years I had been saying to Barry I have this terrible idea I am going to be tortured at death. I felt it was my fate, that nothing could change it. I was so frightened and because the fear was so terrible, I just accepted it and to my amazement went through it. I lay there in complete acceptance. It amazed me that I could be so calm about something so awful.
>
> Barry turned over and I told him what I had seen. Normally I won't discuss the things I see as I cannot bear to think about them. I fell asleep almost immediately which was unusual, and awoke, it seemed, almost immediately. I found myself leaning over Barry. He was black with a very refined, terrifying, majestic appearance; powerful, supreme, unapproachable. The fear left after a while and I lay back down as soon as his appearance returned to normal.

CHAPTER 40

# NO GREATER LOVE

I n February 1980 Julie and I flew to Florida, USA, for six weeks. We were fed up with the cold and wet English weather and thought we'd investigate the possibility of living in that balmy southern state. It was the northern winter and when we arrived in Miami we were in short sleeves, a promising sign. But within a couple of weeks we discovered the draining humidity of tropical Florida and that for much of the year most of the residents lived in an air conditioned environment.

We were staying in a motel and Julie took some weight-reducing tablets. She didn't really need to, for she was slight of build with an attractive figure. But like many women in their late 30s she was concerned about keeping the weight off her thighs. The contents description of the American tablets showed that they were far stronger than was permitted in England. This pleased her since it suggested quick results.

And quick results indeed followed. Within an hour she was on the bed vomiting and sweating profusely. A similar reaction had happened when she took the Pill to ease her period pains at Friday Lane Cottage. Only this time the effect was more violent. After a few hours she settled down but the sweating continued. What follows is a transcript of how Julie described what happened next:

> I put my hand on my forehead and smelt the sweat. 'It's the smell of death,' I thought. This was because when my mother was dying I was kissing her forehead and I could smell something earthy in the sweat and knew it was death. I said to myself, 'Now smell this deeply,' which I did. I remember breathing it into me and I knew that if ever I smelt that again I would know for sure that that person was dying. There would be no doubt. That was my experience with my mother. In Florida, I put my hand with my own sweat on it against my nose and I smelt it and I said to you [Barry], I've smelt death sweat.

Years later I saw a period movie about Queen Elizabeth I. She was thought to be dying. Her physician bent over and smelled the sweat on her forehead. 'She's not dying,' he pronounced.

In a rented car we drove north looking for a less humid spot. This brought us into Georgia and looking at the map of the coastline we were confident we'd find a nice little beach and perhaps a suitable home. But Georgia was also humid. And the coastline, as far as we could discover, was all marshes. Up we went through Charleston, South Carolina, and it was cold. Over the border into North Carolina and it was snowing. So back to Miami we sped to see if we'd made a mistake about Florida. We hadn't. But we decided to make the most of the last week of our holiday in this very beautiful part of the USA with its white sandy beaches, pelicans and tropical flora – all facing the blue sea of the old Spanish Main.

One morning Julie was in bed having a cup of tea. She turned to me and said, 'Feel this. I think there's a lump in my breast.' There was, about the size of a pea, on the right side. We decided to have it examined immediately on our return to England.

Back in London, Julie had a biopsy. It showed positive: cancer. The doctors wanted to remove her breast. 'Never,' she said. 'I'd rather die.' They settled for a lumpectomy, the removal of the lump only – plus 12 cobalt radiation sessions and five electron machine treatments on the breast and the lymph gland in the right armpit. They also irradiated her ovaries to atrophy them and stop the production of oestrogen, a hormone said to be unfavourable for cancer sufferers. And that was without the radiation of innumerable X-rays. She suffered the usual radiation sickness of nausea and general malaise. The doctors were unable to say whether the cancer had been eliminated or not. It was a case of 'wait and see,' they said.

Not long after, her shoulder joint started to freeze up until it was agony for her to try to lift her arm. As far as I was concerned the radiologist in charge had fouled up. He overdosed her. Flesh is different, as people are different, but the medical profession does not seem to know that; so it was fire away as usual and don't consider the obvious consequences. Not everyone gets a frozen shoulder with this treatment. But what can you do when the medicos close ranks? I wrote to one of her other doctors pointing out that their treatments did not consider the whole body. He objected strongly but had nothing to say about the jelly and custard and other rubbish they allowed their patients to be fed in the hospitals. How it is today I don't know.

It didn't help matters that two days after Julie came home from hospital the woman next door, aged 36 with a boy of seven, died of cancer. And just before her homecoming a neighbour two doors down had died of a heart attack. Julie, watching the hearse drive out of Kingsley Place, commented impassively, 'Death always comes in threes. Mine will be next.' She was not the least pessimistic – just saying it as she saw it.

On another morning, as we got up, Julie looked out the window and down into the back garden. 'God,' she gasped, 'that's my grave.' It had been raining all night and a section of a garden bed had collapsed exposing a deep, long oblong trench. Symbols to her were part of the other world and she read them with uncanny accuracy.


I had written Julie a poem called *The Garden*, which meant much to her. Here it is in part:

>Come
>I will show you a garden
>Where nothing dies
>My respite for you
>When day is done.
>Come

I will take you with me
Hold my hand
My love.


Julie loved reading the celebrated English poets. I saw a bookclub ad for a special edition of poems by Byron, Keats and Shelley and sent away for it. I slipped a card inside saying:

> To Julie
>     My apologies for such a tawdry looking edition; the lottery of a bookclub choice, I fear. But please allow Byron to speak for me from the first page I chanced to open:
>
>> How beautiful she look'd! her conscious heart
>> Glow'd in her cheek—
>> Oh Love how perfect is thy mystic art...
>
>     He must have seen your smile
>     Barry


For my birthday in August, three months after her operation, she wrote on a card:

> No greater love has man than to lead the imperfect which was I into the garden of perfection where truly nothing dies – a promise you gave to me and you did not lie. The pain and terror of the earth destroyed my heart. So my soul could see in the darkest night. Always you are there and I shall never be alone, not even in death. The master takes his children home. Each day I wake, I listen, I hear and feel the quality of the garden. I am there, waiting. No greater love has man than to teach divine love. This you do. Thank you always.
>     Julia.


On New Year's Eve, after seeing she truly did not fear death, she wrote this poem:

I shall wait in the silence of my heart.
I shall rest in the peace of your (God's) touch.
I shall face the void with certain heart.
I shall wait for the voice of command.
I shall wait for I have been blessed and truly know.

On the bottom of the slip of paper I scribbled, 'If ever she died and I read her poem and remembered her sweet, pure God-like smile and loving devotion to her God, I'm sure my heart would break.'

In February 1981, to escape the worst of the English winter, I took Julie to Australia for a six week holiday. We stayed with my mother. Over the years both had mellowed and become dear friends. We spent a day with my cousin Judith who read our Tarot cards. The first card she turned up for Julie was the card of death. But then amazingly, in seeming contradiction, she turned up cards indicating a wonderful inheritance for Julie. Julie said, 'That makes sense. That's where I'm going, to my heavenly Father. There is no greater inheritance than that.'

This was also the last occasion I went fishing. As a young man I'd always been a keen fisherman, so keen that at Narooma I used to row out through a calm surf in a leaky old wooden rowing boat, hoping that the sea would not come up while I was off shore. On a couple of occasions it did, forming pretty big breakers. I'd heave to, just outside the breaker line, wait for a lull between waves, take a deep breath and row like mad into the 100 metres separating me from the beach. The rowing boat was not only made of heavy wood but litres of water would start to gather in the bottom unless I bailed it out every few minutes. Even getting the boat started on its way was a laborious feat of strength. The waves, now behind me, would travel far faster and inevitably would churn over the back and swamp me. It was then a case of abandon ship and swim for your life, endeavouring to catch a wave and bodysurf in. As it was a narrow bay the boat would wash in close enough for me to grab hold of it and haul it to the beach. Before attempting to row in, the trick was to lash to the seats in sugar bags the usually considerable catch of fish. But once when I was with a mate we forgot this precaution. As the sea swamped us and we swam for the shore we could feel some of the catch colliding with us in their swim to freedom. It was one of those moments when you couldn't help but think of sharks.

Anyway, the front lawn of Judith's small cottage was right on the bank of the Woronora River, south of Sydney. I hadn't fished for years and there in front of me against the sandy bottom was a huge school of large mullet, gently keeping position against the lazy flow of the incoming tide. This was a sight any fisherman would find hard to resist. So into the house I went, mixed up some gluey dough for bait (mullet love dough), took a line proffered by Judith and promised 'fish for dinner.' I jumped into her little rowboat tied to the bank and pushed off. Down went my baited hook right among the school. I waited for the strike, cast again and waited and waited. The fish ignored me. They weren't on the bite, which is one of those tricks of nature every hopeful must encounter.

The lesson for me as a spiritual teacher: no matter how eager you are to go fishing, they're not necessarily going to be on the bite.

# CHAPTER 41

# WHAT TO DO?

W hat do you do when you discover that the woman you love has cancer?

First, as we did, you turn to the medical profession whose response is usually radical surgery and/or chemotherapy plus radiation. The doctors do their best according to the established medical procedures but soon you sense the limitations of their treatments and start looking for alternatives. These inevitably advocate major changes in diet and habit, such as: no meat, white or red; no smoking or alcohol; no cosmetics or hair dye; no packaged or refined foods and no canned or frozen foods; no artificial applications to the skin; no more salt and a reduced sugar intake; no fried food; no dairy products; and copious volumes of fresh carrot and fruit juices. Also on offer is a bewildering multitude of food supplements in pills and capsules, herbal mixtures and Chinese acupuncture. It seemed to me you would have to be dying to take on the alternative. And that's usually the case.

For us in the early 1980s there wasn't the excess of alternatives available as there is today. We started off by reading every book we could find on alternative methods. There were the American ladies who claimed they'd eliminated their cancers: one by drinking only watermelon juice, the other by an exclusive diet of some other tropical fruit juice.

We learned that in many such cases the cancer was a melanoma type and melanomas were known for their unpredictability – they could suddenly disappear for no apparent reason. Also, amazing remissions happened sometimes, though rarely, with all cancers. These provoked stories of "miracles", which perhaps such remissions are. Nobody, including the doctors, can explain why they happen.

After researching all the alternative literature, Julie found the most convincing and practical method was that developed by Dr Max Gerson MD, an American physician who worked on the totality of the body, restoring its healing ability through detoxification. This involved, among other things, a continuous intake of fresh juices (for enzymes), a high ingestion of essential minerals (the potassium group) and regular coffee enemas to stimulate the liver whose natural function is to discharge toxicity in the body.

In 1946 Dr Gerson became the first physician to demonstrate recovered cancer patients before a US Congressional Committee. The committee was holding hearings on a Bill to find means of curing and preventing cancer. Unfortunately the lobby supporting surgery, radiation and chemotherapy caused the defeat of the measure by four votes. Had the Bill been passed it could have supported extensive research into the Gerson Therapy. After that, Dr Gerson was outrageously pilloried and publicly maligned by the American Medical Association.

So Julie began the Gerson regime. We made carrot juice several times a day, ensuring that she drank it within ten minutes of making, so it did not lose its live enzyme potency. The carrots were supposed to be organically grown, which had me running around London trying to find such a source – and in 20 kilo bags. I found one just down the hill, in an Archway Road health shop, where I was assured their supplies were organic. But our delight at this was short-lived when I saw exactly the same brand of carrots on general sale at the London markets. And of course organic produce was much more expensive. But I must say that the man at the health shop didn't know he'd been wrongly informed and he gave me the tell-tale bag for nothing.

We bought the prescribed Gerson tablets and other medication from Martin Gwynne, a good man in Bloomsbury, London. Martin, a businessman in his own right, helped people with cancer by dealing with the bureaucratic hassle of importing the most important medications, enema buckets and so on from the USA. He did this without taking a profit. Peppermint tea was Gerson's prescribed hot drink and Julie drank quarts of it. Bottles of sprouts we grew in the airing cupboard, taking advantage of the heat from the hot water system.

We were still having check ups with her specialist at The London Hospital but after the radiation was completed there was nothing more he could really offer, other than talking to her. To me, these "monitoring" talks by doctors who usually end up saying, 'You're doing okay,' without any practical supporting evidence, give the patient a false sense of progress.

Each week for several weeks we drove four hours across to Bristol to consult a doctor who had set up a cancer clinic in his practice. Among other things he advised was a programme of laetrile injections. Laetrile, sometimes called B17 or amygdalin, was hailed in some quarters as a miracle cancer cure and condemned in others as a deadly poison. It is extracted from the seed within the stone of apricots, peaches and bitter almonds. Laetrile was available only on prescription and the injection had to be given daily by a doctor.

I rang our local medical centre and asked my doctor for a prescription. 'No way,' he said, 'we can't do that. And nor would we inject it for you. Laetrile has not been scientifically tested enough.'

I hit the roof. 'My wife's dying. You can't do anything for her yourselves but you'd deny her a possible chance.'

'Yes. We have to.'

Julie also had several sessions in London with the world renowned healer, Ted Fricker, but again with no evident result. Her condition was slowly deteriorating and she knew it. Her frozen shoulder joint gave her more pain at this stage than the cancer. She visited physiotherapists and I would massage the shoulder regularly with liniments. But the damage was done and nothing did much to relieve the pain.

She said, 'I'm not afraid of death. I know that on the death of my body I will be united with my heavenly Father which has always been my heart's desire. But I also know that in my body is the desire to survive – and I respect that.'

Around this time I interviewed Julie about her life so that I would have a reliable record to supplement my memory and what she'd told me over the years.

Regarding the deterioration of her body, she said, 'On most occasions the pain is with me, and then sometimes I escape the pain and I am free and I am without pain. I seem to have the same body that I have now... But it is younger and it is free-er and doesn't have any emotional or physical pain in it. It is happy. There doesn't seem to be any attachment in it. It is free and happy, but it is myself.'

One incident she recounted was a vivid dream back in 1967 when she'd returned to her husband for a time because he hadn't got over his attachment to her. The dream, apart from defining the separation from Ken that was happening, turned out to be amazingly prophetic. Here is her description of the dream:

> I dreamt that I was back living the normal life with Ken when I had only just met you. I was told to take my suitcase and go to the church where you were waiting. I was terribly sad to do this because it meant leaving Ken and the children and going to you because I didn't know you, I'd hardly seen you – and Ken and my mother had been everything to me. But I packed my case and went into the church. I looked out of the church window and saw Ken's arm around my mother and them walking away from me together. They were still together and hadn't divided their relationship.
>
> Then I turned round and the church was filled with really beautiful people. They were not like the friends I'd known with Ken or any friends I'd known before. There was such love in these people and there was such beauty. When I woke up I said to Ken, 'I've been in this church with Barry and these beautiful people – and they were not like our friends.' This was before I knew I was going to leave so there was no resistance in Ken. I didn't know that people could be so beautiful.

I asked her how she interpreted the latter part of the dream about beautiful people. She said:

I see that as the people I've met with you and their beauty.
You know the beauty of John Hart and the love I have had with
so many people which I won't name because there are so many
of them – this real beauty of love, spirit. That is what it meant. So
I always attributed those beautiful people being there because
you loved me enough to come and take me away – to go
through that broken marriage and take me away. You loved
enough. So I feel you brought all that beauty.

Julie throughout our time together was concerned about her two children with a love that I can only inadequately attempt to present and
describe. Although fully aware that I represented her love of God in the
world, that I was her spiritual master, and putting that first, she never forgot or got over the anguish of leaving her two young sons – twice. In her
talk with me she recounted the second occasion. That was when she'd
smelt 'strange flowers around the house' and Ken 'phoned and said he
was having a dream of you (Barry) and that he was going to marry Anne,
and I was going to leave.' She said:

> I didn't think I could do it again. My heart was broken and I
> said I didn't think I could leave the children again. And Anne
> begged me. She said that Ken wouldn't marry her if I took the
> children with me. I spoke to you [Barry] and you said I had to
> leave them and I was begging you. I cried and said to Anne, 'I
> never want you to forget this moment Anne. I never want you to
> forget this or think or say to me that I left my children. I want
> you to remember my anguish and my pains forever. I never want
> you to say again that I didn't love them.' Unfortunately over the
> years she forgot – and she allowed Ken to say that I had walked
> out and didn't care about them.

# CHAPTER 42

# JULIE'S WRITINGS

David wrote to Julie and me enclosing a copy of John Hart's latest piece of writing, a couple of thousand words entitled *India*. John hadn't been to India but he wrote about it and the people as though he had. David said there were some 'very beautiful parts mixed with the rubbish' and that he would appreciate my opinion. I enjoyed reading India but I must say I also found parts of it difficult to follow. My reply to David was hardly what he'd asked for – it was not an opinion. My reading of the text somehow triggered my great love of John and I used the opportunity to declare that love:

> Dear David,
>
> You ask my opinion of John's *India*. Then let my declaration echo through your psyche, through the waters of emotion that contain all past and time, let me be recorded in the voice of forever, let me be the first to stand and bare my breast on behalf of love and say:
>
>> Blessed John
>> Your patient ache (to visit India)
>> Is but my knowing
>> That you are India.
>> Are you an ethic, you ask?
>> Yes

Thank God.
Do you still love too much?
Yes.
Thank God.
Blessed John
Your loving goes before you
Spills into the muck-raked vessel
And dissolves the crusting rings
Of self
And search.
Blessed John
Infinite poet
Humble craftsman
Unpretentious man
I would burden you with praise and love
If I could but find one spot in you
On which to lay them.
Let it be known
That The Blessed John is here.
Hallelujah!
Hallelujah!
We are all saved
Again.
I have absorbed The Blessed John
His passion is now mine
Let his words be returned to the chaos.

Meanwhile, John would occasionally visit us at Kingsley Place. But from time to time he would stop taking the suppressant drugs prescribed for him, with sometimes bizarre results. On one occasion he called, mumbling incoherently and shuffling in his movements. He was unable to speak a word of sense to me. Without letting him in I told him to go. I said, 'I don't believe the way you're behaving. I know the truth you are. You're playing some sort of game and I'm not playing; I'm not going to indulge you in this condition. So go, and return when you've come to your senses.' Julie also came downstairs, stood behind me and then walked away.

A couple of weeks later, John wrote to Julie from the Psychiatric Unit of Whittington Hospital on Highgate Hill, not far from Kingsley Place:

I wanted to say that if you wanted to see me or for us to spend any time together I am still at the hospital and when I leave I will be at my old address. I don't feel it's correct for me to call on you – Barry seemed to not want me there at all and on the last occasion neither did you, so there's not much of a basis for me to visit.

Quite how we became so mutually venomous on the last occasion is rather difficult to understand – I wish you only to get well if that's what you want and to continue to love and love life. I hope your treatment is going well and again, if you wish to see me any time, I would be very happy to see you – if not, then not.

Love John

An accompanying poem ended with the line: 'Love bids me write, but not to sing too loud a song.'

I don't recall ever being "venomous" with John; only straight, as I've described, when I refused to go along with what I knew he was not. Anyway Julie went to visit him at the hospital and invited him to come around when he was discharged, which he did.

A few months later, John came to the house to 'thank me" for an experience he'd had a few nights before, while lying in bed beside Mark's ex-girlfriend, Veronique, with whom he had been living for three months. He had again given up the suppressant drugs two months before. John said he'd recently had the urge to experience the 'God' energy or state he entered in 1968–9 when he was teaching Julie and me as the Blessed John. (John had always tried to avoid the word 'God' but now said he knew that state was the God state.)

Lying beside Veronique he entered himself and found the black abyss which he knew as utter isolation. This, he said, was what people draw back from and avoid; but his decision was to jump into it – which he did. He then saw an image of me take form in his consciousness. Then he entered the God state of indescribable love – and knew that this was the source of my love.

I told John I remembered Julie once saying that she would like to provide him with a real woman and that it was significant that Veronique should have come to him through Mark. In a note at the end of John's account of the black abyss I wrote, 'John is God come into the flesh and materiality of men willingly and consciously. John as God emphasises and shares man's pain in the gutter of circumstances which is his ordinary life.'

Julie was now in almost constant pain and it reminded her of the prophecy of the "torture tools" vision she'd had nearly three years before. She wrote, 'All week I had been telling myself there must be a flowering in all terrible suffering.' This flowering she discovered through one of John Hart's bizarre bouts of "madness". She described the experience in a diary entry that began by implying what might have caused the psychic force behind the "torture" vision. She wrote:

> After my realisation in 1966 I was deep in God-love. I really knew no fear. God became such a love that nothing hurt or touched me. I think I later escaped into some kind of unreal reality in which I knew I had not to refer to God. I felt rather lost and confused. I became tearful, weak and at times emotional. Barry caused me much pain in deceiving me with Rita. This made part of me reject him so that I could not be the obedient student any more. Later came dreadful, terrifying psychic forces.
>
> One night I awoke and heavy iron bars were hanging from the ceiling to the bed. Heavy, rusty torture instruments hung from them. I was awake and still they stayed. I lay still, shaking and perspiring. Then the fear became so intense that I just surrendered myself accepting that if terrible torture was necessary I would accept it. It left. But somehow I felt that at my death it would await me. I was amazed I could be so calm after that dreadful sight.
>
> Yesterday I went to see John and knocked on his door. I knew he was in but he would not answer. I was a little afraid of pushing my way in as I thought the consequences might be more than I could cope with. The girl upstairs said John was insane. She said the social workers would not do anything, saying he would come out of it himself. Also he would not talk to anyone and ate all his food out of dustbins. He never used his front door and climbed in and out of the window. Even his brother he would not see. She said she had a court case coming up to get him removed.

I tried again, called out my name and he answered. He opened the door. The flat was quite unbelievable. The whole place was smashed to pieces. Every inch was covered in garbage just as if it were the remains of a derelict house after a fire. John was starving to death. He sat in a chair with this funny woollen hat over his eyes so that I spoke to a nose and a mouth. I felt he liked me there. I went and got him some food which we ate together. We went into the kitchen. John had flies locked up in there feeding off rotten meat etc. He would not let them out. It was grotesque. He said I must not touch anything, that there were things there that could kill me and that he had it all under control. It was awful.

After a while we left the house, John giving me instructions that he was to climb out of the window and I was to wait inside the hall until he came around the front to collect me. He said I was in great danger and to do as he said. I felt and showed some amusement which was soon supplanted by deep love for John, a kind of recognition of inner perfection. To be with him, even in such chaos, is joy.

He was dirty and shouting at everyone in the street. Yet I felt so safe and at peace. Everyone was staring. I told him about the torture cage and tools and he said, 'Be quiet. Don't speak. I know it.' He kept repeating, 'Shut up. It's not a game. You may not have to go there if you be quiet and shut up.' He then said, 'Where did you get that silly voice? I shall leave you to walk this road on your own.' Then I noticed he did not leave; he kept waiting for me. I knew he needed me. He did not know this for if he had he would have left me. I knew my power was equal to his.

We reached a crossing and I joined the people waiting to cross. John, angry, stood in the road shouting at me to come on. I just stood and waited for the lights to change. It was Barry's Wednesday night meeting and I felt it was irresponsible of me to turn up with John. I could not bear to leave him so I contrived a situation of being unconcerned. He started to shout again that he would leave me if I stopped. He was standing still as he spoke so I walked straight past him. He had to walk away or else he would have ended up following me and his strength would have left.

Then something odd happened. My head opened out. I saw I was in a very poor area. The pavements were covered in excreta and even blood. A strange man came towards me with an open book, a Bible, on the flat of his hand. A car blocked another car and there was dreadful abuse between the drivers. There were tramps and poor people everywhere. I saw all this poverty, insanity, violence and filth was personified in John. His great compassion and love had embraced it all. It was there in the flat and all around. It had become him. I knew again that he was the Christ. That is why this strange man who all would reject is so beautiful to me.

I had to walk miles home but saw John in everything. At the meeting that night Peter Dockley came in with a card showing a butcher outside his barred shopfront from which hung dozens of pieces of meat on hooks. Above that, on the same card, was an altar.

Julie's love of God, and the profundity that accompanies that love, was exceptional. Throughout her life with me I would come across writings on scraps of paper tucked in books and drawers with poems and prayers of gratitude to God and observations on life and love. She would write these randomly, using the backs of bills, appointments, cards or any piece of paper immediately to hand – and then forget about them. Sometimes her writings touched on perceptions of the irrational world where John's "madness" originated. Both were true lovers of the Most High, the Most Holy, the Inexplicable. Some examples of Julie's writings follow.

> May I write to thee my Lord a verse of praise.
> Gratitude of life.
> The beauty given of all wondrous sights.
> All is the glimpse of thy perfection.
> My heart did break with great confusions
> Tears and sorrow now soon to seize.
> I reach up through beauty and darkness.
> My God I ask to be truly with thee.
> The earth, strange earth

Hell and heaven cursed by pain.
Love fleeting forever only held within.
My God, my God – silence —
Nothing enters thy vaults of azure skies.
White light. Ah but Lord Lord
Thou alone can satisfy my longing.

To wake in the night, to experience my existence beyond thought.

I hear the mighty wind, my body feels eternal, my hand falls from the softness of cheek to the softness of woman's breast. I understand man's strange need to be with, to love, the infinity of woman. I shall never take advantage of this sacred union.

The stillness and clarity of the night teaches me far beyond the day. At night I return to dimensions I understand. Colours are more vivid. Lumination transforms existing furniture. Sound significant. Instructions obeyed, the immensity of power leaves no doubt of the Power of will. All is held controlled without my participating. I am reduced by my love, my recognition that I am nothing in the light of this vast yet merciful God. This power leaves me a little disdainful of man. I cannot forget this mighty power. The day is filled with symbol and sign. The daffodils shooting up everywhere in December when not a leaf is left on a tree – the sight surprises me. It is love. Yet it is not enough for man to love the divine.

The stillness of night wakes me. Changes occur in my body. Lumination transforms half the room. The power fills me with fear. I tremble and feel totally weak and surrendered to death. Then calm. Love. The vast merciful God. How can I lead a normal life when I have seen a power beyond man's comprehension? How can I love ordinary man who does not seek the divine in his own existence? I am amazed that my own life is filled with vanities and traits of a ridiculous nature when I have seen this immensity of power. I deeply understand the

words, 'Make me whole.' To be made whole is simply to be
without thought, to become real, the All.

My life like a flower feels joy, understands pain, is reborn,
knows and not knows its divine purpose. The stream, the tree,
my feet touching the grass and soothed by its softness; my spirit
beholds the vision and wonder of the earth, its splendour and
freshness. All is God. I select the men with skillful confidence.
Only one kind of man enters my heart, the man born to follow
the path to God. Whatever his guise I recognise him. His eye is
straight, his heart is true, his aspirations simple. He is the holy
man who seeks the divine and when worthy turns and shows his
love with service to the end of his earth days.

The vast expansions of nothing
All is holy there
Silent being.
Yet can I grasp my nothingness
When beauty and love feel real?
Great, Great All.
No love has bound me.
Purity has tempted me.
Stillness has held me.
My ears have heard thee.
Fossilised into a strange shape
I became thee.

I hasten dear God to come to thee.
For in truth there is little beauty in this earth
Although my eyes loved deeply all I have seen.
Thou are the only love.
My heart knows, my voice speaks.
Help me my Lord to be one of those who have loved you most.
Help me my Lord to have only thought of thee.
I have been vain and sought perfection on earth.
Forgive me my vanities.

I care not for loss and offer all to thee.
Please dear God help me to love thee
As much as those who loved before me.
Thy goodness and love cares.
I feel no fear.
Now death cannot daunt me
I am ready for the journey all sages take.
I kiss the divinity in humanity.
I reach an inward place of sanity.
When I arrive it shall be here
Where all men die.

I have arranged to see John, at my request, to see houses in
the Canonbury area. He suggested Wednesday. I agreed but felt
slightly intimidated as if John had made some demand on me.
Wednesday is difficult because it is Barry's meeting night. I
always behave oddly after being in John's company, so I am told.
And I do not like to disturb Barry's group.

After being with John I sometimes find the group not
desperate for the truth; too intellectual. Barry is a perfect teacher,
very patient. All who come benefit. My impatience only confuses.
They cannot understand me. Barry they understand. I must seek
to be more humble. John can teach me this. So have to go
Wednesday and bear the consequences if any. John has given all
love, deep love to mankind. Barry has given all deep love to
mankind. Barry and John give no exclusivity.

I was hugging Barry. My eyes were closed and I saw my
complacency. I opened my eyes and the complacency left,
leaving clarity of space, self-realisation, nothing. I thought death
shall close my eyes; I must be conscious. I realised why those
awful psychic things happen to me when I am most peaceful and
contented. It is a terrible sight, complacency – the smug,
satisfying warmth and comfort of love. I have not earned such
rest, nor ever shall.

A wonderful joy has entered my soul. I know I have absolute faith in my soul. It does know God, I am sure. It has always known the darkness and allies of death, the terrible psychic suffering of tortured souls. The soul does not fear. It is the light of that dark existence. It passes through the dark, living in its own light. It is totally beautiful. I cannot know fear. Such joy to discover this.

The guru has left his chair – gone. The room is empty, still. Silence, emptiness, freedom from talk and verbal lashings. My eye centres on a brass object opposite, beside the guru's chair. It is shaped like a god's skull. A voice deep says, 'Thou shall worship no god outside. I am clarity, wisdom, joy. To need outside is pain.'

Sometimes at the meetings a strange energy would enter Julie, or she would be in a strange place. By strange I mean she would be disdainful of words although she would be using them; and what she said had little relevance to what I was endeavouring to teach the group. I was concerned with people seeing the fact because that alone keeps them out of their emotions and imagination and in turn reveals the truth.

From that strange place Julie would say things that didn't make sense. They were other-worldly and I knew that they came from her deep perception of the other world, the invisible world of spirit which in fact does not make sense and is beyond human understanding. But people can only enter or realise that place when they have discarded the need to understand; when they have true knowledge which comes from the realisation of God or the Most High. I was concerned with getting the group ready for that – if it was to be for them. Talk from that place only confused them.

I would correct Julie and because what she was saying was the truth for her, she would get emotional sometimes and walk out of the room. A remarkable thing was that when she was in this psycho/spiritual state her lips became a sort of unearthly scarlet red. Of a day when we both noticed this phenomenon we would remark to each other that there was likely to be a change in her perception or behaviour. It occurred also at times after she had been in John's presence.

I find this continuous conflict with Barry so deeply disturbing at the meetings. All words lead to Barry correcting what I have said. Statements are not allowed. Only questions and answers are permitted. It causes such anguish in my soul. Yet all other company I find wasteful and indulgent. I went to see John this afternoon. He is a wise man, a humble man painfully aware of humanity. John's humility is the only alternative I have. Have just read Krishnamurti's words, 'Humility is continuous death.' John knows the truth as much as any man. Few know John knows.

People have built a strange philosophy on death. They tell us life is good when death exists. Poverty, sickness, age can all be strangely dismissed. How can anyone doubt the truth, the awareness of soul? How can they seek power instead of true goodness when death shadows everything they do? True goodness gives true awareness of the soul.

# DESPERATE DAYS

Just before Christmas 1981, Martin Gwynne, the man in Bloomsbury, informed us of a woman in Sydney, Australia (of all places!) who had been successful in treating cancer patients. Her method was based on colonic irrigation and a dietary regime similar to Gerson's. We wanted to go immediately but I didn't have the ready cash. And this good man, without any security (apart from a promise to repay him), lent me £3,000 on the spot. All this time I was still earning from the astrology work and with the forward contracts knew that I could repay the loan.

We arrived in Sydney on Boxing Day to be met by my son, Scott, with a huge box of organic greens. We moved in with my mother and arranged for Julie to begin the treatment the following Monday. Even before we started she was in pain. In a diary entry just after our arrival she wrote, 'Woke in the night with a sharp, clear pain in the breast. Seemed to be like a bell. Nausea for three days. Cannot hold enemas with ease.'

The next day another entry said, 'Woke last night. Thought I saw the Christ standing in brown robes edged with red. I've never seen the Christ before. Wondered if I was going to die.'

On the Monday, as we were leaving the flat for the appointment, my mother said, 'Barry, I have a lovely rump steak in the fridge for your dinner tonight when you come home.' Julie had given up meat the year before, but I was still carnivorous.

Connie, the lady responsible for the treatment, showed us around her clinic in Foveaux Street, Surry Hills, which featured six or seven small rooms each with its own independent colonic machine. She sat us down and told us about the diet and her own herbal medicines that Julie would be taking.

'What about you?' she said to me. 'Have you got cancer?'

'No,' I said. 'But I want to be with Julie as much as I can in this so I'll have a couple of colonics to know what it's like.'

She questioned me about my diet and said, 'If you keep going as you are you'll get cancer. You said you wanted to do this with Julie, right?'

'Yes,' I nodded.

'Then I suggest you go all the way... Do a course of colonics; you won't need as many as Julie. And do the full diet together; you'll find it easier that way. And remember, no more meat.'

'No more meat!' I exclaimed. 'For how long?'

'For good. You've been poisoning yourself.'

Oh dear. No rump steak for me tonight – or ever again. In a flash I was no longer a carnivore.

It's strange in a way, but in my spiritual life, as I've mentioned, I haven't had to give up the usual addictive habits. They've been taken from me. When I was 34 I was at a party and had been smoking cigarettes heavily. Dancing with a woman, I breathed in her face and she turned away with a grimace of disgust saying, 'Vile cigarettes.' I said to her, 'I'll never smoke again.' And I didn't. A ploy to maintain my resolve was to declare to my workmates and friends that I would never smoke again. The humiliation for the addicted self to be seen smoking after such a statement can be greater than the pleasure of having a puff.

I'd drunk alcohol since I was about 16 right up until 1980 when we visited Florida. I enjoyed bourbon more than scotch whisky. There in the home of bourbon I was surprised when I lost the taste for it and had to give away the duty free bottle I'd bought on the flight over. The day after our return to Highgate, I walked up to the local pub after work at about 5 pm as had been my custom for years, and ordered a pint of beer. I drank half, couldn't finish the rest and walked out never to drink alcohol again. I haven't had to quit marijuana or recreational drugs (recreational? – what a euphemism for disaster) because I never experimented with them.

Connie put us on a fruit and salad diet with quantities of green vegetables and regular intakes of carrot juice mixed with fresh beet and apple. The lettuce had to be the cos variety because cos had more of something or other. Pawpaw was a natural healer, so there had to be plenty of those. Soon the kitchen of the small flat was bulging with fruit, vegetables and carrots – and a couple of trays of sprouting wheat grass. We needed more wheat grass but didn't have the room to grow it. My son Scott came to the rescue by planting 12 trays at his North Shore home on the other side of the harbour and driving over with a supply each day. I seemed to spend half my days in the local greengrocers' shops.

We had colonics two and three afternoons a week, each session lasting about 50 minutes. The machine was simple but ingenious. It warmed the water and pumped it comfortably into the colon at a pressure the patient could control. The discharge tube had a glass section through which the patient, although lying down, could observe the detritus being washed out. To begin with only current waste matter comes away. But the idea is to irrigate deeper and deeper into the colon to where accumulated and impacted old matter has gathered and narrowed the passage. Some of this matter is said to be many years old and a potential site of cancer. Reaching it takes many sessions. At first the tolerance is low and the water pressure is felt low in the colon. But with repeated treatments the water is felt reaching into the horizontal part of the colon below the stomach, and even over to the right-hand side.

This is what happened to me: I had 29 colonic irrigations at Connie's clinic and what I saw washed out amazed me and convinced me of the efficacy of this treatment. But I have to say that I was on a most radical dietary regime – I lost at least 28 pounds – and this was complementary to the success of the colonics.

Julie had a few more treatments than I. She felt better but the pain in her shoulder was now so agonising day and night that it tended to obscure the improved well-being she may have been feeling. Connie massaged the shoulder with her liniments each time but any relief was passing.

A doctor I spoke to frowned on colonics because he said it also washed away mucus which the body needed; I supposed it was a matter of what the body needed against what the body needed to get rid of. One woman who came to the clinic said she hadn't been to the toilet for three months. Her doctor had sent her.

On the 2ⁿᵈ of April 1982, after three months and with Connie's approval, we left for home. We continued with the same strict dietary regime and Julie resumed the coffee enemas. The weather in England was gradually warming up and I was able to start growing trays of wheat grass on the back patio. Julie was looking more fragile and what I have to call transparent.

She'd been having reactions from the detoxification taking place in her body, as predicted in the Gerson treatment. These made her vomit and perspire heavily. It is said that under the extreme diet and procedures that are necessary for combating a degenerative disease like cancer, the body starts rejecting anything artificial that has been put into it. One day I found her sitting on the hall stairs crying and she said, 'My teeth are falling out.' It wasn't her teeth; it was her fillings.

Despite all our efforts she obviously was not getting any better physically. She never complained and although weak and in pain insisted on doing what she could to help me. To me and to others in the group her quality could only be described as saintly.

I was desperate. We'd heard of the La Gloria Hospital in Tijuana, Mexico, which specialised in the Gerson treatment under the guidance of Dr Gerson's daughter, Charlotte Gerson Strauss, who had worked closely with her father. It was staffed with physicians practising and learning the Gerson Therapy. We decided to go. It cost a £1,000 a week up front and again I didn't have the cash. I asked my mother for the loan of £5,000 for the trip and she telegraphed it over immediately.

I'd picked up the visas which the Mexican Embassy informed me were required and we set off for London's Heathrow Airport. We would fly to Los Angeles and thence to San Diego near the border. After passing through Heathrow Passport Control we arrived at the departure gate ten minutes early. Sitting there I casually made a final check of tickets and papers. To my consternation I couldn't find the visas. We both went through our hand luggage and decided I must have left them back at Passport Control, or I'd dropped them somewhere out of my passport.

I ran back along the interminable Heathrow walkway to the Passport Control desk, eyes skimming the floor all the way. None of the officials had seen the visas and they hadn't been handed in. So with minutes to go before our plane's departure I raced back to where Julie was waiting for me, grabbed her hand and said, 'No sign of them. We're going anyway.' We were two yards from the gate when it closed. 'I'm sorry,' said the lady, 'but the flight has left.'

'It hasn't. You can't do this,' I cried somewhat hysterically. 'My wife has cancer. She's got to get on that plane. It's a matter of life and death.'

'Sorry sir, but there's nothing I can do. The flight has departed.'

I collapsed on the chair beside Julie. I felt finished, wiped out, exhausted, defeated. All my strength and drive had left me. It was as though I'd utterly and completely failed her.

Julie said calmly, 'It's all right Barry. We'll get another flight.'

'What's the good of that?' I said. 'The car from Mexico that's picking us up is expecting us on this flight. They'll think we're not coming.'

'It'll be all right,' said Julie. And it was. The airline got us on another airline's flight leaving 25 minutes later. We got to Los Angeles only 15 minutes behind the original schedule, transferred to the shuttle flight to San Diego, and there was the hospital car waiting for us just as planned. 'No trouble,' said the driver. 'We expect delays when international flights are involved.'

The story of my emotional collapse at the flight gate has a sequel connected with when I was a boy of about six or eight. My dad was training racehorses at the time (as my mum has mentioned earlier) and he had to get up to go to the track at about 4am. I was a very conscientious boy and took on my father's need to be up early. I would wake up in the very early hours, wander into my parent's room and give my dad a shake, 'Is it time to get up Dad?' When I later tried to explain to Julie just how completely deflated and defeated I felt in that moment at the airport, she said, 'Yes, I know. All your racehorses died at once.'

And the final irony: At the Mexican border they informed us we didn't need visas!

# CHAPTER 44

# THE LAST HOPE

Tijuana, Mexico, is 12 miles south of San Diego, California, and La Gloria Hospital is six miles further on. The Gerson Therapy section of the hospital was large and provided accommodation and a dining hall for about 20 patients and their partners/companions. Here is a letter I wrote to my mother shortly after our arrival:

> We left England five days ago and thank goodness we did. On the way out Julie discovered another lump had come up on her stomach and now two others have appeared on her head. But this is a wonderful place and we both feel it's the only place to be if you have cancer. Every detail is looked after. Although it costs nearly £1000 a week, it is not a rip-off.
>
> Fresh made juices, as prescribed by Dr Gerson, are delivered to the room on the hour every hour from 8am to 8 pm. Nurses bring Gerson medications (supplements) and injections. Doctors are on call 24 hours a day and see her every day. The room is cleaned daily, linen changed and all necessities replaced. One gallon of coffee concentrate (Columbian organic only!) is provided in the room at all times for the coffee enemas taken every two to four hours. Gallon jars of distilled water for drinking and enemas are also delivered as often as required. The room

itself has two double beds, one each, and an enema recess with curtain and bathroom – very nice and light and all carpeted.

The food is unbelievably abundant and nutritious. I am actually starting to put on weight after only five days here. Plates of organic fruit are kept in the room at all times and you send for more when they are eaten. Meals are served in the room (for both of us) or in the dining room where everyone tries to go if they are well enough, for it is very beneficial to talk with other patients. All staff are Mexican and very pleasant and helpful; they surprise us by never taking an attitude no matter how much you call on them. The whole building is kept spotlessly clean.

But it is a place of pain and suffering. The patients no longer have any illusions about orthodox medicine and doctors. Their stories are all the same of the ignorance, arrogance and blindness of the medical profession in their posturing over cancer. People come here as the last hope. They soon realise it is the only hope of cancer sufferers.

Some however cannot adjust to the tremendous demands the treatment makes when they return home and they give it up. Many of course can't afford it. But most do not hear about the therapy because the medical profession will not even look at it to see if there might be something in it. Patients here at present are from Canada, the US, Australia (four of us), Singapore and Holland. Julie is having treatment which we could not get elsewhere.

The clinic says her condition is serious but she has a fair chance. We plan to stay here for three weeks and then to go for one week to the "half-way house" over the border near San Diego. This is about half the price and run much the same as the Gerson Institute but you look after yourselves more.

Julie's "main" problem at present is what is suspected to be a cancer behind the right eye and it is causing her ferocious pain from the temple to the ridge of her nose. The Gerson Therapy is supposed to reduce the tumours and as that happens the pain should abate.

I must say as a close observer that the whole therapy as practised here is an extraordinary experience; it is all done so genuinely and professionally. They encourage the cancer patient to bring a companion because the therapy, when they go home, requires another person who understands what is being done. The clinic works very hard to see that both patient and companion are instructed in all aspects.

Julie is now in the cooling-down room after hydrotherapy. She is happy – and so am I. Something real is being done and we both thank you from the bottom of our hearts for making it possible. I cannot speak highly enough of this place. As I say, not everyone has the will to persevere with this treatment for it is rigorous in the extreme. But some do have the will and they should have the chance to consider the Gerson alternative.

Barry, South of the Border, Down Mexico Way.

Mrs Charlotte Gerson gave a weekly talk. She told us that to continue the treatment when we got home would take one person 50 to 60 hours a week. They also said the Gerson Therapy cannot usually succeed if the patient has had chemotherapy or more than 16 cobalt treatments and 40 X-ray treatments. We thought we might just scrape in.

Within a few days Julie was having a severe flare-up as predicted in the programme. Severe headaches, the vomiting up of vile-smelling bile, diarrhoea and spasms in the intestines, sweating with strong smelling odour, muscle spasms in the lower legs, dizziness and a lot of gas. It lasted about three days and she was too weak to get out of bed. She lost her appetite, couldn't stand the juices and had difficulty with the coffee enemas. When the flare-up subsided she felt greatly relieved and was able to eat and drink normally again.

The doctors described the flare-up as a favourable reaction that was part of the healing process. They said it was due to the body's attempt to detoxify.

Notes of encouragement were arriving from members of the group, including this poem from Clive Tempest:

FOR JULIE...

I see you as a light, approaching
The opacity of life.
You are lucent as the stream of blue

At the border of the night.
You are rivers run to secret dew
Where oceans kiss the sky.
You are silver sheen and serve the light
Of gleams in a lover's eye.
I see you as a love transcending
The sensation that we feel.
You are waving in the field of corn
As the foxgloves glance at earth.
You are calling to the still unborn
As you nurse the still undead.
You are weeping for the need of birth
With tears of the blood you shed.
I see you as a sign, acceding
To the fleeting dance of stars.
You are graven in the line of love
At the corner of a smile.
Your touch behind my eyes shall give
The blessing of vanished time.
You spin me, atoms in a spiral
Wave of greeting the divine.

Ten days after the first flare-up Julie had another healing reaction but not as severe. She wrote:

> I am awake lying in pain. Moisture around my head cools and soothes me. Cockerels crow. I like their sound. I think of when I was a child, well and healthy, listening to them, and hearing death-threatening voices calling, 'We are coming, coming.' My sister only ever heard the cockerels.

The following week she reported to the doctor that her vision was slightly awry, out of focus. He made an appointment for us to see an eye specialist in Tijuana. The specialist, after a close optical examination, drew me aside. 'Get her on the first plane home,' he said. 'In a few days she won't be able to travel.' I gathered he had seen the cancer near her brain.

CHAPTER 45

# FINAL DAYS

I got Julie out of Mexico and the USA as quickly as I could and we were back home in two days, on the 27th of July 1982. On the flight to England the plane was half empty and she was able to sleep stretched out along four seats.

I had with me a new US made Norwalk Juicer, recommended by the Gerson programme because it grinds and presses, and £800 worth of Gerson medications – a three months supply. At the Mexican border both the US and Mexican officials, we'd been told, were severe on any kind of drugs going in or out. Edging along in the huge queue of cars stretching back for half a mile we arrived at the barrier. With some trepidation (and I'm sure an unconvincing smile on my part) we watched them look in at us with the usual suspicious faces that you see when you know you may be doing wrong.

'Keys please.'

The boot opened and after a pause slammed shut; they waved us through.

Before leaving La Gloria I'd phoned Mark, now 21, and told him the situation and that we were coming home fast. He said he would get leave or quit his job and move into Kingsley Place to help me look after Julie; he would do this for as long as was needed so that she could continue the full Gerson treatment. And that's what we did. Julie stayed in bed most of the time.

Between us, Mark and I kept up the juicing, in all 12 glasses a day: six carrot and apple, four green leaf, two orange. We prepared coffee enemas every two or three hours, bowls of salad consisting of finely chopped and grated raw vegetables, one meal each day of baked vegetables and steamed potatoes in their skins, and every second day a special vegetable soup of unpeeled vegetables, cooked slowly for three hours and then put through a food processor to eliminate any fibre. We were growing trays of wheat grass for inclusion in the green leaf juices.

Mark didn't drive so I did most of the shopping while he washed the vegetables and fruit, a job that took several hours a day. The Gerson treatment insists on distilled water for enemas and even for the washing of the fruit and vegetables so I bought an electric distilling machine. This was left on in the kitchen overnight and produced about four gallons. We brewed quarts of peppermint tea which were kept in thermos flasks beside Julie's bed. The pain from the cancer, apart from her shoulder, was acute but she would only take aspirin as that was the one painkiller allowed by Dr Gerson.

I would sit beside the bed holding her hand, both of us silent. On one occasion I heard her whisper, 'Please don't take my Barry from me.' Is it possible to hear such words at such a time and not to weep from the bottom of the heart? For me it wasn't. I walked out of the room and wept from the depths of that place.


At the end of August and about four weeks after our return from Mexico, Julie called out for help. We rushed in and she was lying on the carpeted bathroom floor. 'I was walking across to the toilet and my sense of balance went completely,' she said. 'It wasn't normal; it was strange. I just have to lie here. I don't think I can get up without assistance.' Julie and I both knew that this was a serious development. I phoned her specialist at The London Hospital and told him what had happened. 'Bring her in immediately,' he said.

At the hospital she was taken straight to a bed. As well as the cancer behind her eye, two more lumps had appeared on her head. She was now riddled with the disease. Within hours she was paralysed from the waist down. She could not turn over on her back and had to be placed in every position. After a couple days, the specialist told me arrangements were being made to have her admitted to St Joseph's Hospice, Hackney. She knew about the arrangements, he said.

I entered the room and she was sitting up in bed looking very pale and thin. I'd got used to seeing her like this for weeks in the familiarity of our home, but now in the starkness of the hospital she looked so sick. We didn't discuss the hospice move; we both knew what it meant. I just put my head down on her breast and sobbed.

Within 24 hours she was in bed in the hospice. Here is an extract from a letter I wrote to my mother the day after:

> She is sinking and the doctors say she could go at any time from a brain haemorrhage but until that happens she may go on for a time yet. The other danger is an infection suddenly carrying her off. She is quite resigned to death, at peace with her God and man. As you know, we met through God 16 years ago; she had her realisation of immortality and God the first weekend I stayed in her house. This happened even while she was doubting all that I had told her about God and immortality, and before we had discovered our deep divine connection.
>
> So we are no strangers to the necessity of death, as well as to the other side of it which is everlasting life. It's just painful and difficult passing through the death passage which seems so dark and terminal for both the dying and those who love them. But Julie or Julia lives on in me, not just as a memory but as a living consciousness of being. While we keep our loved ones there – there is no death for them or us.
>
> Julie said yesterday with a whimsical smile, 'If there was a miracle and I survived I'd be asking you to take me back to Double Bay for our winter holiday. Tell Gar [my mother] I love her and recognise her great kindness and openness of heart. Tell her please to not see me as a memory but to know that I live in the deepest place inside her, the place where she loves.'

I spent each morning and afternoon with her. She was too weak to receive visitors other than close family. Ken, her first husband came. Mark was a regular visitor but I think she said she wanted Jonathan to remember her how she was and not to come. Rita, who was now living with her husband in England, travelled up to London by train and spent several hours with her each day.

Julie was wonderfully cared for by the Catholic nuns who staffed the hospice. There was also a visiting Anglican nun, Sister Anne, who looked just like my first mystic love, Ann, who had accompanied me to India. Sister Anne, a staunchly devout and serene young lady in her late 20s, would sit with us mornings and afternoons. She would hold Julie's hand and Julie said it gave her a sense of peace and tranquillity.

I had this extraordinary vision of Sister Anne. I realised that she symbolised my first Bhagavati, the original Ann, and that Anne, the symbol, had found her love in God and in selflessly serving the sick with her presence. I saw that she had come in love and knowledge to be with the Bhagavati who succeeded her, and who was now returning to the heavenly father they both adored. I told Sister Anne all this; she listened sympathetically, but I don't know that it could have meant much to her. I had seen long ago that realisations are really only for the man or woman who has them.

All previous emotion between Julie and Rita had vanished. Her emotion over me and Rita also had long since disappeared during her illness. As it became clear that she was dying the emotion gave up and disappeared. I would drive Rita to the train each afternoon but never did we speak of past events.

Julie had always enjoyed a cup of Indian tea but under the dietary regimes of the last two years this tea was forbidden. In the hospice there was a small café and Julie quipped, 'Do you think God would forgive me if I had a cup of tea?' We got her a cup, morning and afternoon.

While Julie was being washed one day I went upstairs to the chapel for the first time. Later I wrote:

> I sat on the back pew in meditation. I became aware that my body was "free-standing". By that I mean my body, which was not my physical body, was standing or erect "on its own". I said in myself something like 'My body is free-standing because the God in me is standing free.'
>
> I then started to speak inside myself – something like giving a lecture. I made two points. The first was that the greatest

privilege in life on earth was for man to be allowed to love God. It was not that man could love God of his own conscious volition. But that God permitted a man or woman to love Him. That was the supreme good for any individual. The other point was that the second greatest privilege on earth was to serve God as action, that is, to serve humanity; for humanity was God in existence. This too was a divine concession but one available to mature man and woman.

I then became aware that I was lecturing the dead. It was my first (conscious) lecture to the living dead. The living dead were there, being taught by I who was on earth. This was a tremendous revelation and I was amazed.

The linking of the two worlds, which in the *Origins* book I describe as the current purpose of life on earth, was now being done in a way I had never dreamed of. Such is the power of divine consciousness that exceeds all parameters of the human mind. From now on, when I speak I will also be speaking to the dead. I, or God (not the speaker), have made the crossing. I remember telling them that while they were where they were, they must install the two points in themselves; because when the consciousness they are projects another body/mind into sense on earth, the knowledge will be in the projection. And then, when a teacher or master here speaks of God, it may awaken the memory of the greatest good I had described.

But, I said, the face of this planet was heavy with self (selfishness) and ignorance. A cloak of material self would insulate the awareness from the flowing love and wisdom which the living dead could now be so much aware of and a part of. The delay in penetrating this layer of self in every body here was what was called time.

All this, and a host of other wonderful revelations which are within me, and which many of the group are having, is due to the virtue being released by the Bhagavati Julia as she slowly vacates her visible presence.

Shortly after entering the hospice Julie started to experience agonising pain from the cancer. She'd been having morphine injections and when one of the hospice's little automatic morphine machines became available they gave it to her. The machine, electric powered, was taped to the arm and delivered regular preset doses of morphine without the rigmarole and discomfort of frequent injections. Julie asked me to buy two of the machines and donate them to the hospice, which I did.

The sheer helplessness you feel when the woman you love is dying and is so close to the end has to be experienced to be known. And her calm acceptance of the inevitable, and utter faith in where she was going, was a lesson and a benediction for us who were with her.

Propped up in bed, paralysed, riddled with cancer in stomach, breast and brain, and with only days to go before her death, she dictated last letters to the people she loved. Here are some excerpts:

> Dearest Ken, [her first husband and father of Mark and Jonathan]
> My situation is that I am deteriorating rapidly day by day and feel I would like to say my goodbyes in case I go at any time in the night. I would like you to know how close and loving I felt towards you when you came to visit me. I shall never forget your dear face and the love in the past that you gave me.
> I believe you have spoken to Mark about the funeral being just for the meditation group and afterwards a personal gathering of just family beside my grandmother's grave where my ashes will be scattered. If you do not want to be there I know you will come sometimes and I shall know.
> Mark has been very close to me and it is a great comfort to know we fully understand each other. I trust the love you once had for each other is possible again. I know that Jonathan is complete with you and Anne and I have written to him. Please take Anne's hand as she is also in my thoughts.
> All letters of goodbye are inadequate because there are no goodbyes. When the heart is in God there is no sadness in dying.

> My Dearest Friend John, [Hart, the Blessed John]
> It appears I shall have no more long walks with you. But just know I shall always love you and those walks and talks being with you never cease. You have always been one of my most loved closest friends on earth. Death I know cannot change this.

I am now hopeful that death will come soon. I hope we both find the same contact after death that we found in life. If loving and caring about you makes these things possible then there is no doubt we shall always be together.

Thank you for all the beautiful poems you have written me, the stories and brilliance you have given me, the sweetness and love that I felt so rarely from anyone else in the world. My dearest John, I love you.

Dearest Jonathan, [her son]

I write this now to make sure we have the opportunity for a few seconds to be together for I could die at any moment and I would like you to know you are always in my thoughts. Never be sad about me if you feel there were things you did not have time to say because it isn't true. Every moment with you was always a special delight for which I was grateful to God. God is everything but we can mostly understand him as love. I will always be there when you think of me because I truly love you.

My Dearest Special David, [White]

Strange we have been so far apart having been so close. Such strangeness we cannot understand. Just in my heart I know I love you and that you are an angel. You have always brought joy in my life. I thank you for the days when the sadness of Mark and Jonathan was so deep in me that you were one of the few people who could make me happy. You were indeed sent by God.

Dying has not been easy. And it will be merciful when death comes, which I pray will be soon. I do not wish to see you as I am very sick and paralysed but wish you to hold the days of beauty we shared in the past and the future that shall come when we shall all be free and love again forever.

I trust your brown eyes keep their intensity and your proud heart remains strong. These are the things I recognise you by.

❧

Dearest Gar, [my mother]

Barry has been coming in and reading to me your sweet loving words. I am now in St Joseph's Hospice. The care here is not to get you better but to make the dying process as easy as possible. I have a free private room where Barry can visit me at any time. He spends many hours with me and the privacy is very important to us both. Some people would prefer an open ward for the company but Barry and I, as you know, enjoy the quiet alone moment. So I am indeed fortunate to have a room to myself. How long it will be now we cannot be sure. The main thing is to love God and leave it, as his time will be the right time.

Barry's meditation group has extended greatly since our return from Australia. The group is working very hard to support Barry going out into the world with his teaching. A new course of public lectures starts Sunday week. Every week the meeting draws about 30 people. Barry is well-loved and has great support around him at this time.

The days I have had in Australia have been so beautiful and I would like you to know how meaningful they are to me now, not being able to walk. Barry and I made good use of that precious time and I shall always be there with you and Barry. Darling Gar, I'll close now. We are very close to you at this moment as we write this and always shall be.

# CHAPTER 46

# JULIE'S RETURN

J ulie entered the hospice on the 31st of August 1982 and started to go in and out of unconsciousness on the afternoon of the 14th of September. She had lost the use of her right hand and arm a few days before and was starting to lose the left arm. That night as I left at about 10 pm she just managed to give me her blessing, kissing me several times on my cheek as I held it against her mouth; and then, as standing at the door I looked back, giving me a feeble and heart-rending little wave. The next day, the most touching moment for me, before she lapsed into final unconsciousness, was when she once again declared to her God, 'Please don't take my Barry. Please don't take my Barry.' And then, 'Please help me to love him more.'

That night the nursing sisters told me she could die at any time. They made up a bed of chairs and cushions with blankets so that I could sleep beside her. Her breathing was heavy and I knew that while I heard that, she was still here. At 11.45 pm a sister shook me awake. 'She's about to die,' she said. I walked round to the other side of the bed. I kept speaking to her, telling her I loved her and to go in peace and love. Several times I kissed her head and face. Sometimes she seemed to groan a response from her throat.

About ten days previously she had gone through a terrible period of feeling there was no God. The God she had loved so intensely throughout her life seemed to have vanished and she repeated over and over how grateful she was for the words of Jesus on the cross, 'My God, why hast thou forsaken me?' She knew the desolation behind his cry. After a final agonising day in which her features were contorted with strain, she suddenly fell into peace. God was there once again. Her countenance became smooth and beautiful. Whereas before she had been praying and asking others to pray for her to die, she now said, 'I want to die but I can wait. All is right.'

On this night of her dying, except for the slightly open mouth, the peace held. The skin was pale but beautifully moulded, clear and glowing. Her closed eyes with their darkened lids and dark skin around the sockets were very beautiful. Since I'd first met Julie and had seen her sleeping with her closed eyes looking like this, or perhaps when she was not well, I'd felt a great impulse of love for her. (I once told her of this and she didn't like it much.) And now her final illness revealed the significance of my odd perception. As she breathed fitfully towards her last, she looked so innocently beautiful, innocent like a baby creature that has no name except 'baby creature of the earth.'

After midnight I observed to her that the new day had come. The ward sister said some prayers and laid a crucifix on her abdomen. I was weeping a lot, snatching for tissues and not knowing what to do with the soggy bundle piled up in my hand and on the bed. I smiled at the sisters and apologised several times for my weeping, trying to say it was only my apparatus weeping and that I knew everything was all right. I'm not sure I was very successful in that communication.

Just before 12.40 am her breathing became even more fitful and guttural, each breath held as though it was the last, only to be released and renewed again. My head laid lovingly on her chest could feel the heart beating faintly. Then came the last breath. It was over. I removed the wedding ring – with its inscription inside, 'Julie you are a Star' – from her finger and slipped it on my little finger.

As she sank towards the end I was holding both her hands. They had been warm throughout. But at the moment of her death I noticed that the tips of the fingers went instantly cold. The rest of the hands remained warm. It was as though that small area of cold signified her withdrawal and departure.

The moment Julie died I stopped weeping. I kissed her forehead and looked upon her dead body for a minute. The sisters said they would bring me a cup of tea in the adjoining room. I walked in there. I was looking at the symbols in front of me – two lights over a picture on the wall. Then I was aware that I had no grief. I realised my grief had evaporated the moment she died. I felt different.

Then I realised that the spirit of Julie, or what I had loved in her, had entered me! She had died into me. She was actually there informing me by her presence. I had spoken often enough about this from knowledge that came from where I did not know. But now I had the living experience. She was closer now than at any time in our life together.

To the sister arriving with the tea I exclaimed with astonishment and delight, 'Julie has entered me. She's here, inside me, now this very moment. She's here.' What we had endeavoured to live in our life was now a consummate fact and truth. At last, union, in death. Eighteen years before in a vision of the Bhagavati, I had been told by the Lord that I would be united with this love. I'd often wondered why that promise had not quite been fulfilled yet. That night it was.

I never wept for Julie again, never knew any grief or sense of separation. Even when I went home amidst all her familiar things, I was at peace, fulfilled and joyous in the living presence of her love in me. It was a miracle to my mind; but to my being it was a perfectly natural event. For death must be the same for every man and woman if they love each other and God enough.

Next morning I went to the hospice to pick up the death certificate. I was exultant and had been all night and it must have showed. As I walked in, one of the sisters, who had been very close to Julie at the end, said 'You came in like a symbol of the Resurrection, your hair flowing and full of spirit.'

The extraordinary thing was that for some time I had been teaching the immortalising of love between man and woman; that the whole purpose of their love was to immortalise it so that in death there would be no interruption. At the end of August the group had circulated a public notice that I would be giving a series of four Sunday afternoon talks, one a month, on immortality. One of the talks, programmed for November, was called 'Woman and Man – Immortalising your Love'.

It seems to me that God-realisation reveals a great knowledge of love, life, truth, death and God. But in this existence only experience makes particular knowledge real. For example, a man who has realised God but

345

who has not realised the love of woman, through loving woman one-pointedly and dying to himself for that love, could not talk about or teach tantric love, any more than a woman (and of course a man) who has not experienced giving birth to a child could communicate that reality.

Six days before Julie's death my mother in Sydney had a remarkable experience. My mother was somewhat psychic by nature and on this morning she arrived at work at Bondi where she had kept house for a doctor for several years. She wrote:

> When I arrived, this uncanny thing came over me which I could not explain. There seemed to be something wrong and something right. On my right there seemed to be a kind of dark small rough cloud; and on the left one that was natural coloured. I seemed to be worried and mixed up. I said to the girl working the computer, 'Dee, I feel terrible, kind of unnatural, like something that has never happened to me before. I can't explain it; it's all around me and I feel so sad and terrible.' Then I started to cry from my heart. I could not stop. I got around doing my work blinded with tears and kept saying to myself, 'What is up with me?'
>
> I then said to Dee amid tears, 'Don't be surprised if I get a call from London today. Something must have happened to Julie. This thing must be a message; it is so queer and I feel so sad and dreadful, please forgive me. I can't help or stop crying.'
>
> Marcelle, my friend from next door, rang the doorbell and I had to go with my red eyes and tears. She said, 'Oh Kay, has something happened to Julie?'
>
> I couldn't say yes or no. I just shook my head: No.
>
> She put her arms around me. I asked her to forgive me, and said, 'This has never happened to me before, all the time Julie has been sick. This thing I feel is not like anything I've ever had. I just can't stop.'
>
> I was in that state for at least four hours. After about 2pm I became very relaxed, the crying stopped and I felt completely at peace and could think about Julie from then on without agony of heart and crying.

Just before you [Barry] phoned to tell me Julie had died, I said to Marcelle, 'I feel now, since that terrible day I had, that when I hear about darling Julie's death I can accept it. I feel completely at peace about her.'

And I was right. When you [Barry] told me, I was still at peace. That's why I know it was her. She came to me so I would not suffer when it happened. Her knowing I may be here in my flat alone (at night particularly) when I got the sad news, and how very upset I would be, she came to me in some kind of way beforehand, during the day whilst I had my work and people around me. I could never have taken the sad news alone at the flat, I'm sure. I was afraid of the time and day when you would phone and tell me, but Julie made it so that it was possible for me to accept it. She knew I would suffer and she wanted to avoid that.

Julia's body was cremated five days after her death. Here is a letter I wrote to my mother describing what happened and an incredible sequel to her death:

The crematorium service was very simple and moving, according to those who attended. It consisted merely of my reading five poems which Julia had asked for. About 24 of the meditation group were present and we kept it as loving and real as we could against the rather awful conventional background of those places with their rather threatening solemnity.

Several people had remarkable experiences involving Julia's spirit before she died and after. Some of them had not seen her before but had just been connected with members of the group. One amazing experience happened early Monday morning, the day before the cremation. It involved Anne, who was once Julie's closest friend and who is now married to Ken, Julie's first husband. They live in the same house where Julie used to live. Anne woke up terrified at 1am. She sensed someone in the room. She knew it was Julie. She saw a figure in a nightdress with small, short puffed sleeves (Julie's nightie). No face. Anne started screaming. The figure didn't disappear but pulled back into the shadows. Ken, lying beside her, tried to pacify her. The whole house awoke to her screams. She felt she was being suffocated; that she had to get out of the house. It was far from pleasant. She thought she was going to have a heart attack; her heart was beating so loudly. They quietened her down.

After half an hour she lay back in bed. The energy was still with her. She thought she had to sort it out. Then she was aware that she had to pray; not just to pray where she was, but to get out of bed on her knees and pray. She felt silly. She thought she must be going mad. She told Ken beside her about having to get out and pray. He said, 'Do it then.' She got out on her knees beside the bed not knowing what she was going to pray. She found herself praying, 'Please Lord give them the strength to let me (Julie) go.'

Anne knew Julie felt that people in the group were holding on to her and wouldn't let her go. Anne said Julie seemed to feel an obligation to stay while they needed her but direly wanted to go to her God. Anne then got up, went over to the Bible and opened it. It was at John 20:17, where Mary Magdalene sees the risen Jesus who says, 'Do not cling to me for I have not yet ascended to the Father. But go to my brothers and tell them.' Anne knew then that she must phone me and tell me that Julie wanted to be free to go to God. (She phoned at 9 am.) Anne hoped that I would tell the group at the cremation what Julie wanted. She felt much better after telling me.

Soon after, I was speaking to Ken and he said he hoped I had taken Anne's experience seriously. I told him I had indeed. He said, 'I was terrified too. I knew immediately who it was, but didn't see anything.'

The weekly meeting of the group had been moved forward to that night and I asked each one present to pray for Julie's release. I gave them this special prayer freeing Julie in love:

Julie or Julia, I free you from within me. Go to your God, the Father, or wherever you wish in love and peace. I free you with love, goodwill and understanding.

I said this was a prayer for all people mourning their departed loved ones, who had not realised that their grief and lamentations were actual-

ly holding back the spirit that had now been freed by death. And
repeated the request at the cremation ceremony next day.

At the meeting I also gave the group a second prayer. I said a new
way of praying was being introduced to the world that night; these were
not only prayers, but a way of communion with the powers of love and
goodwill.

I said, 'You must pray for the world, like this…'

> I pray and commune within me with outgoing love to the
> starving, the poverty stricken and the afflicted in the world. I give
> back to you all that which I as the world within me have been
> withholding, the loving understanding that it is I, and my human
> selfish ways, that have done this to you. I free you from myself.

I said that nothing would be served by just uttering the words as people often did when praying. There had to be a deep sense of
understanding and contrition: understanding that human selfishness and
lack of love alone is responsible for the plight of others; and contrition
arising from the realisation that I, the present individual, am the only one
who can make this spiritual contribution towards correcting the world's
imbalance. For while there is selfishness and lack of love in me, the
external world of people must continue to suffer from those causes. But
when I free myself of these ignorant negativities, the lot of someone,
somewhere in the world, is improved.

The symbol of the success of our prayers releasing Julie was presented to us at the crematorium, although only one of us apparently noticed
it. Sandy, one of the women in the group, phoned me the next night.
She said, 'Did you select the spot where the flowers were laid out?'

'No,' I said.

'Did you see what was on the two brass plaques immediately above
the flowers and card? (The card saying, "To the memory of Julie Long.")'

'No,' I said, 'What did they say?'

'One said "Rejoice! I am free." The other said, "To live in the hearts of
those we love is not to die."'

At home in the early hours after Julie's death I had been woken:

> I will put a ring of gold around your heart. This is not to bind
> you but to allow you to love more profoundly and widely. You
> will now love with the love of Julia as well as your own love.
> Also, when you look into the hearts of others it will be with
> greater loving discernment.

As Julie had requested, I took her ashes down to Sussex, where she was
born, and sprinkled them on the grave of her grandmother whom she
loved so much. Jonathan and Mark came with me and we met Rita, her
husband and her two girls there.

Farewell Julie.

*Barry Long went on to become well known as a
powerful spiritual master. Soon after Julie's death he was
able to devote himself fulltime to teaching. He gave public
talks and classes in London, and then on visits back to
Sydney, and his books were published.*

*In 1986 he returned to Australia and made his home on
the Gold Coast but for the next ten years travelled
extensively, teaching in Europe and America. In later years
his international audience travelled to see him in
Australia. He gave his last public teachings in 2002 and
died on the 6*[th] *of December 2003 of prostate cancer.*

John Hart, David White and Barry having lunch at Kingsley Place. John Hart is engaging Julie who is taking the photo.

Julie, Richard Beim and Barry at Kingsley Place.

Left: Barry with Golden
Anchor, 1979.
"Stay anchored to your
senses."

Below: Mark leaving
home, Kingsley Place,
1979.

Above: Florida, 1980.

Right: Barry on the beach at Double Bay, Sydney, 1981.

Barry and Julie in Australia, early 1982.

Previous page: Julie meditating, Gar's flat, Australia, early 1982.

Back Row (L–R): Clive Tempest, Peter Kingsley.
Front Row (L–R): David White, Peter Dockley, Barry, Peter Kuttner. September 1982.

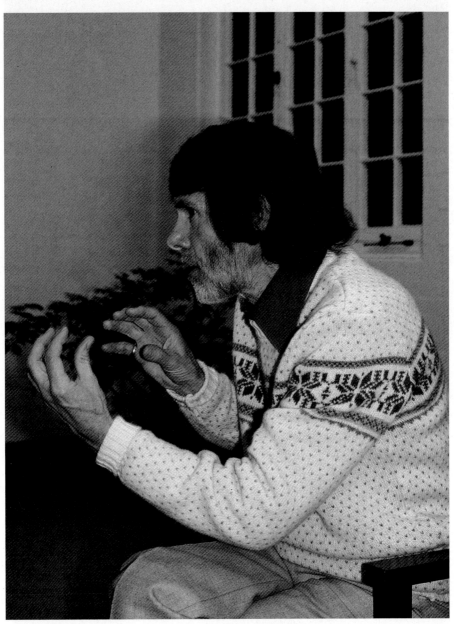

Barry teaching in 1982.

Barry just after Julie's death, September 1982.

# BIBLIOGRAPHIC NOTES

Full and current bibliographic details of Barry Long's works in English and in translation are available at www.barrylongbooks.com.

*Works by Barry Long Cited in this Book*

## KNOWING YOURSELF
Contains the material written in India and following the *Realisation of Immortality* – the manuscript brought to London from India – together with further observations made after the Transcendental Realisation.
[See p. 194]

## WISDOM AND WHERE TO FIND IT
The edited text of the talks given in Wardour Street, London in 1968.
[See pp. 131, 160, 203]

## MEDITATION – A FOUNDATION COURSE
A practical course of ten lessons with exercises to produce more stillness in the midst of everyday life. First edition written 1965–7, and circulated as one of David White's private editions and subsequently in many editions and translations.
[See p. 99]

## A PRAYER FOR LIFE
First written to be recorded as an audio tape, *The End of the World*. Later published with additional material as a book, subtitled, *The Cause and Cure of Terrorism, War and Human Suffering*.
[See p. 291]

## THE ORIGINS OF MAN AND THE UNIVERSE
Barry Long's master-work, containing gnostic revelations about the structure of the human psyche, the Seven Levels of Mind, terrestrial evolution and the *Myth That Came to Life*.
[See pp. 294–6]

## THE WAY IN
A collection of writings from the 1980s including statements made 1980–2 to announce early public meetings and meditation classes.
[See p. 272]

*Barry Long's Songs and Poems*

## SONGS OF LIFE
[See p. 3]

## EPIC SPIRITUAL POEMS
[See pp. 273–6]

## WHERE THE SPIRIT SPEAKS TO ITS OWN
Collected poems with Barry Long's commentary, subtitled The Passion of Spiritual Awakening. Contains the poems and songs quoted in the autobiography, with complete versions of epic poems like "The Pigmy" [See p. 149] and other verses.

*Audio Books*

*The Myth of Life Collection,* read by Barry Long
   Start Meditating Now
   A Journey in Consciousness
   Seeing Through Death
   Making Love
   How To Live Joyously
[See p. 291]

*Other Books by Barry Long*

## STILLNESS IS THE WAY
Based on an intensive meditation class taught by Barry Long in 1984.

## ONLY FEAR DIES
The causes and effects of unhappiness and how to be rid of them.

## MAKING LOVE
The basic message of Barry Long's tantric teaching.

## TO WOMAN IN LOVE
Answers questions from women about love, relationships and the spiritual life.

## TO MAN IN TRUTH
How men can be true to life and love while facing the stress of the world.

## RAISING CHILDREN IN LOVE, JUSTICE AND TRUTH
Detailed advice for parents, children and young people.

All Barry Long titles are published in the English language by Barry Long Books, an imprint of The Barry Long Foundation.

The Foundation holds an archive of audio and video recordings of Barry Long's talks 1986–2002. For current details of the available recordings see www.barrylong.org.

THE BARRY LONG FOUNDATION INTERNATIONAL
PO Box 838, Billinudgel, NSW 2483, Australia
www.barrylong.org
Email: contact@barrylong.org